A BIBLICAL THEOLOGY OF WORSHIP

VICTOR KIM

PUBLISHED BY FASTPENCIL

Published by FastPencil
307 Orchard City Drive
Suite 210
Campbell CA 95008 USA
info@fastpencil.com
(408) 540-7571
(408) 540-7572 (Fax)
http://www.fastpencil.com

Printed in the United States of America.

First Edition

I know no one who rivals Pastor Victor in two areas: pursuit of true worship and connecting the shadows of the Old Testament with the realities of the New (Heb. 10:1). This book converges the two and challenges contemporary worship that is high on style but low on biblical and spiritual substance. His carefully argued points are rooted in sound biblical theology that begins in the Garden and ends in the wedding supper of the Lamb in Revelation. Victor's desire is to see the people of God worshiping Him, not according to the dictates of our culture, but in accordance to how the Lord wants to be worshiped. Don't rush to get through this book; take pauses to reflect and evaluate your heart in light of what God may be whispering as you turn the pages.
Ryun Chang, Ph.D.

❧

ACKNOWLEDGMENTS

I am greatly indebted to John H. Sailhamer who influenced me to read the Pentateuch from the perspective of the author Moses' intention during my M.Div. years at Trinity Evangelical Divinity School in the early 80's. Most of my writing in the first section is based on his books, especially Genesis Unbound.

My biblical theology was greatly shaped by two professors, Meredith G. Kline and G. K. Beale, during my Th.M. years at Gordon-Conwell Theological Seminary in the early 90's. During those years my desire to have a greater understanding of the biblical rationale for the pastoral ministry especially in the area of worship increased.

I believe a person can learn in a greater degree when he is involved in teaching. I am so thankful for the teaching opportunities in the late 90's at Reformed Theological College in Kampala, Uganda and Moscow Bible Seminary in Moscow, Russia where the schools were running on a two-week module system that made it possible for me to take time off from our church's pastoral ministry. During those years, I had the opportunity to apply what I learned while teaching courses on Biblical Theology and the Book of Revelation.

I am thankful for the teaching opportunity at Acts Ministries International Institute that meets for two weeks annually. There I have been teaching on the same subject, a biblical theology with its focus on worship, for the past five years. My colleagues, especially Ryun Chang, who have been relentlessly and patiently reviewing my teaching content and giving me advice on what should be included in my book, have always been encouraging.

I am also so thankful for the recent opportunity to sit through the course, "A Biblical Theology of Worship," by Eric Bolger at the Institute for Worship Studies in Orange Park, Florida at the beginning of my writing sabbatical. It refreshed me to see a kindred spirit, someone who has a heart to apply biblical theology on worship in the context of church ministry.

I cannot be thankful enough for The Remnant Church which I have been pastoring for nineteen years and has constantly challenged me to lay a biblical theological foundation of worship and at the same time put it into practice every Lord's day in the worship service context, never to settle for where we are as a worshiping community but to "press on to take hold of that for which Christ Jesus took hold of [us]" (Phil 3:12). It was these years that gave me the burden to write a book on applying the biblical theology of worship. It was also our church ministry life that helped me to write From Conversion to Discipleship as a D.Min. project at Westminster Theological Seminary.

I thank the Lord for G. Moon that our roads crossed paths before she went to Asia where she has been serving faithfully for over ten years. With her expertise in writing, biblical knowledge and understanding of my way of thinking which often can be confusing, she was gracious enough to proofread all my work so that an average reader could understand what I have written.

I would also like to acknowledge Bryan Kim, Jaean Lee, Daniel Kim and Jihun Kwac for their splendid work on the book design. Thank you!

Lastly, I would not have been able to write if it were not for my wife, Eunice, who has always been by my side to encourage me to pursue what God has placed in my heart during our last thirty years of marriage.

CONTENTS

Part I - Worship in the Garden without an Altar, Tabernacle, or Temple Building ix

Chapter 1   What Is Good 1

Chapter 2   In God's Own Image 7

Chapter 3   In God's Presence 11

Chapter 4   Trusting God Enough to Obey 17

Part II - Worship in the Land at an Altar, without a Tabernacle or Temple Building xxi

Chapter 5   Worship as a Means to Approach God 23

Chapter 6   Worship as Calling on the Name of Yahweh 35

Chapter 7   Worship as Primarily a Service to God for the Redeemed 41

Chapter 8   Worship as the First Priority for Those Who Have Been Called by God 51

Chapter 9   A Stairway from Heaven Resting on the Earth 71

Part III - Worship at the Altar and in the Tabernacle lxxix

Chapter 10   The Tabernacle as a Sanctuary of God 83

Part IV - Worship at an Altar without a Temple Building ci

Chapter 11   Worship and the Prophet's Ministry 105

Chapter 12   God's Holy Presence and Being Mindful of God 119

Part V - Worship at the Altar and the Temple Building cxxxiii

Chapter 13   The Temple Building 135

Chapter 14   Yahweh's Glory Cloud and Fire 149

Chapter 15   The Temple Courts, Where and How the Worship Took Place 163

Chapter 16   The Prophetic Ministry 193

Part VI - Worship in Christ Jesus without an Altar, Tabernacle, or Temple Building ccxv

Chapter 17   Jesus Christ as the Last Prophet, God's Final Word 217

Chapter 18   The New Covenant Worshiping Community according to the Epistle to the Ephesians 241

Part I - Worship in the Garden without an Altar, Tabernacle, or Temple Building

The Place of Worship, the Garden as a Sanctuary

From the very beginning, even at Creation, God had in mind the sanctuary, a place where people would be able to commune with God and have a relationship with Him. Though Moses, the author of the creation account, begins Genesis with an overview of all creation, in the second chapter, he quickly goes on to narrow his focus onto the "land" which had been made on the third day (Gen 1:10). It was in that particular land called Eden that God "planted a garden" (Gen 2:8). Moses gave the location of the land by mentioning the names of the four rivers and their locations, which must have been familiar to his contemporaries. The first two rivers, the Pishon and the Gihon, most likely marked the southern borders of the land, Canaan, while the last two rivers, the Tigris and the Euphrates, served as the northern borders (Gen 2:10-14).

Therefore, the "land" of Genesis 1 that Moses had in mind was the Promised Land, the land God promised and called Abraham to (Gen 15:18, 12:1). Interestingly enough, God gave the perimeter of the land which Abraham's descendants would receive four hundred years later by rivers — "from the river of Egypt to the great river, the Euphrates." The land promise and its location were reiterated by Moses in his last book, Deuteronomy 1:7—"as far as the great river, the Euphrates." Although neither one of the rivers that marked the southern borders was mentioned, most likely the first readers of the Pentateuch (the first five books of the bible written by Moses), the Israelites in the wilderness and the next generation, saw Egypt, from which the Israelites were brought out of and never to go back to, as the southern border of their new promised land, further separated by the Sinai desert between them (Josh 13:3; 15:4).

If the "land" of Genesis 1 was referring to Eden, the Promised Land for the Israelites, then "the garden" (Gen 2:8) was to be a sanctuary where Adam and Eve were to enjoy God's presence and serve Him (Gen 2:15). It was in that garden (sanctuary) that God gave man's primary calling in life to "work" and "take care of" "the garden." It was also in the Garden that God revealed His will for the first man, Adam, which was that the man was to keep and obey God's will (Gen 2:16-17).

1

WHAT IS GOOD

There are three things that should be noted in relation to "good" in the first two chapters of Genesis: 1) nothing can be spoken of as "good" until God makes it good, 2) the biblical understanding of "good" in Genesis is mainly theological, i.e., "good" is equated with God's standard rather than the human standard of a moral goodness (Mark 10:18), and 3) understanding of good in relation to worship.

A Place of Rest

Only on the third day is the word "good" mentioned twice (Gen 1:9, 12); until land appeared, there was no suitable place for man to live. God's creative and handiwork would not be completed until God created man in His own image and there was a suitable place prepared for this man to dwell (Gen 2:1).

The place of rest for Adam and Eve was the Land, where the Garden was planted. The Land, which later the second generation of Israelites would enter, has always been referred to as a resting place (Josh 1:13). But true rest could only be enjoyed when Adam kept God's word in the Garden, or for God's people under the old covenant, when they walked in the way of the Lord (Jer 6:16). But sadly, like Adam who broke the covenant and was cast out from the Garden (Gen 3:23), God's people would also eventually be driven out from the Promised Land, the place of rest, and taken into exile by the Babylonians as Isaiah prophesied (Isa 28:12). Just as the ground was cursed because of the first Adam, the Promised Land, the place of rest, could not enjoy rest until the disobedient people who had been dwelling there but failing to keep God's word were sent away for seventy years in captivity (2 Chr 36:21).

We are able to see God's goodness from the very beginning in that God does not rest until He gives man a place to dwell and rest (Gen 2:2-3). This idea of God giving His people rest can be best seen when God made a covenant with David. Until God provided "a place for" His people, God, like His people, "[did] not [dwell] in a house from the day" God brought the Israelites out of Egypt (2 Sam 7:6, 10). The ultimate true rest would come to all humanity when God would establish His kingdom through the One whom David's son, Solomon, would foreshadow, that is Jesus Christ who "is Lord of the Sabbath" (Matt 12:7) and gives "rest" to those who heed His call (Matt 11:28-29). God sees that our lives are "good" when they are found in Christ and experience true rest.

For this reason, worshipers under the new covenant are called to enter the rest—"Let us, therefore, make every effort to enter that rest" (Heb 4:11). When worshipers congregate together as a new covenant community, unlike the church in Laodicea (Rev 3:15-16), the church must experience the true "rest" of their souls. It is through being part of a worshiping community and the act of worship that weary souls are refreshed.

In the beginning, the Garden was a sanctuary where Adam and Eve were to enjoy rest. In the wilderness, the tent of meeting (=the tabernacle) was a sanctuary where Moses and the Israelites were to experience rest as they were longing for God's promise to be fulfilled in the Promised Land (Exod 33:14). In the Promised Land, rather than worshiping the Lord, God's people polluted the land with idolatry, and as a nation, they failed to experience rest. Although after the seventy years of captivity they were back in the Promised Land, they were still not experiencing rest since the nation was under the Roman Empire. It was a simple reminder that true rest could only be experienced when the Son of God would come and gives this rest to His people by conquering death through His own death and resurrection.

Therefore, whenever and wherever the new covenant people come together as a church and worship, that is where a Christian can truly experience rest.

Serving as Signs, Not Serving Idols

Moses grew up in a culture where worshipping the sun, moon, and stars was very common, yet as he writes the Scriptures, he puts forth a different world view where these are not themselves the objects of worship but rather signs pointing people towards worshipping the one, true God. On the fourth day of creation, God established these lights to "serve as signs to mark seasons and days and years" (Gen 1:14). Their ultimate purpose was to help God's people to remember and know when to gather together to celebrate God's goodness in worship (Exod 23:14-17). When the culture of that time elevated these created things to the position of gods, it became the "not good" sin of idolatry. But originally, when God placed the sun, moon, and stars in their proper places, "God saw that it was good" (Gen 1:18). Just before God brought his people out of Egypt, he sent various plagues, the penultimate being the one of "darkness... over Egypt" (Exod 10:21-22). Through this, God was basically judging the gods of Egyptians, showing himself to be greater than the gods that they were worshipping. But sadly enough, the Israelites, right after crossing the Red Sea, turned so quickly to the same sin of worshipping created things rather than the Creator, this time a man-made god, the golden calf (Exod 32:4), and their idolatry during the forty years in the wilderness was summarized by the prophet Amos—"You have lifted up the shrine of your king... the star of your god" (Amos 5:26).

Useful for Worship

In his description of the location of Eden, in addition to the four rivers, Moses also mentions three things that were prominent in the "land of Havilah"—gold, resin, and onyx (Gen 2:11-12)—all three related to worship in the wilderness journey. Pure gold was used for all the furnishings in the Tabernacle (Exod 25ff.). Although the specific term "aromatic resin" (*b'dolah*) is used in only one other place in the Bible, Numbers 11:7, it reminds us of the various "fragrant spices" that were used to formulate a specific incense for use in the Tent of Meeting where God met Moses

(Exod 30:34-37). "Onyx stones" were used on the priestly garments, mounted on the ephod and breastpiece (Exod 35:27; 39:6). All these were mentioned to remind the reader that God was preparing the Garden in the Land that would serve as a sanctuary.

God originally gave us these precious stones and metals for us to use to love and worship Him. Sadly, in our materialistic culture, we do the opposite, in our greed using God and people to acquire things like gold and jewels. Materialism has taken its toll, and just like the people in the past, we value material things beyond what God had originally intended, and they have become our gods. What do you love? Jesus spoke plainly that we could not serve or worship both God and money (Luke 16:13).

David warned of what idolatry can do to us in Psalm 135:15-18. Idols have form without life. As strange as it may seem, "Those who make them will be like them, and so will all who trust in them" (v. 18). Basically when we worship idols, we become like them in that we may have a physical form but we lose our spiritual sensitivity. Unfortunately, Israel as a nation failed to heed the warning of Psalm 135 and as a result, God's judgment came upon Israel. Before they were taken into exile, the contemporaries of the prophet Isaiah, refused to listen to God's word (Isa 28:10). God's judgment was that they would lose the privilege of hearing God's word—"Be ever hearing, but never understanding; be ever seeing, but never perceiving" (Isa 6:9). Indeed spiritually, they did become like the idols they served and worshiped. (For further reading on this, see Beale's, *We Become What We Worship*)

Living in one of the major cities of the world, New York, where materialism is most rampant, without being aware, Christians are becoming no different from non-Christians as we subtly assimilate into the materialistic culture. As modern worshipers, we can be guilty of not seeking to hear God's word when we participate in a worship service because of our spiritual ears have become deaf. Worshipers must set apart Jesus Christ as Lord in their hearts. As we enter into worship, the Holy Spirit must touch us by helping us to see, "Of what value is an idol, since a man has carved it... it is covered with gold" (Hab 2:18, 19) so that the idols in our hearts can be demolished.

What is really valuable in life? What do we consider precious, more desirable than gold? Making a commitment or promise to the Lord had lost meaning and significance, whether it was in the prophet Hosea's days (Hos 6:4) or Jesus' days (Matt 23:18-22). Worshipers might have had all the right religious lingo, speaking or singing about God, and as long as it did not cost or risk the material possessions they owned, they were comfortable in observing or even participating in worship. Not much has changed since then. In our days, we enjoy worship service as long as the music is culturally relevant and resonates with us emotionally; we are good, attentive listeners when what is spoken of challenges or satisfies our modern curiosity or intellectual mindset during the worship service.

But the question that should constantly haunt us is, besides our time and effort, "Does worship cost me anything?" We still have not learned what David said, "I will not sacrifice to the Lord my God burnt offerings that cost me nothing" (2 Sam 24:24). Worship has always been costly. Nearly two thousand years ago, the Son of David, Jesus, "sacrificed for [our] sins once for all" (Heb 7:27) on Mount Calvary. Indeed worship is costly since it required the whole life of the Son of God.

Worshipers under the new covenant do not approach God with offerings, hoping or assuming their offerings would be acceptable to God, since Christ has offered a perfect sacrifice, once for all. But as strange as it may sound, when the worshipers' minds and hearts are "sprinkled" with the blood of Christ as they "draw near to God" (Heb 10:22; Isa 52:15), when there is a fresh understanding of God's redemptive work through Christ's sacrificial death, for these worshipers, whatever they once considered "valuable" loses its value in comparison to the infinite and eternal value of Christ's sacrifice.

This was the case for the woman who "broke the [alabaster] jar and poured the perfumed on [Jesus'] head" (Mark 14:3). Unlike the others who had a utilitarian mindset and were more practical about the sacrifice (v. 5), valuing the "very expensive perfume… [which] could have been sold for more than a year's wages" (v. 4), the woman valued the person, Jesus Christ - it was just that simple! One should not presume that the woman somehow vaguely knew about the sacrificial death of Christ. But one thing is for sure, what the woman "wasted," a year's wages, can never be understood or accepted by modern worshipers until we understand the gospel (v. 9). As worshipers realize the severity and weightiness of their sins in the light of God's forgiving grace that comes from the ultimate sacrifice of His Son on the cross, they can surrender themselves wholeheartedly in all aspects of their lives, including what they own.

It is no wonder that in another instance, a sinful but forgiven woman did the same thing by breaking an alabaster jar to anoint Jesus (Luke 7:36). Unlike Simon the Pharisee, the woman experienced God's infinite grace of forgiveness through Jesus—"her many sins have been forgiven—for she loved much. But he who has been forgiven little loves little" (v. 47). But who can say they do not need God's forgiveness when we all need to be forgiven (1 John 1:8-10)? How can one's many sins be forgiven? Does a person have to sin more than others to have many sins be forgiven? Herein lies the importance of the realization and awareness of God's forgiveness in worship. Perhaps this is one of the main reasons participating in the Lord's Supper is important for worshipers.

I wonder how modern worshipers would take what the early church practiced. In the early church, "no one claimed that any of his possessions was his own ... [and from] time to time sold them, brought the money from the sales and put it at the apostles' feet" (Acts 4:32, 34-35). Sacrifice is meaningful and "waste" inevitable, only when it reflects the worshiper's heart's desire for, realization of, and renewed appreciation of the infinite grace of God's forgiveness through Christ's sacrifice. Now how much value does gold have? How precious is gold? Is it that the more pure the gold is, the better the gold? The gold from the land of Havilah was "good" because worshipers would use the gold to worship and serve God rather than try to use God to gain the gold.

2

IN GOD'S OWN IMAGE

As long as we can remember, people have always desired to relate to a divine being or visible gods in various forms. But the problem is that God is invisible and does not have any form. We assume we could relate to Him better if He were visible. But if that were the case, then God would no longer be an infinite being but rather be finite and limited to our human reasoning and understanding. We can only know God from how He has revealed Himself through what He has said in His written word, the Scripture. God did not leave it up to our own imagination, speculation or knowledge for us to know Him. God's word is given so that we may walk in it (Deut 29:29).

God specifically forbade making any form of an idol (Exod 20:4-6), knowing that the Israelites, like others, would always be tempted to relate to God by limiting Him to the form of a creature rather than taking on the harder task of relating to Him as the infinite Creator that He is. Any image or form in relationship to God was to be avoided. In line with this principle, when a person was building an altar for God, even dressed stones were forbidden and only uncut stones were allowed (Exod 20:25; Deut 27:6).

Reflecting Christ's Glory

The only image of God we find in the Bible is in human beings until the Second Person of the Trinity would become man (Col 1:15). Since humans were created in God's own image (Gen 1:26-27), their responsibility is to represent God in every aspect of life. Therefore, just as God "rested from all his work" on the seventh day (Gen 2:2-3), the Israelites under the old covenant were expected to cease from their regular activities and rest on the Sabbath. Since God is spirit and does not have image, we as His image-bearers need to strive to grow and conform "to the likeness of his Son" (Rom 8:29). Since we have been created in God's image, like the father-child relationship (the first man Adam is referred to as "the son of God" in Luke 3:37), we need to "be imitators of God" (Eph 5:1). Incomparably more than what Moses experienced under the old covenant, as we turn to the Lord and as the worshipers' hearts are liberated, we reflect the Lord's glory, and our hearts "are being transformed into his likeness with ever-increasing glory" (2 Cor 3:16, 18).

Triune God and Community of Believers

Although God (*elohim*) is one, the word in Hebrew is in a plural form, and different interpretations exist for it. But it is interesting to note that whenever humans were connected with God's image or likeness (Gen 1:26), or when the Bible talks about humans' rebellion against God to assume God's role (Gen 3:22; 11:7), God referred to Himself as "us." And if people ought to reflect the invisible God, could it be that just as the Triune God is the God of community, people must reflect God in the area of relationship, community, and unity? Just as there is a perfect unity in the community of the Trinity, we need "to live a life worthy of the calling... make every effort to keep the unity" (Eph 4:1, 3).

When God said, "It is not good for the man to be alone" (Gen 2:18), what God had in mind was not only the marriage relationship (the purpose of which ultimately would be to reflect the Christ-church relationship under the New Covenant (Eph 5:1, 31-32). From the very beginning, rather than individuals, God's purpose for humanity has always been community. For this reason, although people often approached God alone, once the nation Israel was established under the old covenant at Mount Sinai, worship was always corporate. It was rather inconvenient for the people to gather at a designated place three times annually, leaving their own hometowns (Psalm 121 was sung by the worshipers as they made their annual journeys to Jerusalem). Yet it was in corporate worship that the community of God's people was to experience spiritual unity—"For there the Lord bestows his blessing" (Ps 133:1, 3).

3

IN GOD'S PRESENCE

Before sin entered into the world, there was no barrier between God and man; therefore, there was no need for a temple building, altar, or offering/sacrifice. It is only after the Fall, with man being cast out from the Garden, that for the first time in the Bible we find an offering/sacrifice made to the Lord (Gen 4:3-4). When we come to the last book of the Bible, the reason for the absence of a temple in heaven is given—"I did not see a temple in the city because the Lord God Almighty and the Lamb are its temple" (Rev 21:22).

The temple building was significant because in some way, the worshipers experienced God's presence there. Therefore, the absence of a temple in the Garden reminds the reader that in some way, the very presence of God was in the Garden. In this way, one can say that the Garden was the very sanctuary of God.

For Jesus, the Son of God incarnate, His physical body is a temple (John 2:21) since He is God Himself in human flesh (John 1:14), Immanuel (Matt 1:23)—Jesus' presence is God's presence. Therefore, true worship takes place, before anything, in the very presence of God. For this reason, Jesus said to the Samaritan woman that it is not in a particular setting or place that worshipers can worship, but that it is about a particular moment when the worshipers find themselves in the very presence of God (John 4:21-23, notice Jesus said, "a time... has come"). There, at that moment, the woman was in the very presence of the Son of God. It was there, at that particular moment, that Jesus revealed Himself (John 1:26). Unlike the man healed of blindness who worshiped Him when Jesus revealed Himself (John 9:35-38), the woman did not worship Christ right then and there; nonetheless, she was overwhelmed with joy from encountering this Christ who knew "everything [she] ever did" (John 4:29) and shamelessly gave her testimony to others.

Three things should be noted from the event that took place between Jesus and the Samaritan woman. First, true worship takes place in the moment when a worshiper is gripped with the awareness of the very presence of God. Worship is a natural by-product of and the only legitimate response of the worshiper to an encounter with the supernatural presence of God. Second, through worship, Christ reveals Himself. At every conclusion of worship, worshipers should seek to ask, "How did God reveal Himself today in our worship service to Him?" Third, in worship, a worshiper realizes that no one knows him better than God. In worship there is no pretense, no cover up, but rather the worshiper can be truthful (like the woman) and be liberated from legalism and seek God's grace and mercy in Christ. For this reason, the worshiper under the new covenant has a greater and deeper appreciation of Christ's death and resurrection.

The first human beings, Adam and Eve, were created without sin. Therefore, they were able to be in the very presence of God in the Garden, unlike the high priest who could only enter into the Most Holy place, the inner sanctuary, once a year by sacrificing first "for his own sins" (Heb 5:5). In this sense, Adam foreshadowed the ultimate perfect high priest, Jesus Christ, who sits at God's right hand in the very presence of God (Heb 1:13).

Ministering before God

Adam was placed in the Garden to "work" (*abad*) and "take care of" (*samar*) the Garden (Gen 2:15). Throughout the Pentateuch and Prophets (the one exception being Jeremiah 27:6), the word "work" or "serve" is used to signify serving God or other gods. In other words, what Adam did, his work in the Garden, was considered "serving" God. Before the Fall, there was no distinction between the holy and the common. Although humanly speaking, when there was an "automatic sprinkler system" in the Garden (Gen 2:6) and the ground was not yet cursed, one wonders what real work there was for Adam to do. Yet calling what Adam did "work" highlights how the distinction we make today between "secular" work (i.e., our jobs) and ministry (i.e., "serving God") was unheard of in the Garden. Even under the old covenant, priests were working in the temple on the Sabbath, and it was not considered breaking the Law (Matt 12:5). What was considered as normal work outside of the temple (which was prohibited on the Sabbath) was considered "ministry" when done in the temple by the priests, even on the Sabbath.

If we were to ask Adam what he thought God's calling upon his life was, I presume he would say, "Giving glory to God by working the Garden." The word "secular," which means that something has no religious or spiritual basis, was completely foreign in the Garden. Adam "ministered" (served God) in the "sanctuary" (the Garden) by taking care of the Garden. Once sin entered the world and Adam and Eve were cast out from the Garden, what was once "work" through which Adam served God became a "painful toil" (Gen 3:17).

This work-ministry in the Garden was to be restored by the coming of the woman's offspring, Jesus Christ (Gen 3:15). For this reason, presently "creation waits in eager expectation for the sons of God to be revealed" (Rom 8:19). Although the children of God have not been fully sanctified and all of creation is waiting in eager expectation for " a new heaven and a new earth" (2 Peter 3:13), God has already begun the work of new creation in the heart of every person who is in Christ (2 Cor 5:17).

Therefore, under the new covenant in Christ, the distinction between what is holy and common, "ministry" and career/secular work, or clergy and laity becomes blurred when it comes to serving the Lord. Although 1 Corinthians 10:31 — "whether you eat or drink or whatever you do, do it all for the glory of God," — primarily has to do with edifying the body of Christ, it leaves little room to dichotomize between what is sacred and secular, or what is for Christ and for ourselves. For this reason, for believers, in every area of everyday life, whether the government-citizen relationship (Rom

13:1) or the master-slave (in our days, employer-employee) (Eph 6:6), the lordship of Christ should be the governing factor. Just as the covenant with Adam (Hosea 6:7), of which "the tree of the knowledge of good and evil" was a visual representation, was to serve as a reminder of God's kingship over Adam who was a regent king, the believers should be reminded in every aspect of their lives of the new covenant in Christ because they are "God's workmanship, created in Christ Jesus to do good works" (Eph 2:10).

Instead of using the body to indulge in sexual immorality, Christians should "honor God with [their bodies]" (1 Cor 6:20). In a similar manner, Paul, after concluding his theology of God's sovereign grace with a doxology, urged people "to offer [their] bodies as living sacrifices... this [was their] spiritual act of worship" (Rom 12:1). The words "spiritual act of worship" (logikos latreia) can also be translated "reasonable service" (more preferable since another word, proskyneo, is more specifically translated as worship, i.e., John 4).

Some have misunderstood and misapplied Romans 12:1, assuming that whatever they do for the Lord is their "spiritual act of worship." Thus they see their time serving the Lord with their own career or other means of work as validly replacing actual Sunday worship service with a church, and they do not see the need for being committed to a church body and participating in corporate worship. Romans 12:1 is followed by an encouragement to Christians to participate in doing church work with different "gifts," which everyone has received primarily within the new covenant community (vv. 3-8), but this should not be a replacement for participating in the corporate gathering of Sunday worship. Perhaps, in our utilitarian and performance-oriented mindset, it seems more reasonable or worthwhile to do something practical than just to pause long enough to stand in awe in the presence of the Lord (Hab 2:20; Luke 10:41-42).

Regarding Christians' careers, the line of distinction between what is sacred and what is secular has indeed become negligible since Christ has redeemed not only who we are (identity) but also what we do (responsibilities) in this secular world. At the same time, although there is diversity in terms of gifting and responsibilities both within the church and outside of church (secular), since the world has not yet been fully redeemed, there is a special purpose for Christians corporately gathering, especially for Sunday worship which is of foremost importance for a church. The two primary reasons for coming together as a church are to worship in celebration of God's goodness and to edify one another through the means of different gifts. Whatever we do, both in the sacred community and secular world, we do in the name of Jesus, but every believer has the responsibility to glorify God in worship, together in unity, as part of a community.

Intimacy with God

When God promised Moses liberation from the bondage of slavery in Egypt, He promised that the Israelites would worship in the place where Moses encountered God for the first time (Exod 33:12). Just as God was preparing the land and planted the Garden so that Adam and Eve would worship Him there, God was delivering the Israelites out of Egypt so that they would worship God in the Promised Land. Likewise, God has brought His new covenant people out from the bondage of sin through Christ (Matt 1:21) in order that they might worship and serve the true living God (1 Thes 1:9). Christian worship, therefore, is grounded in God's redemptive work through Christ's death and resurrection.

Just as the tent of meeting ("anyone inquiring of the Lord" in Exodus 33:7) and later Solomon's temple were places for the Israelites to encounter and have fellowship with God, the Garden was a place that God designed where Adam and Eve were to enjoy His presence and obey Him in faith. We are, in a way, given more information about what mainly took place in the Garden by reading Numbers 12:4-6 as we get a glimpse of what took place between God and Moses in the tent of meeting. As a faithful servant of God, Moses enjoyed an intimacy with the Lord that no other prophet among the Israelites had.

Under the New Covenant, when Christians come together to worship in a particular place, God's promise of His very presence is fulfilled in Christ, not in a tabernacle or a particular temple building, but among God's people, who are God's children, since "we are the temple of the living God" (2 Cor 6:16). The author of Hebrews gives a clear distinction between Moses under the Old Covenant and worshipers in Christ under the New Covenant in relation to intimacy with God (i.e., the degree to which they experience His presence) in Hebrews 3:5-6; Moses was a faithful servant *in* God's house, but Christians are referred to as *being* God's house, themselves being the very hosts of his Presence.

4

TRUSTING GOD ENOUGH TO OBEY

If it is God's will for people to obey His commands, He would never make His will so complicated that it would be difficult for us to understand. Rather, he would make it simple. That was how it was in the Garden. God's command was simple, and there was only one prohibition, do "not eat from the tree of the knowledge of good and evil, for when you eat of it you will surely die." Adam had not witnessed or experienced death at that time; therefore, although God's command was simple enough for anyone to understand, it was also impossible for Adam to obey without trusting, having faith in what God said, His word. For this reason, Moses later said to the generation who would be going into the Promised Land that God's commands could only be obeyed in faith (Deut 30:11-14).

Just as we enter into and begin our Christian life by confessing that we come to believe in our hearts the gospel message of Jesus Christ's death and resurrection, (Rom 10:6-10), the first man, Adam, and the Israelites were to have trusted God and His word. Sadly, rather than trusting in what God had said, Adam and Eve trusted in their own physical instincts and considered "good" in their own eyes (Gen 3:6). Like the first man, Adam, the first generation of Israelites in the wilderness failed to enter into the Promised Land, Canaan, because they failed to trust in God's word—"For we also have had the gospel preached to us, just as they did; but the message they heard was of no value to them, because those who heard did not combine it with faith" (Heb 4:2).

Therefore, from the very beginning in the Garden where the first Adam failed, there was a longing and anticipation of the Promised One, Eve's offspring, who would destroy Satan (Gen 3:15) when the second person of the Triune God became the man, Jesus Christ. Just as the first man, Adam, was placed in the Garden to worship and obey God, the last Adam, Jesus Christ (1 Cor 15:45), was also in the garden (kepos) (John 18:1) for His final battle to obey. But unlike the first Adam, the last Adam overcame the temptation in submission to the Father—"not what I will, but what you will" (Mark 14:36) and "became obedient to death—even death on a cross" (Phil 2:8). And just as the first generation of Israel was led into the wilderness, Jesus Christ was also led into the wilderness to be tested in the area of worshipping God (Matt 4:1). But unlike the first generation of Israel who failed and fell into idolatry in the wilderness, the true Israel overcame the temptation by keeping God's word—"worship the Lord your God, and serve him only" (Matt 4:10).

For this reason, unlike Matthew's, Luke's genealogy of Jesus concluded with the first man, Adam, in order to make the connection that Jesus was the last Adam when he overcame temptation in the following section. What Adam in the Garden and the Israelites in the wilderness failed to do, the last Adam and true Israel succeeded in doing by overcoming the temptation in the wilderness during the forty days (Luke 4:1-13). In other words, Jesus Christ is the only One who can replace our failure and disobedience with His obedience, God's righteousness.

Every Lord's Day, Sunday, on the day which Jesus Christ conquered death, Christians around the world congregate together to worship Him. Wherever Christians commit themselves to meet regularly at an appointed time, that congregation is called a "church," and the place where they come together to worship is called a "sanctuary." In the sanctuary, before God's presence, worshipers are expected to place their faith, not in their own merit or self-righteousness (Luke 18:9), but in Jesus Christ and what He has done to demonstrate God's righteousness (Rom 3:26). For people who have been created in God's image, the only legitimate identity for Christians is Christ. Therefore, worship is a great equalizer, since through worship, worshipers are reminded of their true identity in Christ—"and have put on the new self, which is being renewed in knowledge in the image of its Creator. Here there [are] no Greeks... slave or free, but Christ is all, and is in all" (Col 3:10-11). In this way, the true spiritual unity of a congregation takes place when the worshipers place their faith in God's redemptive work through His Son Jesus Christ (Eph 2:14-18).

Part II - Worship in the Land at an Altar, without a Tabernacle or Temple Building

An Altar as a Place to Approach God

The first form of worship appears in Genesis 4 when Cain and Abel brought the fruits of their labor to the Lord as "an offering" (vv. 3-4). Although the exact word "altar" is not mentioned in this first appearance of worship (and in fact does not appear until Noah "built an altar" in response to God's saving grace (Gen 8:20) through which he and his family "were saved through water" in 1 Peter 3:20), it is most likely that Cain and Abel did use an altar when they made their offerings to God.

5

WORSHIP AS A MEANS TO APPROACH GOD

Since there is a separation, a chasm between God and mankind, after the Fall, people could only approach God through worship with an offering. Worship is the way man responds to and expresses acknowledgment of God's grace upon the fruit of man's work. It was never left to the worshiper to decide the form of worship but rather the worshiper had to approach God on God's own terms. Because God sets the terms of engagement in worship, one cannot assume all worship to God is acceptable. It is expected of the worshiper and it is his responsibility to know whether God approves or disapproves of, accepts or rejects the worship. It was in the context of worship that God still spoke to mankind even after the Fall. Therefore, worshipers ought to seek to hear what God has to say—"Guard your steps when you go to the house of God. Go near to listen ... God is in heaven and you are on earth, so let your words be few" (Ecc 5:1-2).

Although God is omnipresent, God has graciously invited us to approach Him. When sin resulted in a broken relationship with God, He provided a means through which we could approach Him, which was worship. Throughout history and in every culture, though specific beliefs about gods or spiritual beings may have differed, human beings have always been worshipers, and they brought some form of offering to a designated place (usually a place known as spiritual or sacred) for their gods. A sacrifice was offered either to please the spirits or coerce the gods to do what the people could not do with their own power (i.e., protect their families or village from other bad spirits, etc.). Sometimes an offering was offered in the hopes of having some type of spiritual communication or seeking the spirits' response. It is a deeply embedded principle in human religious culture that relatively powerless human beings cannot approach a higher power or spirits without an offering or the right "formulas" (methodology). Religious people in general have always felt obligated to do something for or give something to their gods if they were going to be on good terms with their deities.

Bridging the Gap between God and Man

Offerings and worship in the bible are fundamentally different from any other kind of religious worship. The starting point for biblical worship, rather than being man seeking God, is God graciously inviting people back to Himself in order to restore the broken relationship through the means of worship. When the covenant was broken and Adam and Eve were "banished [them] from the Garden... the east side of the Garden" (Gen 3:23-24), we are still able to see God's grace; they were cast out from the Garden in order to be kept from being in the sinful state forever by taking "the tree of life" and "liv[ing] forever" (v. 22).

Until the coming of the true reality when the woman's offspring would break down the barrier of sin between God and man once and for all, God, in His grace, provided a way called "worship" that foreshadowed this reality. Sinful people could not just approach God who was holy, but through worship, they could approach God to restore and continue to have a relationship with Him and experience His presence.

Although God was always invisible, whether in or outside of the Garden, people could still approach God in worship to have a relationship with Him. Worship existed before the Fall, but after the Fall, specific requirements of offering and sacrifice became necessary elements if one were to approach God. Yet it was not so much the offerings themselves but rather faith expressing itself through obedience to the God who required such offerings that was key. Unless there was faith, clearly recognizing the separation between the holy God and sinful man, man would continue in his own presumptuousness, expecting God to be obligated to give man what he wants and meet man's expectation of how God should be.

Man's Response to God's Grace

Now the ministry, serving God or worship, was separated from work (Gen 4:2). Unlike in the Garden, we could assume it was labor-intensive, whether tending flocks for Abel or farming for Cain; surely life in the land that had been cursed by God was toilsome (Gen 5:29). Before, in the Garden, their whole life was dedicated in service to God, whether they ate, drank, or worked. Now in Genesis 4, people had to work for the harvest in order to sustain their lives physically. Part of their happiness in life came from enjoying the fruit of their labor. But unless man recognized that being able to enjoy the result of his hard work came from God, the true life-giver and the Creator of all things, he would not be able to truly enjoy God's general grace to all mankind—"A man can do nothing better than to eat and drink and find satisfaction in his work. This too... is from the hand of God" (Ecc 2:24).

For this reason, both Abel and Cain brought offerings, the fruits of their labors, to the Lord (Gen 4:2-4). What they brought to the Lord was a reminder of God's grace upon their labor. Therefore, worship is a form of expression recognizing and in response to God's grace upon the worshipers' life. In that sense, for Christians there is no distinction between how we serve God in the new covenant community, church, and outside of church in a secular world, being faithful to what God has given, our so-called "secular" careers. Worshipers give offering to the Lord in response to what God has been doing in their lives, especially in their work, whether sacred or secular.

Walter Kaiser commented on the grain offering from Leviticus 2 in the following:

The idea that the grain offering was a "memorial" also signifies that one purpose of an offering is to jog memories. We often think of an offering only in the task oriented sense; that is, we put money in the offering plate to pay for the church expenses, to feed hungry people, to send the youth choir to choir camp, and so on. In other words, we tend to think of offerings as means to get things done… but Leviticus suggests that one of the most basic reasons we make offerings is not so that something will get done but so that something will be brought to mind. (*The New Interpreter's Bible*, p. 1020)

Although both Abel and Cain approached God with their fruits, for some reason there was a distinction made between the two worshipers. Many have undertaken to come up with and have mistakenly given the reasons behind the distinction. One of the common errors lies on wrongly focusing on the offerings themselves rather than the worshipers. We need to note, it was not just Abel's offering or Cain's offering that God had accepted or rejected—"the Lord looked on Abel and his offering… Cain and his offering" (Gen 4:4-5). Prior to any offering that is accepted or rejected by God, it is the person, the worshiper and his relationship with and standing before God that takes precedence.

Hebrews 11:4 interprets and gives us the clear reason for the distinction that was made—"By faith Abel offered God a better sacrifice than Cain did. By faith he was commended." Basically Abel had faith in God while Cain did not. We can assume that Cain did have faith about God—a belief in His existence and his (Cain's) religious obligation and duty to that God, but this was not enough. Just as in Genesis 4, the author of Hebrews places emphasis on the two worshipers rather than on what they offered.

What was it that made the person Abel and what he offered accepted by God? It was Abel's faith by which "he was commended as a righteous man" (Heb 11:4); again the emphasis is on the person with faith. Basically, Abel was relating to God in faith while Cain approached God without any relationship with Him. Perhaps, Cain did not really believe God was the source of all blessings on this earth, especially the fruit of his hard labor.

Two verses down in Hebrews 11:6 it says, "And without faith it is impossible to please God, because anyone who comes to him must believe that he exists and that he rewards those who earnestly seek him." We can see this verse as a summary describing the faith of the two men mentioned just previously. The language of the first part of the verse about pleasing God connects it to Enoch who is described in verse 5, and the reference to coming to God in the second part of the verse connects it to Abel who is described in verse 4 as doing just this when he brought his offering to God.

Both Abel and Cain approached God in worship with offerings; the right form and right offerings were there. But what was really missing in the person Cain was the faith that believed God "exists" and "rewards those who earnestly seek him" (v. 6b). In other words, Abel believed God was the creator (Heb 11:1-4) who sustained and the giver of all good things (Acts 14:17). Abel did not approach the altar just to fulfill his religious duty but really believed there was a living relationship between himself and God. For Abel, it was never a monologue or one-way relationship, but a dialogue; just as we respond in worship to God's grace upon our lives, God also responds to our faith in Him. Like Enoch, Abel was commended for his faith in God.

This really strikes at the heart of worshipers in our days. On the average given Sunday morning, much of the church gathering has become a theatrical institution; the congregation is more interested in hearing a "good" sermon and singing culturally trendy songs than expressing a worshipful response to God's grace shown during the weekdays of their busy working hours. One does not need such a recognition of God's grace in order to get excited about and participate in listening to a sermon, engaging in singing in worship, or giving ten percent of their earnings. Like the people of northern Israel, perhaps those are the things we "love" to do (Amos 4:4-5).

A person has to be redeemed first to be a true worshiper of God. Paul and Barnabas were preaching "the good news" to the people in Lystra, "telling [them] to turn from... worthless things to the living God" (Acts 4:15). There is God's general grace given to all mankind (v. 17). But like David in Psalm 19, it takes faith in God's written word (vv. 7-11) for eyes to see that God is the author and creator. When a person, through the preaching of the gospel, places his faith in the Savior Lord Jesus Christ who was cursed on our behalf on the cross (Gal 3:13), his eyes will be opened, and he will turn from darkness to light (Acts 25:18). Like Abel who had the eyes to see the invisible are those who have received the special grace of revelation so that they might give a legitimate response to God's grace in worship.

Approaching God on His Terms

For some reason, Cain knew his life was not pleasing to God (like some irreligious people might feel thinking if there were a God, the way they live might not be pleasing to him). When Cain knew that "The Lord… did not look with favor," he responded to God's response in anger. God spoke to Cain as though it was given that anyone who approached God in worship had the responsibility to know the kind of worship mandated by God. We can see God graciously correcting and reminding Cain—"If you do what is right, will you not be accepted" (Gen 4:7). The fruit of Cain's labor was on the altar, and perhaps he had the form of the worship right. But the acceptable offering was the offerer in his right standing with God. The true right "form" in worship was in the person who was performing the service to God.

Similarly, God rejected Saul "as a king over Israel" not because he failed to bring "the best of the sheep and cattle to sacrifice to the Lord" (1 Sam 15:15) but had "rejected the word of the Lord" (v. 26). Worship must flow out from the worshiper's heart of obedience to the Lord. This was the reason the prophet Samuel rebuked Saul, saying, "Does the Lord delight in burnt offerings and sacrifices as much as in obeying the voice of the Lord? To obey is better than sacrifice" (v. 22). It was not what Saul and others thought was better but rather what had clearly been revealed in the written *Torah*, that is, how God required to be worshiped on His terms.

God had clearly shown from the very beginning that He was interested in the person who was making the offering before the offering itself. Interestingly enough, there is a parallel between Cain and Saul in relation to worship and their lives afterwards. Cain thought if he got rid of his brother Abel, his competitor, that it would eliminate his problem of being rejected. Sadly Cain's understanding of worship was not vertical but rather limited to a horizontal, man-centered understanding. After God rejected Cain and his offering, Cain ended up becoming the first murderer in the history of mankind.

As with Cain, God also rejected Saul and his offerings. Although David was not exactly Saul's competitor in worship, Saul did want to keep his kingship and saw David as a new competitor for the throne (1 Sam 18:8). Therefore, Saul until nearly the end of his life ended up going after David's life, although God would not allow Saul's attempt to succeed (1 Sam 23:14).

Unlike the gods of this world, God cannot be manipulated by man's performance or offering. People cannot just assume that as long as their motive is "pure" and "right" and they give their best for some reason that they and their offerings would be accepted. This is so since God is foremost interested in receiving the worshipers before anything else is placed on the altar (Mat 5:23-24).

Why was God so meticulous about how He wanted to be worshiped? Why could God not leave it up to us humans to approach Him as we wish as long as we give our best? Rather than obeying and following God's word, naturally in our sinful nature, we gravitate towards following our own minds, hearts and instincts which often contradict God's will. If the choice were to be given, we would choose to serve ourselves and serve God out of our own convenience.

For this reason, later in Israel, having a "family shrine" or an individual one was strictly prohibited. The Israelites' worship of the Lord had to reveal and express God's kingship and complete obedience to His word, but they failed to do this after they entered the Promised Land. Interestingly enough, the Book of Judges ends with two tragic stories that begin with "In those days Israel had no king; everyone did as he saw fit" and concludes with the same reminder (Judges 17:6; 18:1; 19:1; 21:25). Those two tragic stories have their roots in idolatry, false worship and a Levite who was responsible for helping the priests to serve God rightly in matters of worship but failed to do so. It is a reminder that in order for us to serve and worship God, we must serve God as our King and follow His instructions, His word, regarding worship.

In our modern day Evangelical worship, three things typically have been highlighted: the message, music, and an emphasis on giving. In the city, what people especially are looking for is a message that is intellectually challenging and logically coherent without being offensive (i.e., politically correct and sensitive). The music has to be culturally relevant, engaging, and compatible to the modern pop music culture. As long as one can be attentive, engaged in, and committed to a regular giving in a Sunday worship service, the person safely assumes he has worshiped "well." Rather than constantly being taught by God's word regarding worship, worshipers are expected to just simply follow the worship service schedule and format. If the first activity that was described as being done by man after being cast out from the Garden was worship, then does God not have a say about worship in the Scripture? There is no greater need for the church today than learning about and pursuing the biblical worship that God has mandated for worshipers.

God's Acceptance of Our Worship

We do not know exactly how Cain knew his offering was not accepted by God, but somehow he knew it to the point that it got him upset and discouraged (Gen 4:5). We find something similar in nature for the contemporaries of the prophet Malachi in their days. There was much weeping and wailing from the worshipers since God was no longer paying attention "to [their] offerings or [accepting] them... from [their] hands" (Mal 2:13). Again, the text is not clear on how they knew, but they felt the worship and all its regulations and offerings were burdensome. They had lost sight of the great name of the Lord Almighty. As a result, they, especially the leaders who were supposed to control the quality of worship, did not take worship service seriously (Mal 1:11-13).

God's people before the new covenant were forgiven based on what God would do by sending His Son Jesus Christ "as a sacrifice of atonement" (Rom 3:25-26). In that sense, both those who are under the new covenant and those who came before are forgiven on the same ground, Christ's death and resurrection. What the people after the Fall and under the old covenant did, their worship rituals, was a "shadow of what is in heaven" (Heb 8:5). The true reality is Christ's perfect sacrificial death "once for all" (Heb 10:10).

For this reason, Moses by "faith... kept Passover" (Heb 11:28) knowing one day God would "raise up... a prophet like [him] from among [their] own brothers" (Deut 18:15) and ultimately bring the true exodus for His people through the cross (Matt 2:15; Luke 9:30-31).

Every Sunday Christians around the world gather together in different designated locations with the particular community of faith they are committed to called "church." Whether they know it or not, the worship they are offering to God in Christ's name has been already accepted based on what Christ has done on the cross, offering Himself to God the ultimate sacrifice. Anyone who has faith in Jesus Christ can "approach the throne of grace with confidence... by a new and living way opened for us through the curtain, that is, his body" (Heb 4:16 and 10:20).

Therefore, for the people under the new covenant in Christ, the issue is not whether or not God accepts their worship but rather do they have faith in Jesus and the God who "forgave... all... sins" (Col 2:13)? The greatest reward for those who earnestly seek Him in worship is being fully assured that their worship to God has been accepted because of Jesus Christ.

But sadly, modern day worshipers rarely consider the importance and deep appreciation of God graciously accepting our worship on the ground of Christ's perfect sacrifice. Instead, we are more concerned about a message focusing on "how to" and music that can stir up our emotions. Through worship, we seek to hear how to succeed in our society while God, who is spirit, seeks to find "true worshipers" who would "worship the Father in spirit and truth" (John 4:23).

In order for the true worship to take place, worshipers must have faith in Christ and His atoning sacrifice—the faith that does not rely on his or her own merits. On any given Sunday, worship should not take place in an atmosphere of uncertainty (i.e., "let's wait and see if God accepts or not"), but it should be a place where believers congregate themselves and have assurance, gratitude and a celebration of God accepting the believers based on the cross.

Although we know very little about Abel of Genesis 4, Hebrews 11:4 tells us that "he was commended as a righteous man," which is to be understood in the context of worship. How can a person be righteous when he is a sinner exiled from the Garden after the Fall? It is impossible unless there is God's favor, grace like Noah—"found favor in the eyes of the Lord... Noah was a righteous man, blameless among the people of his time" (Gen 6:8-9). In other words, like Noah, Abel was "commended as a righteous man" because he approached God believing God would accept him, not based on what he did or offered but based on God's promise of the woman's offspring (Gen 3:15); Abel approached God with this kind of faith; he lived like Noah's father, Lamech, who was waiting for God's comfort (Gen 5:28-29) by the coming of God's Son.

God Speaks in Worship

Just as God spoke to man in the Garden, the first time God spoke to man after man was banished from the Garden was in the worship setting. There were two ways God spoke to worshipers, especially to Cain: at the moment when the offering was made to the Lord, and after (Gen 4:5-6). Although God did not speak directly, the first instance possibly had to do with Cain's "inner conviction" while the offering was made; he somehow sensed that it was not being accepted by God. The second instance had to do with God reminding Cain of something he was supposed to know. Therefore, when God spoke, it was Cain's "inner realization" of something Cain already knew about the worship mandate.

Overall, God continued to speak to people - not to everyone, but to a small number of people, especially the line of Seth in Genesis 5. Individuals to whom God spoke specifically were called "prophets" (in Gen 20:7, for the first time in the Pentateuch, the word "prophet" appears referring to Abraham). We can say generally that prophets were the people to whom God spoke. We find in the Bible the main people God spoke to after the Fall were Cain and Noah, although it was most likely God spoke to Seth's descendants also.

Either during or after Cain's offering was made, God spoke regarding the need for living a right life and warning about the power of sin in Cain (Gen 4:7). Although this was not the only time God spoke, since our interest is in God speaking to man in the worship context, we will limit our discussion to Genesis 4:7 for Cain.

Through worship, the Holy Spirit in us gives us certain realizations through God's word that has already been planted in us. Not only is living "a life worthy of" (Eph 4:1) God's calling prior to worship important, but also after worship, living a life according to what God has spoken through the Holy Spirit during worship. Someone once said that worship that was not worthy of living out was a painted lie. Whenever God speaks through worship, it must bring us to change the way we live, bring us to repentance or an awareness of sin's proximity that is much closer than we think it is. Unfortunately, Cain did not repent or take God's warning seriously enough to struggle with sin but ended up letting sin take its toll.

Being convicted of our sins is inevitable in worship when we experience God's holiness (Isa 6:5) and see the purity of Christ (2 Cor 5:20). The result of having such conviction does not bring us to a place of being overwhelmed by guilt but rather to a deeper appreciation of the cross and a greater desire to become like God's children who would want to model after their God the Father (Eph 5:1) as God has spoken, "be holy, because I am holy" (Lev 11:44). What a privilege and honor—"Both the one who makes men holy and those who are made holy are of the same family. So Jesus is not ashamed to call them brothers" (Heb 2:11). This verse should be understood in the context of worship according to the following verse 12. In other words, in worship, we are reminded of who we are and made to become, the children of God.

6

WORSHIP AS CALLING ON THE NAME OF YAHWEH

The first form of worship in the Bible was performed by individuals rather than as a community. Perhaps it was still an early stage of the human population on the land. G. Ch. Aalders sees Genesis 4:26, "to call on the name of the Lord" as a "public worship" based on other Old Testament references (Pss79:6;116:17; Jer 10:25). Aalders goes on to say,

"The emphasis must fall on the public character of this worship. Naturally we are not to think of a highly developed liturgy such as was established by the Mosaic laws. It was something far more simple and elementary. This development of communal worship was, moreover, also a further indication of the advance of culture. But among the Sethites this cultural development took an entirely different direction than it did among the Cainites." (G. Charles Aalders, *Bible Student Commentary*, pp.135-36)

Culture and Subculture

The first instance of worship with Cain and Abel was about whose worship was accepted by God. Now Genesis 4:16-26 tells us of a subculture (vv. 25-26) within a dominant culture (vv. 16-24), a contrast between Cain's and Seth's descendants. Although God specifically said that Cain would be "a restless wanderer on the earth [*eretz*]" (v. 12), most likely in order to avoid this very wandering, Cain went to the east of Eden, "lived in the land of Nod" and became a city builder (vv. 16-17).

In a way, the first city that was built by Cain was another form of man's struggle against God's judgment (the "cursed ground" and becoming a "wanderer"). The city revealed man fighting to live apart from God; building the city was man's attempt to prove that he could live without God for a "better" and more "secure" life.

We do not have all the details, whether or not Cain's parents, Adam and Eve, went together with him, but the author Moses does make a clear distinction between Cain and his other brother Seth of verse 25. It is another reminder that in this world, there is a main, dominant culture that is very much prevalent but secular, without the awareness of God, but there is also another culture, a subculture, less visible; in the mainstream society, this subculture oftentimes goes unnoticed because it is considered unimportant by the dominant culture.

These two cultures have always coexisted with one another. The mainstream society's moral decadence is highlighted with the conclusion of Cain's descendant Lamech— how he avenged with murder and viewed God's judgment (vv. 23-24). It is interesting to note that Lamech is recorded as the seventh generation from Adam. Unlike the descendants of Seth in the following chapter, the length of number of years is not mentioned for Lamech and his descendants. It could be that the author Moses was making another sharp contrast between Lamech and Enoch, who was also from the seventh generation from Adam (Gen 5:18-24). This shows that living a godly life with an awareness of God, like Enoch did, does not take an ideal environment; it can take place within a secular culture.

Like any other modern city, the city that Cain built had much of man's ingenuity and cultural advancement—domestication, music and technology (vv. 20-22). Domestication is a necessity for the food we eat. Music is a form of art that expresses what is on our hearts and minds, touches our emotion and imagination; it brings us to an appreciation of beauty. Technology grants us convenience and more efficiency of labor. Yet with all these that are helpful for us to live a better life, if God is absent from our culture, we are not living up to the full potential of the way God originally intended for us to live in His image. Surely, "man does not live on bread alone but on every word that comes from the mouth of the Lord" (Deut 8:3)!

We can appreciate beauty and experience pleasure through the means of music. But there is a beauty beyond what music can produce and a satisfaction beyond our experience of pleasure through music. If music can serve as an aide for us to serve God in worship, "to gaze upon the beauty of the Lord" (Ps 27:4), then we are fully utilizing what God has given to us so we can live up to the primary purpose of mankind, finding pleasure in worshiping the Creator.

Although not much is written about their cultural contribution to the society, the subculture that is represented by another group of people, Seth's descendants (vv. 25-26), nevertheless fulfilled the purpose of what God had intended in creation, that is, worship. Unlike the culture of Noah's days that was spiritually mixed because of the attractiveness of other peoples' physical beauty and strength (Gen 6:1-2), Seth's descendants did not try to adopt or assimilate into the secular culture; rather, they were known as a worshiping community.

It is most likely that the worshiping community was in close contact with the city that Cain started or lived right in the heart of the city. They were part of the mainstream society, yet they continued to maintain their subculture, worship, which was never replaced with the main dominant culture.

Today, especially in the major cities, the art of worship has been replaced by simply art. The beauty of the invisible Lord has been replaced with external beauty apart from moral purity. The musical worship has been gradually replaced by musical concerts. There is much confusion about the spiritual experience with people assuming whatever emotional experience they go through is spiritual. When art and technology are put together to design and make instruments that would help the worshipers seek His face, the subculture controls and protects the unseen spiritual condition of the society; it offers a completely different counterpart for a moral standard of living.

When domestication, art and technology have already been part of the main cultural development, it is imperative that church must maintain the subculture and their identity as a worshiping community. When a church loses saltiness in her society, there is no clear right or wrong moral standard, and she presents no alternative to the society that she is a part of.

Worship as Declaration, Confession

Prior to Genesis 4:26, it was a person who brought an offering to the Lord, but in the time of Seth and his descendants, "people began to call on the name of" Yahweh. Although we see later that Noah, Abraham and other individuals approached the altar alone, in Genesis 4:26, the emphasis is placed on a community. Just as God is triune—unity in the community of the Trinity—when a community comes together to worship in unity, that worship reflects the Triune God. Therefore, "people began to call" is crucial to understanding that worship has to be done corporately if it is supposed to reflect who God is.

How can a sinful heart confess the holy name of God, Yahweh? Unless there is a cleansing of our hearts, we will just merely give lip service to God as the prophet Isaiah prophesied, "These people come near to me with their mouth and honor me with their lips, but their hearts are far from me" (Isa 29:13). James warned us that what we say and confess comes from our hearts. Therefore, if it is a true confession from the heart, then it would be utterly impossible to "praise our Lord... and curse men" from the same heart (Jas 3:9-11). The only way that blatant contradiction would be possible is if what we say does not come from the heart. Therefore, to "call on the name of the Lord" in Genesis 4:26 should be taken as the corporate confession that Yahweh is the only true living God, and this Creator God whom Seth and his descendants served and worshiped is the same God whom the Israelites were called to serve and worship.

In Zephaniah 3, God speaks of the future judgment on both Israel and the rest of the nations in verses 1-8. At every level of leadership and in every area of the city of Jerusalem, Israel's center for both worship and politics, corruption was rampant (vv. 1-5), affecting both the religious sphere and the society at large. But as strange it may sound, God's judgment is followed by God purifying "the lips of the peoples, that all of them may call on the name of" Yahweh (v. 9). This purification of the peoples would only be possible when the Son of God would come and take on God's wrath upon

Himself - then "the offerings... will be acceptable to the Lord" (Mal 3:1-4).

The temple and worshipers would be cleansed when Jesus Christ as the "Lamb of God... takes away the sin of the world" (John 1:29). As a prophetic act, Jesus clears the temple (John 2:13-22) two times, in the earlier and latter parts of His ministry, foreshadowing what His death would bring in reality. To cleanse the physical temple means to cleanse the community of believers. For this reason, the author of Hebrews tells us, "Through Jesus, therefore, let us continually offer to God a sacrifice of praise—the fruit of lips that confess his name" (Heb 13:15).

Worship is about speaking forth "Jesus is Lord" from the heart by the work of the Holy Spirit (1 Cor 12:3), and singing praise is calling on the name of Christ melodically (Eph 5:19-20; Col 3:16-17). Through worship, the redeemed community, the church, declares Jesus is Lord and no other. In this sense, one of the words used to describe worship is connected with bowing down (shachah). The first time the word is used in the Bible is Genesis 18:2. Although Abraham was unaware that the three visitors were angels and one of them was Yahweh appearing in human form (theophany), Abraham "bowed low to the ground." Most likely not knowing they were angelic beings, Abraham was greeting and welcoming them (Heb 13:2) with the bowing gesture, which was typical in that culture (Gen 19:1; 23:7). But interestingly, one of them (Gen 18:22) could have been Yahweh.

In worship we declare Christ's lordship. We renounce all other competing members, the idols in our hearts, and renew our commitment to the Lord and Him only—"Who may ascend the hill of the Lord?... He who has clean hands and a pure heart, who does not lift up his soul to an idol" (Ps 24:3-4). For this reason, the message that is preached during the Sunday worship service has to be God-centered and affirm Christ's lordship. It should remind and guide the worshipers who have to practice their faith in the secular culture to keep themselves "from being polluted by the world" (Jas 1:27) by submitting to God's will.

Rather than trying to balance our time and energy between work and ministry, as we work in a secular environment and do ministry in the new covenant community, the church, we need to make every effort to "be holy" in the society. God's calling upon the church is being the "salt of the earth… the light of the world" (Matt 5:13-16). Does this not presuppose the world that we live in is decaying and dark in the eyes of our Lord Jesus Christ? Rather than spending our energy trying to assimilate into our mainstream culture or making the gospel relevant to the current culture, the church needs to maintain her "subculture" and continue to proclaim and "call on the name of the Lord" in worship.

7

WORSHIP AS PRIMARILY A SERVICE TO GOD FOR THE REDEEMED

In the Garden, it being the sanctuary of God, whatever man did, in a way, was a service to God. Therefore, there was no separation between work and ministry. When the covenant was broken and man was cast out from the Garden, man could only approach God with an offering before an altar. In that sense, the altar (or for that matter, the tabernacle or temple building) served as a reminder that there is a barrier and separation between God who was holy and the sinful man. Although the Garden was guarded to keep man from having the access "to the tree of life" (Gen 3:24), God in His grace allowed and invited man to have access to the true and living God through making sacrifices to the Lord in worship, with the hope that one day there would no longer be any barrier between God and man—"I did not see a temple in the city, because the Lord God Almighty and the Lamb are its temple" (Rev 21:22); just as the Garden was God's sanctuary, in the future, the entire city, the heavenly Jerusalem, will be God's sanctuary, the fullness of God's presence in all of its splendor and glory—"Now the dwelling of God is with men, and he will live with them. They will be his people, and God himself will be with them and be their God" (v. 3).

Covenant of Works and Covenant of Grace

The life of worship, service devoted to God in the Garden, for Adam was the result of a covenant relationship between himself and God. This covenant was based on Adam's work; Adam was supposed to keep God's word and not break the covenant by eating from the tree of the knowledge of good and evil (Gen 2:17). God's calling on Adam's life was to serve Him by working the Garden. Therefore, worship, serving God by working in the Garden, was Adam's daily life activity because Adam was in a covenant relationship with God.

Once man became sinful, the covenant with God could no longer be based on "work" since no man in his sinful state could keep such a covenant; when the human "heart is deceitful above all things and beyond cure" (Jer 17:9) and love and commitment are "like the morning mist, like the early dew that disappears" (Hosea 6:4), our relationship with God can only be established and sustained by God's grace and faithfulness.

Until the Woman's Offspring, the Last Adam, the Son of David would come and live a perfectly obedient life, establishing a new covenant which is also based on work (like the First Adam) – this work being Christ's work, not man's – God's covenants with Noah, Abraham, the nation Israel through Moses, and David could only be based on God's grace, God's promise apart from man's work. Those who approach God in worship must see the whole act of worship as not an end in itself but only a shadow of the reality, Christ's perfect sacrifice (Heb 9:13-14).

It is interesting to note that prior to God establishing a covenant (*berit*) with Noah (Gen 6:18), he was introduced as someone who "found favor in the eyes of the Lord" (v. 8) rather than one who had merit; therefore, God's covenant with Noah was based on God's grace. Noah was warned about the "floodwaters" though most likely he had never experienced or seen rain coming down from the sky. In other words, Noah had to have faith; he had to trust God enough to prepare, making the ark for the coming judgment of God.

Clean, Pure or Unclean

It would have made more sense to bring only the "clean" animals into the ark, but God commanded Noah to "take... seven of every... clean animal, a male and its mate, and two of every kind of unclean animal" (Gen 7:2). The word "clean" (*tahor*) is used to describe animals, people, things (especially gold), places or the dietary law in the Pentateuch.

God had told the first high priest, Aaron, "You must distinguish between the holy and the common, between the unclean and the clean" (Lev 10:10). Just as the word "holy" carries the meaning of being set apart for God, the word "clean" should be understood in the context of dedication to the Lord rather than as some kind of intrinsic cleanliness. For this reason in the New Testament, when Peter responded to the Lord in his vision experience, "I have never eaten anything impure or unclean," God told Peter, "Do not call anything impure that God has made clean" (Acts 10:14-15). Later at Cornelius' house, Peter said, "God accepts men from every nation who fear him and do what is right" (v. 34-35). Therefore, the biblical understanding of "clean," like "good" in Genesis 1-2, especially in the Pentateuch, should be understood in reference to things, animals, or a person who is set apart, to be dedicated for the purpose of God's acceptance.

Once again acceptable worship is not just about acceptable offerings but how the worshipers themselves and their lives must be dedicated to and set apart for God since God's people under the new covenant in Christ "have been made holy" (Heb 10:10). Christians are called to "honor God with [their] bod[ies]" (1 Cor 6:20). We worship God with faith, believing that God has accepted us based on Christ's death that brought us to God (1 Peter 3:18). We are "a new batch without yeast... the yeast of malice and wickedness, but with bread without yeast" (1 Cor 5:8). Therefore, our worship has to be sincere and truthful.

God's Response to Worship

When God told Noah to bring clean animals into the ark, He had in mind that some of those clean animals would be used for burnt offerings (Gen 8:20). Here for the first time a specific type of offering appears in the Bible, the burnt offering. We do not know exactly how the offering was offered to God prior to Noah. But in examining burnt offering we seek to answer the following questions: 1) Why was worship in the form of burnt offering the first thing that Noah did after coming out from the ark? 2) What is it about worship that pleases the Lord? 3) How does (or should) God's covenant with Noah give us a model to follow in the way we worship?

The burnt form of offering was probably the most popular way of offering at that time and continued to be until the time of Jesus in the Middle Eastern religions. In the Mosaic Law, at the very beginning of Leviticus, meticulous prescriptions for how the burnt offering should be offered were given. Unlike other types of offerings, the emphases of the burnt offering are on offering its totality and creating smoke that one could both see and smell (Lev 1:3-17).

Just as God "remembered Noah and all the wild animals and the livestock that were with him in the ark" (Gen 8:1), Noah must have remembered God's saving grace and "built an altar to the Lord," offering a burnt offering to Yahweh (v. 20). Noah knew why God made a clear distinction between the clean and unclean among the animals. In a way, one can say that the primary purpose for the clean animals to be in the ark was for them to be reserved and saved with Noah through the flood in order to become the offerings to the Lord. For this reason, as Noah, by God's grace, experienced salvation from judgment, the first thing Noah did was worship by building an altar and offer burnt offerings to the Lord.

Just as the water/flood was the form of God's judgment for the entire world in the Noah's days, later the Red Sea would serve as God's judgment upon Pharaoh and his army when the Israelites came out of Egypt (Exod 14:27-28). Just as Noah's family members were saved with Noah (with whom God established a covenant) since "Noah found favor in the eyes of the Lord" (Gen 6:8), the Israelites were identified with Moses in the Exodus, went through the Red Sea with Moses, and "they all ate the same spiritual food and drank the same spiritual drink" (1 Cor 10:3-4). All this is to say that the two great events of God's judgment with water foreshadowed how God in the Last Days would save His people—"These things happened to them as examples and were written down as warnings for us, on whom the fulfillment of the ages has come" (v. 11).

Noah and his family, "only a few people, eight in all were saved through water, and this water symbolizes baptism that now saves you also" (1 Peter 3:20-21). Just as Noah and his family and the Israelites were saved, not by going around, avoiding the flood or the Red Sea but rather going "through water," the people under the new covenant in Christ went through the final judgment of God on the cross as they have been identified with Christ (Gal 2:20) when they have placed their faith in Christ, which is one of the main meanings of baptism.

Just as Noah offered burnt offerings on the altar after experiencing God's salvation, the Israelites after witnessing God's salvation of Exodus and having gone through the Red Sea, "Moses and the Israelites sang" the song of salvation (Exod 15:1-18). It should be the same song, the song that needs to be sung in every Lord's Day worship service, for those who have been redeemed by the blood of the Lamb. This was the exact same worshipers of the new covenant the apostle John saw in his visionary experience —"... God's wrath is completed. And I saw what looked like a sea of glass mixed with fire and, standing beside the sea... they held harps given them by God and sang the song of Moses... and the song of the Lamb" (Rev 15:1-3)—the sea and fire all remind of God's judgment and His wrath.

Of course not every song that is sung in worship should be limited to the cross, but every song should have its reason and be grounded in Christ's cross and resurrection. The only reason Christians can worship and why worship is the foremost activity as a community of faith is because they have been redeemed and have experienced the incredible work of God's salvation on the cross. It would be unthinkable for us to try to engage in any form of worship, whether with spiritual songs or the message of God's word, without such gratitude and faith in Christ. Worshiping God is the most natural response of the redeemed to God who is the author of the supernatural redemptive work.

Worship that Pleases the Lord

Why is the aroma from the burnt offering in Genesis 8:20 described as the "pleasing aroma?" Surely it was not that the smell of burning meat was pleasant! The best way to understand this is to see it from the worshiper's experience while the burnt offering was offered since the worshiper was given specific instruction on how it should be offered to the Lord. It would not just be an act of imagination for the worshiper, but through his act of service to God, the worshiper would be experiencing the sight, smell, and sound of the burnt offering. Just as the black burning smoke was rising upward into the sky, visually the worshiper was experiencing and being reminded of how important it was for his service to God to reach and touch the footstool of God; it was also a visual way of experiencing God accepting the worshiper's service to God. This is so since human beings are very much sight- and sound-oriented.

Whatever was placed on the altar for a burnt offering was to be burned up completely. It was a reminder of the importance for the worshiper to have a complete, nothing reserved, full dedication to God. Christ's death is the burnt offering par excellence —"Be imitators of God... and live a life of love, just as Christ loved us and gave himself up for us as a fragrant offering and sacrifice to God" (Eph 5:1-2). When we lay down our life for God and for others just as Christ has done, completely surrendering and in obedience to God, there is no greater love and sacrifice (John 15:13).

Was there anything for Noah to hold back before God when he and his family had just experienced and survived an unimaginable catastrophe? When Noah came out from the ark, he saw a world that had been completely destroyed, no sign of human beings or the remains of their belongings. Before anxiously getting busy to find a location to find a haven of rest after being confined to the ark for nearly a year, Noah gathered stones and taking "some of all the clean animals... sacrificed burnt offering on it" (Gen 8:20).

Noah had witnessed the depravity of humanity for six hundred years before he entered the ark. Based on God's warning and promise, he had faithfully preached for a hundred and twenty years while the ark was being built (Gen 6:3). What more could he have done? Build up another shelter or tent that would eventually be worn out?

Every Lord's day, as we enter into worship, as we gaze upon the cross, we see life's paradox in Jesus—"Whoever finds his life will lose it, and whoever loses his life for my sake will find it" as Jesus has said (Matt 10:39). After having lost everything, in a way, the only thing Noah could do was to worship God in complete surrender, including his life, on the altar. Worship becomes a unique opportunity for us to continually commit to live a life of surrender to the One who gave up His life for us.

Hearing the Heart of God

As the smoke from the burnt offering was rising up into the sky and the burning fragrance was permeating the air, Noah was hearing God's heart that God would never again destroy "all living creatures as [He has] done" (Gen 8:21-22). Just as God blessed the First Adam after Adam was created, now God blessed Noah with the same blessing, with some elaboration (Gen 9:1-17). Just as Adam was given a command to keep, now Noah was again given a command that revolved around the importance of the fact that man has been created in God's image (vv. 4-6).

If the tree of the knowledge of good and evil in the Garden served as a sign of God's covenant with Adam, the rainbow would serve as a sign of God's covenant with Noah and "all life on the earth" (v. 17). Just as God established a covenant with one man Adam in the Garden that included all people, living creatures and the land, God's covenant with Noah included "every living creature on earth" (v. 9-10).

In this sense, the new covenant, which is the covenant between God the Father and God the Son, Jesus Christ, based on Christ's work (John 17:4), made all those under the new covenant included in Christ and therefore righteous (Romans 5:18-19). Christ's life of complete obedience on earth from the beginning of His earthly ministry (Matt 3:15-17) to the end (Heb 5:7), ultimately "obedient to death—even death on a cross" (Phil 2:8), becomes the sign of the Father and the Son's faithfulness to the covenant.

In the Lord's Supper, the worshipers are drawn to the table, hearing the very heart of God—"This is my Son, whom I love; with him I am well pleased" (Matt 3:17). As the worshipers participate in the Lord's Supper, they are reminded of Christ's faithfulness and obedience, how because of

His death, they are made righteous (Rom 5:19); they stand in the very presence of God not as the condemned, but righteous. As the worshipers remember Christ's sacrifice, see the elements, touch and break the bread, taste and drink the cup, as strange and mysterious as it may sound, a real spiritual fellowship takes place between God and His people that the world would never know. No wonder Jesus said, "Do this in remembrance of me" (Luke 22:22:19).

The covenant with Noah, that never again would the world be destroyed by a flood, was God's unconditional commitment to His covenant apart from man's work. The covenant with Noah was supposed to serve as a sign of God's faithfulness to His promise, and human beings were expected to trust God's promise and be secure in Him rather than attempt to live apart from God like the people of Babel did in Genesis 11:4.

In worship, worshipers like Noah have the privilege to hear the very heart of God. All Christians have experienced God's faithfulness that was climactically shown on the cross. It does not end there, however, but continues on. Based on God's redemptive work, our souls are continually nourished through God's faithfulness to His promise—"he who began a good work in [us] will carry it on to completion until the day of Christ Jesus" (Phil 1:6).

As we look around the world, can anything be fully trusted or guaranteed? Our future looks awfully dim "under the sun" in the absence of God (Ecc 1:14). Although life in general has become more convenient and comfortable thanks to the ongoing advancement of modern science and technology, they have also resulted in new problems like the unusual change in the climate due to global warming and pollution, and we continue to struggle for a better life and improve our living condition, without an awareness or acknowledgment of God's faithfulness to the future or having an eternal perspective in mind.

Human history continues to move in one direction, which the Sovereign God has ordained. Ever since the death and resurrection of the Son of God, the Last Days have begun (Acts 2:17). There is God's ultimate grace —"in these last days he has spoken to us by his Son… sustaining all things by his powerful word" (Heb 1:2-3). Can there be anything more secure than God's word and His faithful promise? Life is sustained by Christ who is the very "image of the invisible God... in him all things hold together" (Col 1:15, 17). Noah had but a glimpse of God's faithfulness to His promise in comparison to the full revelation of God in humanity Jesus Christ, who is highly exalted and sitting at God's "right hand until [God makes his] enemies a footstool for [his] feet" (Ps 110:1). In the midst of a constantly changing and unstable world, the unchanging God is faithful to His promise—who can but worship Christ?

8

WORSHIP AS THE FIRST PRIORITY FOR THOSE WHO HAVE BEEN CALLED BY GOD

In the case of Cain and Abel, the issue was whether man would worship in faith or simply out of a religious duty, without faith or a relationship with the living God. In the case of Cain and his descendants who represented the mainstream secular culture versus the line of Cain's brother Seth who had formed a subculture, the issue was whether man would acknowledge God and call on the name of Yahweh in worship or whether they would live in the absence of God. After the people of Babel were scattered and by the time we come to Abram in Genesis 12, the readers are led to assume that the people believed in different gods while at the same time being somewhat familiar with Yahweh, the One who called Abram to leave his country Haran (Gen 11:31, 12:1).

As we continue our study on worship by looking at the way God related to Abram, we will examine the following questions: What was God's purpose in calling Abram to leave his people to go to the "land" that God would show him? What was the reason behind Abram's regular practice of building an altar? Why did Abram continue to move from one place to another rather than settle down? Why did Abram give a tenth of what was recovered to the kingly priest Melchizedek? What is the relationship between worship and making a covenant? Why was Abram's faith tested?

God's Calling Back to the Land

Geographically, if people were to have tried to get back to the Garden, they would have had to move towards the west (Gen 3:24). When Adam and Eve were cast out from the Garden, they moved toward the east. Cain did the same (Gen 4:16), and the people after Noah also continued to "[move] eastward ... [and] found a plain in Shinar and settled there" (Gen 11:2). Abram's father Terah was from Ur of the Chaldeans (Gen 11:28). Along with Shinar, Ur was one of the farthest points east of Canaan mentioned in Genesis 11.

For some reason, Terah and his family "set out from Ur of the Chaldeans to go to Canaan. But when they came to Haran, they settled there" (Gen 11:31). As we often find in the biblical narratives, many of the details, especially regarding the reason behind the decision or action, are left out. We do not know exactly why Terah decided to leave for Canaan but ended up settling in Haran. But readers have the entire story of the Pentateuch, from Genesis to Deuteronomy, as a backdrop which can help provide a better understanding of reasons behind various decisions or actions made therein.

God had prepared the Land and placed Adam in the Garden where Adam and Eve were to serve/worship and have fellowship with God. Although they were later banished from the Garden, they were still in the Land and supposed to seek relationship with Yahweh and worship Him only. But people, who wanted to live apart from God, continued to move eastward, farther away from the Land, Canaan, the land which God had prepared, farther away from that land God originally blessed Adam and Eve, and Noah to fill by being "fruitful and increas[ing] in number" (Gen 1:28; 9:1).

We are able to see this movement back towards Canaan in the funeral procession for Jacob that went from Egypt to Canaan in Genesis 50. Eveson's comment is insightful:

"This pilgrimage to Canaan was an acted prophecy of what would happen when they would eventually leave Egypt. The route they took was a long and cumbersome one. They did not enter from the south into Canaan but went round the Dead Sea area and crossed over the Jordan near to Jericho [from the east]. We are not told why they did this. In the providence of God it anticipated the Exodus route. There is an ultimate homecoming, when God's people from all nations will come to the mountain of the Lord (Isa. 2:2-4)." (Philip Eveson, *The Book of Origins*, p. 571)

It is very likely that the fact that Terah died in Haran on his way to Canaan (Gen 11:32) foreshadows how the first generation of Israelites who came out of Egypt to go to the Promised Land, Canaan, would die in the desert and never make it.

God called Terah's son, Abram to "leave ... and go to the land [God would] show" him (Gen 12:1). This time, unlike his father, Abram and his family "arrived" in Canaan, and his story unfolds within the Land of Canaan. God spoke to and called Abram "while he was still in Mesopotamia" (Acts 7:2). It was not every day that God called someone. It was not a common thing to hear God's voice. Later God referred to Abraham as a "prophet" (Gen 20:7), and this is where the word appears for the first time in the Bible. Surely, hearing God's voice as a prophet was a rare thing, just as it was in the days of Eli in 1 Samuel 3:1.

We no longer have prophets in our days in the sense of there being individuals who are called, inspired and used by God to write His word, the Bible. But was there not a conviction from the Lord within each one of our hearts when we each heard the gospel and accepted Him —"those he predestined, he also called" (Rom 8:30)?

There could have been many people who heard the voices of the gods or spirits of the religions of Abram's days. How was Abram supposed to know that it was Yahweh who spoke to him? Could it be that the Creator God, the One who "created the heavens and the earth" and prepared the Land and Garden for people to dwell in to have fellowship with and serve Him, was the Yahweh who called Abram (and perhaps his father Terah in the past) to the land that He had in mind? And the Creator God and His creation story would have been continued to hand down from one generation to another. If so, it is no surprise for Abram and also the readers to see Abram being called into the Land, Canaan, to serve and worship God; in this way Abram is no different from Adam and Eve in the Garden, Abel, Seth's descendants, and Noah in the Land.

Not much has changed since Abraham's days. In our days, we have countless religions, different forms of religious practices, and beliefs in spirits and gods. In our pluralistic and spiritually diverse society where the rights of the individuals and their beliefs are to be respected, can there be one true God? If the Creator God in Genesis chapter one is the only true God and no other, then when one "hears" God's or a god's voice, how can the person have spiritual discernment and know the truth from falsehood or deception? Are our hearts longing to serve and worship the one and only true God of the Bible? Do we sense the separation between God and us because of the severity of sin? Do we believe in the woman's offspring about whom Moses later wrote (Deut 18:15) who is the divine being in humanity, Jesus Christ? It is He who said, "a time is coming when you will worship the Father neither on this mountain nor in Jerusalem... and has now come when the true worshipers will worship the Father in spirit and truth... I who speak to you am he [Messiah]" (John 4:21, 23, 26). Peter in one of his earlier encounters with Jesus could not help but to "[fall] at Jesus' knees" because he could not stand in the presence of Christ's holiness (Luke 5:8). Once Jesus revealed who He was to a blind man whose sight was restored and who was longing to believe in Christ, the man confessed that he did believe in Jesus and "worshiped him" (John 9:38).

So it is not about whether or not a person is religious or has some deep spiritual experience. It is not even about the knowledge a man has about gods which could be based on his own logic, assumption or speculation. God never asked us to figure Him out with our own minds and feelings. If that were the case, Abraham would have stayed in Haran and never obeyed God's call to Canaan. But by "faith Abraham... obeyed and went, even though he did not know where he was going" (Heb 11:8). "By faith [Moses] left Egypt... he saw him who is invisible" (v. 27). Like Abraham, now is the time for you to place your faith in the One who has died on the cross for your sins, Jesus Christ. The God who called Abraham out of Haran is the same God who has called us to worship—"that you may declare the praises of him who called you out of darkness into his wonderful light" (1 Peter 2:9).

Worship in Response to God's Revelation

Even though the author does not mention that God continued to lead Abram after he arrived in Canaan (Gen 12:6), we can safely assume that that was what happened with Abram since from earlier in the chapter it is clear that Abram would not have known exactly where he was going unless God showed him (v. 1). Just as when later God told him to "go to the region of Moriah... one of the mountains I will tell you about" (Gen 22:2), roughly the area was mentioned, but the exact location was not given until he arrived there after the three-day journey (v. 4).

When a person comes to know Jesus Christ, not all of his questions will be answered. We do not respond to God in obedience because everything makes sense to our human logical understanding, but we decide to follow because of our faith in Jesus Christ. Trusting in God is beyond human reasoning. We do not come to trust God because everything makes sense to us. Quite the opposite, there is faith in our hearts against all odds, requiring an audacity to say, "Yes, Lord, I believe!" Initially in the early stage of our Christian walk, we are given a big picture of becoming disciples, followers of Christ. We may not fully understand what the discipleship entails, but daily, we deny ourselves, take up the cross and follow His lead (Matt 16:24). And that was how it was for Abram, not knowing exactly where he was going (Heb 11:8).

Interestingly enough, although the first specific place that God led Abram to was "the site of the great tree of Moreh at Shechem" (Gen 12:6), the emphasis of the passage in which this information appears is not so much on the place, describing what it was like, etc., but rather on the fact that this was where God revealed Himself ("appeared to him") to Abram (v. 7). The location of the second place where Abraham built an altar to Yahweh is just described as "the hills east of Bethel" between Bethel and Ai" (v. 8 and also in 13:3) which is somewhat ambiguous. It would be the area where later God would reveal Himself to Abraham's grandson, Jacob, in a dream (Gen 28:19, and again in Gen 35:3). During the prophet Amos' days, God spoke to Northern Israel, saying, "Seek me and live; do not seek Bethel,... Gilgal... Beersheba... Seek the Lord and live" (Amos 5:4-6). It is another reminder to all of us that contrary to pagan religious beliefs, with Yahweh, no place is intrinsically sacred; rather, it is wherever God reveals Himself that is sacred.

God called Abram, and Abram responded with obedience in faith. God appeared to Abram "at the site of the great tree of Moreh at Shechem" and promised him the land that he was called to. In response to God's revelation of His promise, Abram "built an altar to the Lord and called on the name of the Lord" (Gen 12:6-7). Later Abram came back to the same place where he had built the altar and "called on the name of the Lord" (Gen 13:3-4).

One should not make any connection with building an altar and "the great tree of Moreh... the great trees of Mamre" (Gen 12:6; 13:18). It is true that many pagan religious practices were performed under special "sacred" trees. Later as a nation, the Israelites would prostitute themselves, serving idols under "the scared oaks" which they had adopted from the practices of other religions (Isa 1:29). The spiritual apostasy of the nation Israel, especially under King Ahaz, is described as their offering sacrifices "under every spreading tree" (1 Chr 28:4). God warned through his prophet, Isaiah, that the nation of idolaters would be taken into exile because of the idol worship they performed under the oak trees they regarded sacred (Isa 6:13).

In contrast to the Canaanites around him, Abram worshipped God under a tree, not because the tree or site itself was sacred or spiritual, but simply because God revealed Himself to Abram at that place. It was one of the first lessons Moses learned when God revealed Himself in the burning bush—"take off your sandals for the place where you are standing is holy ground" (Exod 3:5). Moses most likely covered his face by bowing his head to the ground out a reverent fear (v. 6). Wherever and whenever God reveals Himself, that place and moment must be regarded as sacred; like Moses, in response to an encounter with the holiness of God, we worship God.

In every Sunday worship service wherever the gospel is preached, that is the place God is expected to reveal Himself. Every Sunday, worshipers are reminded of God's promise to His people—"no matter how many promises God has made, they are "Yes" in Christ. And so through him the "Amen" is spoken by us to the glory of God" (2 Cor 1:20). If the act of worship is in response to God's great revelation, then placing the preaching of the Word at the beginning of the order of worship, before anything else, could be most appropriate. This may be unconventional for most evangelical churches in America since especially after the Reformation, preaching, the ministry of the Word, has become the highlight of most modern Protestant worship services. The preaching of God's Word first can help us to avoid wrongly focusing on the music rather than its content, the lyrics; it can also help us avoid failing to make a distinction between public and private prayers which need to be grounded in God's word,

Usually a word of instruction is given at the beginning of the Lord's Supper in order to properly guide the congregation in participating in the Communion. In the same way, the sermon in a Sunday worship service context should help the worshipers to properly engage in worship. In preaching, there is a place for helping and being aware of the modern day listener since some may have little to no background knowledge of the bible, or even never have heard the gospel message; newcomers may also be unfamiliar with the way a particular local community of faith worships. But at the end of the day, it is a gathering of the redeemed to worship God. The primary focus of the ministry of God's word is Christ and the gospel. Through the ministry of God's word, we anticipate that even unbelievers or those who are not accustomed to the way we worship can "fall down and worship God, exclaiming, 'God is really among you!'" when the Holy Spirit convicts them in their hearts of sin (1 Cor 14:24-25).

The Life of the Worshipers of God

Although Abraham lived in the Land of Canaan for a hundred years, God "gave him no inheritance... not even a foot of ground" in the Land (Acts 7:5). The Land would be given to Abraham's "offspring" (Gen 12:7) after the Israelites first spent four hundred years in Egypt (Gen 15:16). As Abraham left his country, he probably realized that when God made him this promise at the beginning of this new spiritual journey, it was about more than just merely possessing a Promised Land. The promise was becoming a "great nation," God making Abram's "name great," becoming a "blessing" to others, and people being blessed being hinged upon Abraham (Gen 12:1-3). His nephew, Lot, should have chosen to stay with Abraham through whom all nations would be blessed, even if it meant to forsake his possessions (Gen 13:5-7), but instead Lot "chose for himself the whole plain of the Jordan and set out toward the east" (Gen 13:10-11).

For Abraham, the true blessing was beyond the Land itself "flowing with milk and honey;" it was in the receiving of God's promise (Gen 13:14-17) and "walk[ing] before [God Almighty] and be[ing] blameless" (Gen 17:1). After Abraham, his grandson Jacob had to come to grips with the fact that "every good and perfect gift is from above, coming down from the Father of the heavenly lights, who does not change like shifting shadows" (Jas 1:17), before he crossed the Jordan river to enter the Land from the east. After a long struggle with believing that he had to pursue material possessions to be blessed, Jacob finally realized only God could bless and that he needed to be blessed by God and God alone—"I will not let you go unless you bless me" (Gen 32:26).

Although Abraham acquired so much wealth and received the Land promise for his descendants, Abraham (and his son, Isaac, and the next generation, Jacob) "by faith… made his home in the promised land like a stranger… lived in tents… For he was looking forward to the city with foundations, whose architect and builder is God" (Heb 11:9-10). For this reason, Abram did not build a city and name it after his own son (Gen 4:17) or "make a name for" himself (Gen 11:4). For what, when God promised Abram that He would make his name great (Gen 12:2)? Rather than building a city, he built an altar wherever he went; wherever God revealed Himself to Abraham, there he would worship God.

Sadly, later the nation Israel in the prophet Jeremiah's days failed to live by God's promise but rather placed her trust and life's security in the Land and the temple building (Jer 7:4), and as a result, "the house, which bears [God's] Name, [became] a den of robbers" (v. 11).

Abraham never looked for a chance to settle down in one particular place. In a way, Abraham was constantly on the move (Gen 13:17-18). In the first two chapters of his life in the Land, for Abraham, no matter where he was, the priority in life was worshiping Yahweh (Gen 12:7, 8; 13:4, 18). Worship was his first main activity in the Land, and it would be through worship that the final test of his faith would come; would Abraham worship God or would he worship and idolize his son, Isaac (Gen 22:1-19)?

There is a great dichotomy for modern day worshipers, which would have been completely foreign to Abraham and the way he lived his life. Many of us regularly and consistently attend weekly Sunday worship. But our lives, lifestyles, and what we pursue in life during the week in the secular world could be completely contrary to our confession and service to God in our Sunday worship service. What are we really seeking in life? Do we pursue things of this world because they are of great value or worth by the standards of this world? Or by the way we live as sojourners like Abraham, does our life become a living testimony such that it can be said of us, "the world was not worthy of them" (Heb 11:38)?

The Eternal Kingly Priest

"After Abram returned from defeating Kedorlaomer" and other kings, the king of Sodom and the king of Salem "came out to meet him in the Valley of Shaveh" (Gen 14:17-18). Our focus will be on Melchizedek, king of Salem, and how he ministered to Abram as a "priest of God Most High," since the mentioning of priesthood, priestly ministry, and giving are all related to worship. And what is even more significant is that Melchizedek had a dual role—king and priest. We do not know of anyone else in the Bible, especially in the Pentateuch, who had this dual role. Aalders proposes that Jethro also had a similar dual role:

"This dual role need not surprise us, for there are other instances of this. Moses' father-in-law, Jethro, is called priest of Midian in Exodus 2:16 and 3:1, while he obviously also was the political ruler of one of the Midianite tribes." (G Charles Aalders, *Bible Student Commentary*, p. 289)

But this is highly doubtful since there is no record of Jethro as being any type of political ruler, let alone possibly a king.

The word "priest" (*kohen*) appears in Genesis 14:18 for the first time in the Pentateuch. Although we have no previous mention of priests or priestly service up to this point, culturally in Abram's days, the priestly role was most likely already widely recognized in that part of the world (Gen 41:45). For those who believed in Yahweh, however, the formal establishment of the priestly office does not come until Aaron from the tribe of Levi under the old covenant (or Mosaic covenant).

Although we do not have much information about Melchizedek, we have enough to conclude that he in some way resembled and foreshadowed the "woman's offspring" in the kingly line of David, the Son of David, Jesus Christ. Because the Bible does not give any information other than what we have in Genesis 14:18-20, it is natural for us to raise some questions and draw some conclusions. Where did Melchizedek come from? He is like the Son of God "without father or mother, without genealogy, without beginning of days or end of life" (Heb 7:3). For this reason we can say that his priestly duty foreshadowed the eternality of Christ's ministry as the great high priest—"Therefore he is able to save completely those who come to God through him, because he always lives to intercede for them" (Heb 7:25; Ps 110:4).

Melchizedek was the king of Salem which was an old name of Jerusalem. In the Book of Psalms, God's dwelling place is often referred to as Jerusalem or Zion. It is the city of God where the nation Israel gathered together to "praise the name of " Yahweh (Ps 122:4). There, in the sanctuary of God, were "the thrones for judgment" (v. 5) of which Yahweh was seen as the King. Psalm 76:2 uses the older name of Jerusalem to describe God's dwelling place—" His tent is in Salem, his dwelling place in Zion." All of these references connecting to the kingly priest, Melchizedek of Salem, lead us to conclude that Jesus Christ is not only King Yahweh but also the Eternal Great High Priest.

Several things should be noted from the above. The pagan religions of Abram's days were not the only ones that had priests; at least one person from Salem was the priest of the same God that Abram served, "God Most High" (Gen 14:18-20). Although there is no biblical record that the priest served as a mediator on behalf of the worshiper, Abram, and others before him, Abram nevertheless acknowledged Melchizedek's priesthood by giving "a tenth of everything" to him (v. 20). There could be a significant connection between the fact that Mount Moriah, where Abraham's faith would be tested through worship, was located in Salem and that this encounter with

Melchizedek from Salem showed that even someone like Abram needed a mediator. There is also a parallel between "the Lord... God our Savior, who daily bears our burdens," who came down "into his sanctuary... [and] received gifts from men" (Ps 68:18-19), and the king, Melchizedek, receiving a tenth of what Abram recovered, hence, another way to see King Melchizedek foreshadowing Christ Jesus.

Culturally, in the days of Abram, the ability to hear the gods' or spirits' voices was limited to a certain type of people called "prophets." Similarly, it was widely held that approaching a deity or the spirits required a special, trained or professional individual, usually having some knowledge of the "spiritual" realm, to serve as a mediator to the gods to offer sacrifices. The sacrifices had to be prepared and performed according to certain prescribed regulations, which were handed down through tradition. No average Joe could just approach the altar and make a sacrifice; a mediator, i.e., professional priest, was needed.

Unlike the other pagan religions at that time, Abram built altars and approached God on his own. Until the establishment of Israel as a nation, having a separate priestly duty or priest was a foreign concept in the patriarchic and pre-patriarchic periods. Interestingly, at the same time Abram was going from one place to another, worshipping God before altars he built without a priest mediating for him, there was a king serving as a priest to the same God as Abram's God, in the same Land though in another city, Salem. All this leads the readers to conclude that even Abram needed this mediator between God and man, but that would not be fully realized until the coming of the Eternal Kingly Great High Priest, Jesus Christ.

Until then, Melchizedek, the shadow of the reality, Jesus Christ, momentarily blessed Abram like Aaron and his descendants would continue to pronounce blessings upon the Israelites (Num 6:22-27) until the coming of the Eternal Priest and mediator (1 Tim 2:5-6) through whom all blessings would come (John 1:16; Eph 1:3). What Jesus said once to the Jews is worth contemplating—"Abraham rejoiced at the thought of seeing my day; he saw it and was glad" (John 8:56).

On one side of the religious spectrum, we have religious people everywhere continuing to seek out a mediator since most of them are convinced that they themselves cannot or know not how to approach the gods, and so they have to rely on others. On the other end of the spectrum are the people who believe that no one should need a mediator, that anyone could tap into the spiritual realm and acquire spiritual experiences; after all, they believe that they are all gods. Some of the traditional beliefs of the Old Church are no different; some still believe they need mediators, i.e., Mary and saints.

There are at least two grave mistakes modern worshipers tend to make. One has to do with receiving "God's grace in vain" by becoming forgetful of "God, who reconciled us to himself through Christ" (2 Co 5:18; 6:1). The other has to do with failing to "approach the throne of grace with confidence" despite the fact that "we have a great high priest who has gone through the heavens" (Heb 4:14, 16).

No one can approach God without Christ who "entered the Most Holy Place once for all by his own blood, having obtained eternal redemption" (Heb 9:12). Every Sunday, the new covenant community is invited to enter the Most Holy Place, the very presence of God, in worship. But sadly, this has not been the aim of worship, being in God's presence and having intimate fellowship with God. Could it be that we have taken God's grace for granted? Oh, how worshipers need to have a deeper and renewed appreciation of God's grace, the price for which was fully paid with the death of His Son Jesus Christ! The closer we approach the Holy God, the more we get to see our true selves. And when we do, we are in desperate need of the Savior more than ever before. So we continue to hold on firmly to what Jesus said —"I am the way and the truth and the life. No one comes to the Father except through me" (John 14:6).

The Assurance of God's Promise

God continues to speak or appear to Abram in visions and dreams, reiterating His promise regarding Abram's offspring and the Land (Gen 12:1-3, 7; 13:14-17; 15:4-5, 7). In response to God's promise of offspring, the Bible says "Abram believed [Yahweh], and he credited it to him as righteousness" (Gen 15:6). But in response to God's promise of the Land, Abram responded with a question, "O Sovereign [Yahweh], how can I know that I will gain possession of it?" (v. 8) One must not assume that Abram asked this question out of doubt, especially since he had just fought in battle and defeated four kings. It is more likely that Abram asked this question out of a desire to strengthen or confirm his faith, just as God's repeated reminders of His promise were not to cause Abram to doubt the promise but rather make his faith in it stronger.

Abram worshiped God in response to God's revelation. The previous four times, Abram, out of his own will, built an altar to the Lord in response to God's faithful promise. But here, in Genesis 15, in response to Abram's question of how he would know he would acquire the land, God was the One who told Abram to prepare certain animals in order to do a covenant "ceremony" (v. 9).

What was so unique and unusual about the way this particular covenant was expressed and confirmed (v. 17)? A covenant involves two parties —in this case, it was God and Abram. In the ancient world, two parties entered into a covenant by walking between the animal pieces as a reminder that if one of the parties were to break the covenant, that party, like the animals, would be destroyed. In this particular case, the covenant was made without Abram having to pass through the pieces; only God alone passed between the pieces in the manifestation of " a smoking firepot with a blazing torch" (v. 17). It must have been a spectacular sight, but for Abram, it was also much more; the significance of what he saw was that Yahweh alone, apart from Abram's ability, would be the covenant-keeper, and this made Abram's faith in Yahweh stronger than ever before. For Abram, God's promise could never be nullified because of man's weakness. Therefore, Abram's faith was all the more strengthened.

What else could Abram have done? Should Abram have raised a greater military army to prepare for another battle, just in case for the future? But Yahweh "came to Abram in a vision" and said "Do not be afraid, Abram. I am your shield, your very great reward" (v. 1). How in the world would Abram's barren wife, Sarai, have a child? How was Abram going to serve Yahweh in the Land and possess it when the Canaanites were already occupying the Land? The promises of offspring and the Land were utterly impossible for Abram to achieve. The only way those things would have been possible were if and only if they were accomplished apart from Abram's work; God alone would fulfill them, and Abram would receive them in faith. For this reason, God first reiterated His promise to Abram

(vv. 1-5), then gave the assurance of His promise through a covenant (vv. 9-17), and finally reiterated His promise to Abram again (vv. 18-21)—all the emphasis is on God's promise. How true it is that "it does not, therefore, depend on man's desire or effort, but on God's mercy" (Rom 9:16)!

In the Lord's Supper, we hear, "This is my blood of the covenant, which is poured out for many for the forgiveness of sins" (Matt 26:28). The bread, the wine, the table, they may not be as spectacular as "a smoking firepot with a blazing torch." But what is and should be beyond spectacular is God's faithful promise of forgiveness through His Son Jesus Christ. Our faith in Jesus Christ is strengthened because our hearts are overwhelmed by God's grace revealed in Christ who was completely obedient as the covenant keeper. We are encouraged to "draw near to God with a sincere heart in full assurance of faith, having our hearts sprinkled to cleanse us from a guilty conscience and having our bodies washed with pure water" (Heb 10:22).

Our Faith Is Tested through Worship

During my college years when I was taking a course on child psychology, at the very beginning of the class, the lecturer used the story of Abraham offering his son, Isaac, to illustrate how infanticide was very prevalent and much easier to do in those days (though for that matter, our society today is not much different as in the name of "pro-choice" we have made it possible to have the freedom to take life). I noticed a few Christians in the class were very uneasy about the way the lecturer wrongly painted the background with one of the most popular stories in the Bible. Although the American Christian culture is rapidly dissipating and being replaced with pluralism and secularism, many of us who were brought up in the Christian culture of an America past are somewhat familiar with the Genesis 22 story. But I believe it is one of the stories that has been moralized and wrongly applied the most.

First of all, when God told Abram to offer his son as a burnt offering, Isaac was most likely in his mid-twenties (based on previous events and the following chapter). Child sacrifice may have existed as early as Abraham's days among the Canaanite religions, but it was certainly not required or even condoned by Yahweh—"Whoever sheds the blood of man, by man shall his blood be shed; for in the image of God has God made man" (Gen 9:6).

In order to understand the intent of the author Moses, which is also God's intent, in this story, we need to familiarize ourselves with the following: 1) what it means for God to test Abraham, 2) what other passages in the Bible, especially the New Testament, say about this particular story, and 3) how the story foreshadows the Son of God. Once these issues have been dealt with, we should be able to properly apply and make the connection to our main topic, worship.

There are several things about God that have been revealed in the Bible. Contrary to the tempter devil, God does not tempt anyone for the purpose of making people sin (Jas 1:13), but he does test them. God did not place Adam in the Garden just to enjoy fellowship with Him; because of his covenant relationship with God, Adam's faith, commitment, and obedience were tested in the Garden, and in the same way, so would Abraham's faith be tested at "the region of Moriah."

Yahweh is omniscient; there is nothing that God is unaware of, and His knowledge is not limited to time since God is the one who created "time." Since God already knew the faith in Abraham's heart and how he would respond to God's command, we can say that the test was not really for God to know the level and quality of Abraham's faith but more for Abraham himself to know. Abraham did not know it was a test.

In Adam's case, he was given a clear consequence regarding what would happen if he broke God's command, but what would have happened if Abraham had not obeyed? Would there have been another curse? Surely not, since the covenant with Abraham was not based on work but grace. In that sense, Abraham's faith was being tested or purified through hardship as with all those who would come after him as his spiritual descendants—"he has preserved our lives and kept our feet from slipping. For you, O God, tested us; you refined us like silver" (Ps 66:9-10).

When Abraham first believed in God's promise regarding the Land and his offspring, God "credited it to him as righteousness" (Gen 15:6), but that did not mean Abraham completely obeyed God from that point on. Although Abraham's faith was never shaken fundamentally, nevertheless, Abraham was unclear on how God would accomplish His promise regarding the Land (Gen 15:8). Because this "how" was unclear to Abraham, he yielded to the suggestion of his wife by taking Sarai's Egyptian maidservant Hagar in the hope of fulfilling God's promise through this method (Gen 16:1-14). Later, even after God revealed "how" He would fulfill His promise (Gen 17:15-16) and confirmed His covenant with Abraham (v. 2), Abraham was still fearful because of his wife Sarah and again lied about his wife in the same way he had done throughout his journey in Canaan (Gen 20:11-13).

God called Abraham. Abraham left in faith. God promised Abraham the Land and offspring, and he believed and his faith was credited as righteousness. And throughout his life's journey as a believer of Yahweh, God encouraged, confirmed, reminded, reaffirmed, challenged, and finally refined, "tested," the faith in Abraham. In a way, Abraham witnessed God's power of resurrection "even though he was past age—and Sarah herself was barren... from this one man, and he as good as dead, came descendants as numerous as the stars in the sky" (Heb 11:12). "Against all hope, Abraham in hope believed... he faced the fact that his body was as good as dead... and that Sarah's womb was also dead" (Rom 4:18-19).

Just as Abraham experienced God's power of resurrection by having Isaac from his wife Sarah, we also have experienced this power of resurrection continued to work in us—"his incomparably great power for us who believe. That power is like the working of his mighty strength, which he exerted in Christ when he raised him from the dead" (Eph 1:19-20). Just as Abraham was tested of his faith, so our faith will continue to be purified through various trials in life as we continue to trust God; He who raised Christ from the dead, "will raise us also" (1 Cor 6:14).

Because of his belief in "resurrection," that God could raise the dead, when Abraham was tested of his faith in God, he was able to go through the test. On the one hand, Abraham had experienced God's faithfulness to His promise through the birth of his son, Isaac, whom Abraham received as God's promise, "through Isaac ... your offspring will be reckoned." On the other hand, Abraham was given a command, to "sacrifice his one and only son." Between the two apparently opposite "wills of God" of which only one could be true if God's promise were to be true, "Abraham reasoned that

God could raise the dead, and figuratively speaking, he did receive Isaac back from death" (Heb 11:17-19).

Abraham witnessed God's faithfulness to His promise for twenty-five years and received Isaac. Perhaps another twenty-five more years after Isaac was born, Abraham had been continuing to witness God's faithfulness. But even after fifty years all together, Abraham still needed to be sanctified; his faith needed to be refined and mature. God, the One who had called Abraham, was faithful (1 Thess 5:23-24). Therefore, the testing of Abraham was a way of God faithfully dealing with the one He had chosen. But the main purpose of Abraham's story and faith would not be complete without Jesus Christ—"The words, 'it was credited to him' were written not for him alone, but also for us, to whom God will credit righteousness—for us who believe in him who raised Jesus our Lord from the dead" (Rom 4:23-24). Only then are we able to properly apply God's word as the foundation for worship.

The command to Abraham to offer his son Isaac as a burnt offering and the story that took place on Mount Moriah, which has been believed to be the present day Jerusalem, Mount Calvary to be exact, can be fully understood in the light of God's Son and His sacrificial death on the cross and resurrection. It was on that mountain/hill that Jesus Christ, the Son of God, offered Himself, yielded to His Father's will, for our sins, and God's justice was demonstrated (Rom 3:26) and "the many will be made righteous" (Rom 5:19).

The test was for Abraham himself to know, for his faith that needed to be refined through the whole process of the sacrifice (=worship); in the same way, God demonstrated His justice and His own love for us: "while we were still sinners, Christ died for us" (Rom 5:8). As a result of Christ's death, God will continue to refine our faith in Christ so that our offerings of praise would be acceptable to God (Mal 3:3-4); our faith needs to be refined/purified for us to offer our service to God.

If it were just a test in the way we often think of it and nothing more, then after God stopped Abraham, he could have just come back down from the mountain with Isaac. But the offering had to be made, and the offering had to be the one God provided (Gen 22:8, 14), and Abraham "took the ram" that Yahweh provided and "sacrificed it as a burnt offering instead of his son" (v. 13). And that was how it was for Christ. Instead of living a perfectly obedient life for thirty-three years and finishing his work without the cross, Christ had to die on the cross "and give his life as a ransom for many" (Mark 10:45); the offering had to be made.

It was on Mount Moriah that God demonstrated His faithfulness to Abraham, and it was at that place that Abraham's faith was vindicated and refined (Gen 22:12). After the sacrifice was made, God reaffirmed all the promises He had been speaking to Abraham throughout his spiritual journey (vv. 15-18). And just as Abraham was greatly encouraged by God's vindication of his faith through the offering of his son Isaac, "we who have fled to take hold of the hope offered to us [would] be greatly encouraged" (Heb 6:18) through the Son of God who offered Himself on the cross. We are greatly encouraged as we worship God who has demonstrated His faithfulness through His Son Jesus Christ and His ultimate sacrifice on the cross.

Yet it is not only through facing "trials of many kinds... [that] the testing of [our] faith develops perseverance" (Jas 1:2-3 and also 1 Peter 1:6-7), but every Sunday worship, our faith is tested and renewed. Just as Christ had to choose in the desert during the forty days of testing whether to bend his knee to the promise of "all the kingdoms of the world and their splendor" or to "worship the Lord... and serve him only" (Matt 4:8-10), Abraham had to decide whether he would choose the gift of his son Isaac over and against the giver of all gifts, God who was faithful. Just as Christ was placed in the Garden to choose between his will and his Father's, Abraham was invited to Mount Moriah to choose between his son Isaac and his God, the God of Abraham.

Every Sunday God invites us to worship Him. We are able to gather together as churches and expect our worship to be accepted by Him because of His Son, Jesus Christ. Often Christians can equate "faith in Christ" with just a commitment made once at conversion or something that everyone has to do in order to have the assurance that their eternal life is secure, but this should not be. We do not enter into worship, "business as usual," fulfilling our weekly duty as Christians, but rather each week, once again, we place our faith in Jesus Christ who is "the author and perfecter of our faith" (Heb 12:2). In our worship, we seek to be purified by the blood of Christ (1 John 1:9). Our desire to be like Jesus, holy and true, is rekindled by the Holy Spirit as we worship Him. Once again, our hearts are cross-examined in worship; who or what are we going to worship? Are we going to serve materialism or God? Jesus said, "No one can serve two masters... You cannot serve both God and Money" (Matt 6:24). Abraham's faith was vindicated and demonstrated that the Yahweh who called Abraham was faithful. God was not wrong or granting beyond what was due when Abraham believed in God's promise and God "credited" it to him as righteousness" (Gen 15:6). Likewise, in worship, as we surrender ourselves and renounce any competing members for our devotion that dare to stand alongside God in our hearts, may the Holy Spirit give us the assurance and words of conviction, "Now I know that you fear God," because you have surrendered all to me (Gen 22:12).

9

A Stairway from Heaven Resting on the Earth

From the very beginning of creation, God always took the initiative when it came to man serving/worshiping Him. It was God who prepared the sanctuary, revealed Himself and promised blessings. Man, only in response to this revelation of God, worshipped Yahweh. Although much of Isaac's life is portrayed as seemingly just a retracing of his father's footsteps, this was to show how God's blessings were handed down from one generation to next and how God faithfully fulfilled His promise through the one whom He had chosen (Gen 27:33). Isaac, like his father Abraham, "built an altar... and call[ed] on the name of [Yahweh]" when God "appeared to him" and reiterated the promise that was given to his father Abraham at Beersheba (Gen 26:23-25).

God continued to reveal Himself to Isaac's son Jacob. Although by nature, Jacob had some character flaws (Gen 27:36), God nevertheless chose Jacob "in order that God's purpose in election might stand: not by works but by him who calls" (Rom 9:11-12). Like his grandfather

Abraham, Jacob's faith was eventually vindicated, at Peniel—"Your name will no longer be Jacob, but Israel, because you have struggled with God and with men and have overcome" (Gen 32:28, 30). At the end of Jacob's life, God's irresistible grace finally paid off as Jacob "when he was dying, blessed each of Joseph's sons, and worshiped as he leaned on the top of his staff" (Heb 11:21).

For Jacob, like all others before him, worship was the first response when God revealed Himself at Luz, which would be known as Bethel from that moment on. Worship was also the last service Jacob would offer to Yahweh as he rallied the last ounce of energy within him on his dying bed. The Archbishop of Canterbury, William Temple (1942-44), wrote:

"Worship is the submission of all of our nature to God. It is the quickening of conscience by His holiness, nourishment of mind by His truth, purifying of imagination by His beauty, opening of the heart to His love, and submission of will to his purpose. And all this gathered up in adoration is the greatest of human expressions of which we are capable."

In relation to worship, Jacob's first encounter with God (Gen 28:10-22) deserves our attention because of the following elements: the stairway that connected heaven and earth, God's presence, and the pillar. Although other events are mentioned elsewhere in the Bible, this particular event at Bethel is unique since it foreshadowed Christ's redemptive work, worship in relation to an "open heaven" (John 1:51), and God dealing with our change of character into His Son's image.

When God Reaches Down to Where We Are

In the past, God spoke to certain individuals who were known as prophets (Gen 20:7) through the means of dreams, visions (Gen 15:1), or simply words (Gen 12:12, later known as prophetic words). The prophet Joel prophesied concerning the Last Days that not just a few particular individuals but now all God's people would be "prophetic" (Joel 2:28-32). In the Last Days, God's people under the new covenant in Christ experience hearing God's voice as His written word is being illuminated in their hearts through the three means mentioned above.

God could have simply just spoken to Jacob, the way He had with others, but here in a dream, Jacob saw "a stairway resting on the earth, with its top reaching to heaven, and the angels of God ... ascending and descending on it" (Gen 28:12). We do not know how much Jacob knew about the significance and meaning of the dream. Usually when one dreams a dream that is from God, the person relies on others for the interpretation which ultimately comes from God. The classic cases would be Joseph (Gen 41:16) and Daniel (Dan 2:19, 27-28) to whom the spirit of interpretation was given; simply put, God has to reveal the meaning of the dreams in order for us to know.

Jacob was not given the interpretation of the dream. But in the dream, God spoke and elaborated further on what Yahweh had been saying all along to Abraham and Isaac. In a way, nothing was really new other than God assuring Jacob's safe return home to Beersheba (Gen 28:28:15), but Jacob had to personally hear from the Lord God's promise. We can assume Jacob was told of Yahweh's promise from his father Isaac rehearsing God's faithfulness as he was growing up (Ps 78:2-7), but a time came when Jacob had to hear it directly from the Lord for himself.

God, who is unchanging, reveals Himself to us with His covenant promise, whether through the preaching of the gospel in the worship setting or the worship itself that is grounded in the gospel message, and our faith in Christ is renewed as we experience a greater degree of appreciating God's faithfulness. That was how it was for Jacob. The God whom Jacob had been hearing about all his life, the God of his father, Isaac, and his grandfather, Abraham, was now going to be the God of Jacob as he renewed his commitment to Yahweh.

In a way, what Jacob saw in his dream (Gen 28:12-13) was the elaboration of how Yahweh would ultimately fulfill His covenant promise (vv. 13-14). God's revelation through His word is progressive, which means that God did not reveal everything at one time in history but continued to reveal His will through different times and places. We do not know how much Jacob knew about the meaning of the dream he had. But the imagery (vv. 12-13), the reiteration of God's promise (vv. 13-14), and His immediate assurance of His presence in the situation Jacob was in (v. 15), were enough to put him in awe and holy reverence to worship Yahweh (vv. 16-19) and renew his commitment to Yahweh as his God (vv. 20-22).

About two thousand years after, the final revelator, the Son of God, gave the interpretation of Jacob's dream in His early encounter with Nathanael (John 1:47). What Jesus said about Nathanael being "a true Israelite, in whom there is nothing false," and that the true Israelite would "see greater things... [seeing] heaven open, and the angels of God ascending and descending on [Christ]" (vv. 50-51) help us to understand Jacob's dream and have a greater depth of understanding of the meaning of Christ's death.

Jacob had been known as a "deceiver" until we come to Genesis 32:28 where he finally surrendered, bent his knees before Yahweh, acknowledged his own physical frailty before God, and became the first "Israelite." In his dream, Jacob actually witnessed vaguely that only God could truly change a person inside out, and it is through Christ's death that a person takes on the form of a new man, conforming to the image of God's Son, "in whom there is nothing false," who is "the faithful and true" (Rev 3:14). Only through the Son of God who came down to our lowly place on earth would our spiritual channel be opened and connected with the true and living God such that we can have fellowship and intimacy with Yahweh in the same way as the first man, Adam, had in the Garden.

Nathanael was amazed by the fact that Jesus of Nazareth really knew him the way Yahweh knew him. Therefore, as surprising it may seem, at that moment, Nathanael confessed with his mouth what he believed in his heart to be the inevitable truth—"you are the Son of God; you are the King of Israel" (John 1:49). And Jesus promised and prophesied that Nathanael and others would experience "greater things" which would be accomplished through Christ's death. What Jacob dreamt in his dream, with all the awesome imagery, would become a reality and tangible experience for all those who would be under the new covenant in Christ.

At the very beginning of Jesus' earthly ministry when He identified Himself with the sinners by being baptized with the baptism of repentance, "he saw heaven being torn open" (Mark 1:10) which was another prophetic event and the continuation of Jacob's dream of what the believers would experience through the cross. Therefore, magnifying and preaching "Jesus Christ and him crucified" (1 Cor 2:2) is imperative in the Sunday worship service. It is through that worship that we are being sanctified taking on more of Christ's image, and we experience intimate relationship and fellowship with God as Christ's death tore heaven open for us.

When God Makes His Presence Known

In those days, people generally believed that gods dwelt in a particular place or territory. For this reason, certain places or things or areas were considered to be spiritual and to have some type of spiritual power in them. In a culture where gods were believed to have power over but also be limited to certain territories, Jacob may have been all the more startled and awestruck that the God of Abraham and Isaac was there at the place where he slept. As Jacob was running away from his brother and leaving his family at Beersheba, he probably never expected Yahweh to be there at Luz— "Surely [Yahweh] is in this place, and I was not aware of it" (Gen 28:16).

Although Jacob's grandfather, Abraham, had built an altar by "the hills east of Bethel," and the old name for Bethel, "Luz," first appeared in the Pentateuch in Genesis 28, Jacob was most likely the first one to build an altar there, at this place which was unfamiliar to him. Therefore, Jacob never expected God to be there at Bethel. If God's appearance to Jacob at that place were not enough, Yahweh also gave Jacob the assurance of His presence, that He would never leave Jacob until He fully accomplished what He had promised to Jacob (v. 15). Unlike other gods who were limited to a particular location, the faithful Yahweh God would never withdraw His presence from Jacob; wherever Jacob went, God would go with him.

The moment Jacob's heart was filled with the indescribable presence of the holy God, the very place where he dreamt became "the house of God... the gate to heaven" for Jacob (v. 17). Jacob did not build a house or pitch a tent, but out in the middle of nowhere, the place where God appeared and spoke to him in a dream was God's dwelling place and also the way ("gate" or entrance) through which one could experience "heaven on earth." Later, the author Moses would experience a similar type of God's presence when Yahweh appeared to him in a burning bush—"for the place where you are standing is holy ground" (Exod 3:5).

Everyone knows that a church is not a building but God's people who are committed to come together at a particular time and place to worship and for spiritual edification. We all know the temple, God's house, is not a building but the church where God has chosen to dwell among His people (2 Cor 6:16). The holiest moment should be when the community of God's people experience God's holiness in the worship service. When the new covenant community of believers comes together and testifies, "exclaiming, 'God is really among you'" (1 Cor 14:25), that is the most sacred moment for the Christian community. There is no greater opportunity to experience God's holy presence than when believers come together to seek His face. God is awesome in His sanctuary (Ps 68:35) where God makes His presence known through the proclamation of His word and praises of His people.

When God Is Remembered in Our Mind

It was the first time the word "pillar" (*matzevah*) appeared in the Pentateuch (Gen 28:18). For the Canaanite religions, setting up a pillar often had associations with pagan idolatry (Exod 23:24), and a drink offering could have been one of the ways they made offering to their deities (Ps 16:4). Even in Asia, using wine in ancestor worship in the form of "drink offerings" has been a part of the culture for thousands of years. But unlike the Canaanite religious practices, in the Pentateuch, for God's people, a pillar was set up to symbolize an agreement between two parties (Gen 31:45-53), to represent God's people, the nation (Exod 24:4), or to simply be a monument (Gen 35:20).

For Jacob, his intention of setting up a stone pillar was not to worship it. As matter of fact, it was the stone that he had used to lay his head to sleep on (Gen 28:18). Jacob did not set up a typical altar, which was a common practice to offer burnt offerings, since he was on his way to his uncle Laban's place in Haran, and Jacob did not have anything to use as an offering other than water and oil. The pillar was appropriate to use for a drink offering, and so he "poured oil on top of" the pillar that he set up.

God, as He promises, would bring Jacob back to the Land. And when God does, Jacob would again "set up a stone pillar" and pour out a "drink offering on it" (Gen 35:14). After twenty years in Haran, Jacob had acquired much wealth in the form of flocks which could have been used for a burnt offering. Although Jacob told his family members, "let us go up to Bethel, where I will build an altar to God, who answered me in the day of my distress" (v. 3), his setting up a stone pillar in the place of an altar was Jacob's way of worshiping God in remembrance of Yahweh's faithfulness to him.

Although the drink offering was a common religious practice for the Canaanites, Jacob was the first one in the Pentateuch to offer a drink offering to Yahweh. Once the nation Israel would be established and one of the instructions for the covenant stipulations on worship would be the drink offering, it would no longer be poured on a stone pillar but on the altar (Exod 29:38-41).

While the burnt offering was a reminder of one's total and complete surrender to Yahweh, the emphasis of the drink offering was a "pouring out" completely, with nothing reserved, like the woman who broke the alabaster "jar and poured the perfume on" Jesus' head (Mark 14:3). Paul in the New Testament compared the way he lived his life with a drink offering (Phil 2:17; 2 Tim 4:6), which reminds us that our life needs to be poured out (used up) to offer ourselves to the Lord.

When the community of believers comes together to participate in the Lord's Supper, we remember. Our minds make a deliberate and intentional effort to think once again of the meaning of Christ's broken body (Isa 52:14; 53:10), his suffering on the cross. As we drink from the cup, our minds are filled with what took placed on Calvary where Christ's blood was shed —"This is my blood of the covenant, which is poured out for many for the forgiveness of sins" (Matt 26:27-28). As we take the cup and remember the salvation day, what took place on the hill far away, we are challenged, and our commitment to live a life in the manner of making a drink offering, poured out for the One who is faithful, is renewed. Our memory is refreshed as we remember this truth anew: since we could not go up to where God was, the Son of God came down to where we were, "while we were sinners" (Rom5:8). At the moment we are reassured of God's promise of salvation and sanctification through the proclamation of God's power displayed on the cross, we like Jacob, are in awe, and like David, say, "You are awesome, O God, in your sanctuary" (Ps 68:34-35). Through worship, our minds are engaged in consciously remembering God's faithfulness to His promise.

Part III - Worship at the Altar and in the Tabernacle

The Tabernacle as a Sanctuary of God

Although the Israelites were officially established as a nation at Mount Sinai and entered into a covenant relationship with Yahweh at that time, they did not get to actually enter the Promised Land until forty years later "because those who heard did not combine it with faith" (Heb 4:2). The Law was given to God's people through Moses as a covenant stipulation (John 1:17). This "Mosaic covenant" was the only covenant God would ever make with an ethnic group of people (in this case, Israel). Yahweh was their true King; His words and instructions addressed every aspect of life for the people of Israel, from public health to social and religious spheres. Once again, as it was in the Garden, in the Promised Land, God's people were to live without making a distinction between secular laws (which were often administered by a state governor or king) and sacred, religious laws. There was no separate moral law that was distinguished apart from social or ceremonial law since everyone was ultimately morally accountable to Yahweh, whether a person had a career in the social world or was called to serve God regarding the "religious" matters in the Land. Since the entire nation was under the covenant with Yahweh, anyone who broke a religious law, i.e., the Sabbath, would receive a capital punishment (Num 15:32-36). Although the covenant was broken by the Israelites' idolatrous worship of the golden calf during the very time that Moses was up on the mountain receiving the Law (i.e., the covenant stipulations), originally God's call for the entire nation Israel was to be God's "treasured possession… a kingdom of priests and a holy nation" (Ex 19:5-6).

The Law covered a variety of aspects of life. The first two and a half chapters (Exodus 21-23) had to do with social law, but Exodus 23 to 40 discussed predominantly worship matters. For God's redeemed people, their primary purpose, responsibility and service to Yahweh who brought them out from the bondage of Egypt, was worship (Ex 3:12). The Israelites were to worship Yahweh and Him alone (Ex 20:2-6), "call[ing] on the name of Yahweh" in worship rather than misusing His name (v. 7). Therefore, one of the primary purposes of the Law was to establish guidelines for worshiping Yahweh. This shows how it was almost as though God could not wait until the Israelites entered the Land to establish worship. Even while they were still in the wilderness, as they continued to travel from one place to another like the patriarchs of the past, for forty years, they were to worship Yahweh in the way He meticulously prescribed for them. Since they were constantly on the move, all the furnishings related to worship were easily transportable.

10

The Tabernacle as a Sanctuary of God

Until the establishment of the nation Israel, individuals had built altars at various times and worshiped without a building or a mediator, priest. Yet the principle behind this practice has been grossly misapplied in our highly individualistic society today. These days, with the recent New Age movement (another form of Eastern religion, mainly Hinduism in Western dress) in America, we are encouraged to have religious or spiritual experiences without a mediator or organized religious institution; anyone can tap into the spiritual realm on their own terms, apart from any specific religious regulation.

But Yahweh God is the God of Trinity, God of community. Therefore, God did not leave it up to the individuals to decide how and when they could approach God in worship, perhaps at their own convenience. Since man has been created in God's image, the act of worship should reflect the invisible God, and therefore worship should be corporate rather than individualistic. Other aspects of the heavenly spiritual realm were also to be reflected and expressed in the visible world through worship. In this way, the meticulous instructions related to worship given in the Pentateuch were only a "copy and shadow of what is in heaven" (Heb 8:5). Even our prayer lives should reflect heavenly activities—"your will be done on earth as it is in heaven" (Matt 6:10).

Various Aspects of the Worshipers' Activities in Worship

In the Pentateuch, the meaning of the word "worship" (*chwh*) is not limited to a bowing down to worship. It is also commonly used to mean a gesture of greeting which was first used in Genesis 18:2 (and also 19:1) unless the object or context tells us otherwise (Gen 22:5; 24:26). The word "worship" first appears in Exodus in the people's response to Moses and Aaron testifying to how Yahweh "was concerned about them and had seen their misery, they bowed down and worshiped." Until the formal establishment of worship at Mount Sinai, approaching the altar to offer sacrifice or a simple gesture of bowing down to Yahweh in response to His faithfulness and goodness were both "worship."

Another aspect of worship is music. Music was first mentioned in the Pentateuch in Genesis 4:21 as having originated from Jubal, a descendant of Cain, perhaps among the people who were not known as worshipers of Yahweh. But the words "to sing" (*shyr*) and "song" (noun form of "to sing") first appear in Exodus in response to the people witnessing God's judgment upon the Egyptian army through the Red Sea (Ex 15:1). While the first music/musical instrument may have been found in a secular culture, the first singing of a song in the Pentateuch was for praising Yahweh. Any attempt to make a distinction between secular, worldly music and sacred praise by style of music ends up being highly subjective, especially when the subjectivity is based on a person's cultural background. Such a distinction should instead be made based on the lyrical content of the songs. This is so since music touches primarily our emotional aspect, which often can be subjective, while the content or lyrics of songs first touch our minds which are more objective.

Although the rest of the Pentateuch elaborates on how Yahweh ought to be worshiped by approaching the altar and how the service to Yahweh should be performed in the tabernacle, simply put, as in the past, worship is either offering sacrifice to Yahweh and/or bowing down before Him as a gesture of giving homage to Him, or singing praises as an offering/service to

Yahweh, which is another way of "calling on the name of Yahweh" in singing.

A typical modern-day Protestant worship service, especially if the format is more liturgical, has aspects similar to worship in the Pentateuch. We worship in response to God's word, the Bible, which is God's written revelation, through its reading and preaching. We give offering as an expression of our trust in God's faithfulness and provision and as a reminder that everything we have has just been entrusted to us as His stewards. We offer various kinds of prayers and praises to God and to one another. Simply put, through the entirety of the worship service, the worshipers are expected 1) to listen and respond, and 2) acknowledge in faith and offer/give. But these activities mainly have to do with what we do as worshipers. We turn now to consider not so much our "doing" but what God does and the spiritual fellowship that takes place between God and the worshipers in worship.

The Earthly Tabernacle as a Copy of the Heavenly Sanctuary

Countless attempts have been made to allegorize and spiritualize the meaning and significance of the tabernacle and its furnishings which Yahweh commissioned Moses to make with the voluntary offerings made by the Israelites in Exodus 25:1-9. In order to avoid over-interpreting the tabernacle and missing the Holy Spirit's intended meaning, we need to limit ourselves to what God has said elsewhere in His written word, the Bible, regarding the tabernacle. Three things need to be considered in this passage in relation to worship: 1) God's promise of indwelling among His people, 2) the result of His people's offering to God, and 3) the visible sanctuary that would be a copy of the true invisible heavenly sanctuary (Heb 8:5).

In Creation, God prepared the Garden, the sanctuary of God, for man to dwell in and have fellowship with God whose presence was there. When Adam and Eve were cast out from the Garden, they were banished from God's presence. Afterwards, the only way they could meet and have fellowship with God was to build an altar to offer sacrifice and approach God in worship. Now, once again, God, like in the Garden, is preparing a sanctuary, a tabernacle so that God might "dwell among" the Israelites (Ex 25:8) even though He is omnipresent. At Creation, God alone prepared the Garden before placing man there, and man was supposed "to work it and take care of it." But in Exodus 25, the people themselves are also involved in preparing this sanctuary as God gave specific instructions for it to be built with the offering from anyone "whose heart [prompted] him to give" (v. 2).

In Exodus 25 to 31, God spoke to Moses about the tabernacle and its furnishings, while in chapters 35 to 39, Moses communicated to the Israelites about the instructions he received from Yahweh, and then the people carried them out. How were the people able to give and make the tabernacle according to the heavenly blueprint? In the second half of Exodus (chapters 25-40), the tabernacle was built by the people whose hearts prompted them to give (Ex 25:2; 35:21, 29), and who were "filled... with the Spirit of God, with skill, ability and knowledge" (Ex 31:3; 35:30-35).

The word "to prompt" (*navad*) of Exodus 25:2, outside of the Pentateuch, besides referring to "freely giving gifts to God," is also used to describe volunteering oneself "for the service of Yahweh" (Judg 5:2, 9; 2 Ch 17:16), or simply doing something for God (Neh 11:2). More than anything, worshiping, serving, and giving should be done with a willing heart and not as an obligation or as an act of religious duty. The offering is just an external, visible expression of the person wholeheartedly being dedicated to God for His service. For this reason, before mention of what could be given to Yahweh for the freewill offering (Ex 25:3), emphasis is placed in the previous verse on the willing hearts of giving. Prior to the making of the actual offering itself, the person who gives the offering and his heart should be dedicated to the Lord. Let us remember it was Yahweh "looked with favor on Abel and his offering" (Gen 4:4).

Although Yahweh was the One who specifically gave the design and specifications for the tabernacle and its furnishing materials, Yahweh chose certain individuals by filling them with His Spirit to actually build the sanctuary (Ex 31:1-11; 35:30-35). Without the Holy Spirit's working in the hearts of the people, the worshipers' own willingness would be inadequate and not enough for the work of preparation and serving the Lord in the tabernacle. Another way of looking at this is that people can never suffice to serve God with their "natural talents" alone; there has to be a "filling of the

Spirit" in order for talented people to become God's instruments and used by Him.

We do not serve God with our talents alone. We may take great pride in our giftedness and ability to do so much. But we need to be reminded of the condition we were in when God called us—"Not many of you were wise by human standards; not many were influential; not many were of noble birth. But God chose the foolish things of the world to shame the wise" (1 Cor 1:26-27). We did not come to know the Lord with our human wisdom; the message of the gospel could only be accepted by faith. For this reason, Paul continued on to say in his letter to the church in Corinth, "my message and my preaching were not with wise and persuasive words, but with a demonstration of the Spirit's power, so that your faith might not rest on men's wisdom, but on God's power" (1 Cor 2:4-5). Church work is not done by a group of talented people. This really strikes at the heart for those gifted people who sincerely believe that with their willingness and abilities, they could do so much for God but are not desperate in seeking God or to be filled with the Holy Spirit.

Some of us are so self-absorbed, intoxicated with God's given talents, and we take great pride in what we were born with, somehow thinking that God cannot accomplish anything without our help. But we need to take our eyes off of our talents and what we have and deny ourselves to seek Him "who is invisible" (Heb 11:27). Like Moses who "refused to be known as the son of Pharaoh's daughter" (Heb 11:24), we need to look ahead to "win the prize for which God has called [us] heavenward in Christ Jesus" (Phil 3:14). Moses could have thought about staying in Egypt, taking on the role of being the second Joseph, to be used by God to protect and save his own people. Why not? After all, it was in God's sovereignty that Moses was drawn from the Nile River and grew up as a son of Pharaoh's daughter, receiving all the finest education and training in Pharaoh's palace (Acts 7:22). But Yahweh had a different plan; unlike Joseph in the palace, Moses would be used in the desert for forty years.

All kinds of precious jewels, stones, fabrics, oil and incense were dedicated to the Lord for the tabernacle and its furnishings. What was the purpose behind choosing skillful and artistically talented people to actually build the tabernacle and its furnishings (Ex 31:1-11)? So the worshipers could seek out the tabernacle for its aesthetic beauty? Surely not! Later, it was Moses who desperately sought God's presence—"If your Presence does not go with us do not send us up from here ... show me your glory" (Ex 33:15, 18). The whole purpose of willingly offering the finest and fully dedicating themselves to God's work was to do things exactly the way God had prescribed and to see Yahweh "dwell among them" just as it was in the Garden; "there, above the cover between the two cherubim that are over the ark of the Testimony, I will meet with you and give you all my commands for the Israelites" (Ex 25:22).

It was not the tabernacle or a temple building they were supposed to seek; after all, it was built according to the pattern that Moses would see upon the mount of God (Ex 25:9). The tabernacle in the wilderness would continue to serve as God's dwelling place until the Son of God would become flesh and make His dwelling (tabernacle) among His people (John 1:14).

The Tabernacle and Tent of Meeting

The word "tabernacle" (*mishkan*) that has its root in the word for "to dwell" is used for the first time in Exodus 25:9. Another name that was often used for the tabernacle is the "tent of meeting" (*ohel moed*) (Ex 27:2). Sometimes in order to emphasize what was contained in the tabernacle, it was called "the Tent of the Testimony" (Num 9:15; 2 Ch 24:6). Once the tabernacle and its furnishings were built, the Israelites were "to camp around the Tent of Meeting some distance from it" (Num 2:1). God had said that He would dwell among the Israelites, and the tabernacle was a daily reminder of God's faithfulness to the promise of His presence.

There is a connection between the tabernacle and observing the Sabbath in Leviticus 26:2—"Observe my Sabbaths and have reverence for my sanctuary. I am [Yahweh]." The purpose of the Sabbath was not just to have a day of inactivity in the name of "rest" (i.e., to just not do anything on that day), but rather that man, who has been created in God's image, should reflect who God is since "God rested from all the work of creating that he had done" (Gen 2:3). Since the Land or sanctuary where God dwelt and all its inhabitants were created in six days, man ought to enter into the Sabbath, the sanctuary where God dwells, with gladness and thanksgiving. For this reason, towards the end of Leviticus 26, although the ground was "cursed" because of the first Adam, if the Israelites had "reverence for" God's indwelling presence in the Land, "the ground [would] yield its crops and the trees of the field their fruit" (v. 4); Yahweh would grant "peace in the land" (v. 6); God would make them "fruitful and increase [their] numbers" (v. 9). All those are the reminders of the Land, Garden, and sanctuary before the Fall. And now, God gives this promise if they obey Him in the Promised Land: "I will put my dwelling place among you... I will walk among you and be your God, and you will be my people" (vv. 11-12).

Unfortunately, when the Israelites entered the Land, they ended up desecrating it by tirelessly worshiping idols when God had so clearly warned them against it (Lev 26:1). Simply put, because the idolaters polluted the Land, the Land could not experience the Sabbath until once again God would cast out the people from the Land towards the east, to Babylonia— "The land enjoyed its sabbath rests; all the time of its desolation it rested, until the seventy years were completed" (2 Ch 36:21).

What Israel as a nation failed to do, the true Israel, Jesus Christ succeeded in when he completely obeyed and perfectly kept his covenant with God the Father. Therefore, the people under the new covenant in Christ as "the temple of the living God," living in "the time of [God's] favor... in the day of salvation," have the privilege to experience the fullness of God's presence as God living with us and walking among us (2 Cor 6:2, 16). Therefore, at the end of the passage, Paul says that in the light of such great promises, we are called to "purify ourselves from everything that contaminates body and spirit, perfecting holiness out of reverence for God" (7:1). For this reason, the new covenant worshipers must be aware of God's presence in and among the community of faith. They are to seek God's holy presence in worship. The worshipers must purify themselves to be compatible to God's holiness since they are in the very presence of God.

Until the building of the first temple by his son Solomon, David often emphasized Yahweh's dwelling in the book of Psalms (Ps 68:5). Though there was no temple building in his days, throughout David's life, he continued to seek the sanctuary or house of Yahweh (Ps 27:4). The closest thing they had to a "house" or "dwelling place" for God was "the ark of the covenant" (2 Sam 15:25). Other than being overlaid with pure gold, the ark of the Testimony was not all that lavishly decorated. The beauty was not in the detailed decorations bur rather in God's promise—"There, above the cover between the two cherubim that are over the ark of the Testimony, I will meet with you" (Ex 25:22). Likewise, no matter how beautiful or majestic the grandeur of the temple building would be, it would be no comparison to the beauty of Yahweh. David sought God's dwelling place, the sanctuary where Yahweh would meet him.

The tabernacle was often referred to as the "tent of meeting" (*ohel moed* in Ex 27:21). This phrase is used over thirty times just in Exodus alone. The main purpose of having a "dwelling place" for God was so that the worshipers could meet God at an appointed time. Unlike in the Garden, where there was no barrier between God and man and therefore no need for an appointment, with the tabernacle/tent of meeting, worshipers were limited as to how often they could meet God. They could not just go to God whenever they felt like it. It was another reminder of the sin that caused there to be a barrier between God and sinful people after the Fall. As the matter of fact, for the Israelites under the old covenant, only one person, the high priest on behalf of the whole nation, could actually enter the Most Holy Place where the ark of the Testimony was, and this was only once a year.

In our days, some worshipers tend to take a casual attitude towards Sunday worship service when it comes to preparing their hearts and minds beforehand. They can have a habit of tardiness, but in their minds, it is permissible as long as they do not miss the sermon. Or if they do miss the sermon, they can always get it from the Internet later. If other "more important" appointments come up at the time of their regular weekly-appointed service, that week, they can choose to attend worship at another church, meeting at a more suitable time, thereby fitting worship into their schedule (which, to give credit where credit is due, is better than skipping altogether) instead of arranging their schedule around their commitment to meet God with a specific body of believers. We really need to rediscover biblically what it means to be in God's dwelling place as a community of worshipers. And before anything, our attitude towards the Sunday worship service should be of having an appointment with God. For this reason, being committed and accountable to a local church is imperative in order to keep us from falling into the temptation of serving the Holy God at our own convenience.

Under the old covenant, the tabernacle continually served as the shadow of what was to come, "an annual reminder of sins" (Heb 10:3) for the worshipers until the coming of the Great High Priest, Jesus Christ (Heb 4:14). When He came, "the blood of Christ... [would] cleanse our consciences from acts that lead to death, so that we may serve the living God" (Heb 9:14). Now, under the new covenant, it is no longer just the one high priest who can enter the Most Holy Place once a year, but through the Great High Priest, "who has gone through the heavens," all God's people can "approach the throne of grace with confidence" ("between the two cherubim") (Heb 4:16).

Prior to Yahweh giving the instructions for making the tabernacle/ tent of meeting, Exodus 33:7 tells us about another tent of meeting which Moses put up from time to time—"Now Moses used to take a tent and pitch it outside the camp some distance away, calling it the 'tent of meeting.'" The tent of meeting in Exodus 33 should not be confused with the tabernacle. Sailhamer's comments should help us to think about the tension between God's dwelling place being among the Israelites but at the same time God being set apart.

"After the incident of the golden calf... the narrative tells of another 'Tent of Meeting.' This 'tent' was not the same as the tabernacle. It was a meeting place with God that was 'outside the camp some distance away'... at this point in the narrative the tabernacle was not yet built... The original idea of a 'Tent of Meeting' by which God would dwell among his people had now become one of the means whereby God had been set apart from them." (John Sailhamer, *NIV Compact Bible Commentary*, p.100)

The tent was supposed to serve as a visual reminder of how God's holy presence was in their midst but at the same time how sin separated God and the Israelites. We do not know whether both the tabernacle and Moses' tent continued to coexist or whether it was that Moses' tent was eventually replaced by the tabernacle which would also be called by the same name ("tent of meeting"), though the latter is most likely. But biblically, the mentioning of Moses' tent comes after the golden calf incident from the previous chapter, and the tabernacle was yet to be built; therefore, it further emphasized how God's presence manifested visually by "the pillar of cloud" (Ex 33:9) moved "outside the camp" (v. 7). Kaiser comments on how the Israelites could no longer enjoy God's holy presence in their midst because of their idolatry:

"It [the tent of meeting] may have been one that Moses set up outside the camp as sort of a second home and the only place where the presence of God would meet him (the presence of sin in the camp handicapped that function there). One thing is certain: this could not have been the Tabernacle itself... the important point was that God had withdrawn His presence, and He had visibly removed Himself from their midst. Moses was the only remaining point of contact for the grace of God in their lives." (Walter Kaiser, *Quest for Renewal*, p.48)

Several questions readers are led to ask are worth pondering. It says, "Anyone inquiring of the Lord would go to the tent of meeting outside the camp" (Ex 33:7). How often did individuals encounter issues in life that led them to seek Yahweh at the tent of meeting? Everyone had the privilege to approach Moses' tent of meeting, while the only time a non-priest could be in the tabernacle courtyard was when the person was offering a sacrifice to Yahweh. Did the Israelites continue to seek God's answer at the tabernacle as they had done with the Moses' tent? Or did they just focus on offering sacrifices to God as a part of their religious duty? Long after, David prophesied about the Son of David, Christ's perfect sacrifice versus the sacrificial system under the old covenant—"Sacrifice and offering you did not desire... Then I said, 'Here I am, I have come—it is written about me in the scroll.' I desire to do your will, O my God; your law is within my heart" (Ps 40:6-8).

Since the altar and tabernacle sacrificial regulations were the shadows of the ultimate sacrifice of Christ's death on the cross, the ultimate goal of worship was supposed to be that through the means of the sacrificial system, the worshipers were to find a grace of approaching God and learning God's will. And so it is for the new covenant worshipers—being able to approach God because of the perfect sacrifice offered on the cross, and seeking His will as the Holy Spirit illumines God's word in their hearts. Has that become the main goal in our worship?

What Actually Took Place in the Tabernacle

Yahweh repeatedly told Moses that the tabernacle, which was to be built was a pattern or model of what God revealed to Moses upon the mountain (Ex 25:9, 40; 26:30). The tabernacle was never the end itself but the means through which worshipers were to seek Yahweh. Therefore, rather than trying to see the tabernacle and its furnishings as having some type of symbolic or spiritual meaning behind them, one needs to see if their purposes were given in the book of Exodus and also if the New Testament says anything about them.

The author of the Epistle to the Hebrews describes the tabernacle, listing its furnishings, but does not assign any symbolic or spiritual meaning to them. Rather than "discuss these things in detail," his main concern is that through the tabernacle, "The Holy Spirit was showing by this that the way into the Most Holy Place had not yet been disclosed" (Heb 9:8). The author goes onto to say, "this is an illustration for the present time, indicating that the gifts and sacrifices being offered were not able to clear the conscience of the worshiper" (v. 9). The main purpose of the worship in the tabernacle was for the worshiper whose "conscience" had been cleansed to be able to "enter" into the very presence of God. The old covenant sacrificial system may have cleansed the worshiper "outwardly," but it was necessary for the Son of God, Christ, to come and die on the cross in order to "cleanse our consciences... so that we may serve the living God" (vv. 13-14). Therefore, our main concern for the worship at the tabernacle should be the significance behind all the activities that took place at the courtyard and in the tabernacle.

Although the ark of the Testimony, which was placed in the Most Holy Place, reminded the worshiper that the purpose of worship was to "meet" Yahweh (Ex 25:22), only once a year was the high priest to be in the very presence of God. The worshipers who approached the tabernacle, as they were entering the courtyard, were expected to believe they were approaching Yahweh as the Levites were ministering/ carrying out their responsibilities before His presence. For this reason, the bread in the Holy Place was called "the bread of the Presence" (v. 30), which was another reminder of God's faithful promise that He would be there.

The purpose of the lampstand in the Holy Place was to "light the space in front of" the curtain that separated the Holy Place from the Most Holy Place (Ex 25:37). It was one of the daily priest's responsibilities "to keep the lamps burning before [Yahweh] from evening till morning" (Ex 27:21). Although the daily responsibilities in the tabernacle mainly consisted of keeping the lamps and incense burning and replacing the bread with a fresh loaf, the priest was ready to serve Yahweh in the lighted space at all times. Ministering before Yahweh was a continuous activity as referenced in Revelation: "they are before the throne of God and serve him day and night in his temple; and he who sits on the throne will spread his tent over them" (Rev 7:15). The last psalm of the "song of ascents" series speaks on this, "Praise [Yahweh], all you servants of [Yahweh] who minister by night in the house of [Yahweh]" (Ps 134:1).

The priest was supposed to "burn fragrant incense on the altar every morning... [and] again... at twilight so incense [would] burn regularly before [Yahweh]" (Ex 30:7-8). In such way, the worshipers' prayers were to be offered continuously. Much later, though most likely David was not in the Holy Place, he described his petition before Yahweh by comparing it with the incense of the Holy Place (Ps 141:2). The apostle John in his visionary experience saw the descriptive activity and result of "the prayers of all the saints" going up before God (Rev 8:3-5).

One can imagine that all the activities that took place in the Holy Place served as visual aids for the worshiper to experience prayer on a physical level—the fragrance, smoke rising up, the bread, and the lamp to light the space. Just as real as what the worshiper experienced physically was the invisible activity happening in the spiritual realm, the physical experience becoming a point of contact for the believer's faith.

How should knowing they are in the presence of God and that the prayers of worshipers have a direct impact on what is happening in this world affect those who gather for service on Sunday? Are we as worshipers conscious of the fact that worshiping is ministering before God?

The curtain in the tabernacle served as a barrier to limit how "close" a person could come to Yahweh (Ex 26:33). The tabernacle itself was a reminder that there was a clear distinction between the priests and the Levites. Whenever a worshiper entered the courtyard that was marked by curtains, he was reminded of the difference between what was common the outside the curtains and what was holy in God's presence within. The only business the person had entering the court was to worship by either offering a sacrifice or giving gifts to Yahweh. The courtyard was as far as an average non-Levite could come into the presence of Yahweh. There could have been a longing in their souls, wanting to be closer to Yahweh. While some had the privilege of being in "the sanctuary of God" and confessed, "it is good to be near God" (Ps 73:17, 28), the majority of the Israelites did not have such a privilege, let alone that of ministering in the Most Holy Place.

Jesus Christ came and through His death broke down the further barrier between the Israelites and the Gentiles; through Christ "we both [Israel and Gentiles] have access to the Father by one Spirit" (Eph 2:18). By "the law with its commandments and regulations," some people were "far away" from the Most Holy Place, while others were "near" to the temple (vv. 15, 17). By the blood Christ, worshipers under the new covenant enter the Most Holy Place, the very presence of God—"we who worship by the Spirit of God, who glory in Christ Jesus" (Phil 3:3). For this reason, we approach God with "our hearts... strengthened by grace" (Heb 13:9) because of God's redemptive work through Christ's death. We come to the table, "an altar from which those who minister at the tabernacle have no right to eat" (v. 10); we eat and drink, not because of our own merit but because of what Christ has done on the cross, for after all, the Lord's Supper is for those who have been forgiven by the blood of Christ.

How shall we worship? Who or what ought we to seek in worship? Who has the right to approach God in worship if it is not those who are wise, influential, or of noble birth (1 Cor 1:26)? Ultimately, whom do we worship?

Why do we approach God in worship anyway? To answer this question, it is worth noting the design of the priestly garments. Aaron was the first high priest, and his role was to approach God on behalf of the people of Israel (Ex 28:29). The whole purpose of the "breastpiece" was "for making decisions... [to] bear the means of making decisions for the Israelites" (vv. 15, 30). The decorative stones, although they may have been precious and costly, had one purpose: to help the people to know God's will as the priest approached Yahweh on the Israelites' behalf in the Holy Place. Because of the light, the beauty of the various stones mounted on the breastpiece was visible. Without the light transmitting and reflecting off of the stones, they would be just stones. Again the visionary experience of the apostle John deserves our attention—"the Holy City... shone with the glory of God, and its brilliance was like that of a very precious jewel... the city does not need the sun or the moon to shine on it, for the glory of God gives it light, and the Lamb is its lamp" (Rev 21:10-11, 23). The list of stones mentioned in Revelation 21:19-20 is reminder of the list of stones in Exodus 28:17-20. Just as it was for Aaron to approach God and God revealed His will to Aaron, as the worshipers of the new covenant approach God in worship, just as "everything exposed by the light becomes visible," the worshipers are called to "understand what the Lord's will is" (Eph 5:14, 17).

This approaching of God to hear and know His decision and will may not be the attitude of modern worshipers. David wrote about his desire to worship God in "the house of [Yahweh]" (Ps 122:1). As David approached Yahweh in worship, his view of Yahweh was God as a judge (v. 5). Basically, he understood God's original intention for worshipers as they were in the presence of God. Just as it was in the Garden, before the altar, and in the Holy Place, worshipers ought to approach God expecting His assessment of and decisions for our lives. Yet for many of us today, it seems just the opposite as we come to God already having made our decisions and simply expecting Him to meet our needs. C.S. Lewis once wrote the following worth pondering:

"The ancient man approached God (or even the gods) as the accused person approaches his judge. For the modern man the roles are reversed. He is the judge: God is in the dock. He is quite a kindly judge: if God should have a reasonable defense for being the god who permits war, poverty and disease, he is ready to listen to it. The trial may even end in God's acquittal. But the important thing is that Man is on the Bench and God in the dock" (C. S. Lewis, *God in the Dock: Essays on Theology and Ethics*, p. 244)

The meticulous details given by Yahweh on Mount Sinai regarding the tabernacle and its furnishings in the book of Exodus could easily bore a reader, and this is not the only place in the Bible where this happens. Later when Solomon built a temple building for Yahweh, its decorative details and furnishings were carefully described in 1 Kings 6-8. The modern reader may not appreciate such detailed descriptions, but the majority of the Israelite worshipers would never have had the Holy Place experience. For this reason, God graciously invited His people to read His revealed written Word and get a glimpse of the beauty of God's holy presence. Of course there were many other manmade structures or objects that could have far outshone the physical beauty of the tabernacle or ark of Yahweh. But could it be that God limited the visible description of the tabernacle so the worshipers would take their eyes off the external beauty and focus their hearts and minds on the true reality, the beauty of Yahweh? All the details should not lead us to seek some type of spiritual meaning behind them but rather lead us to be immersed in our imagination of the beauty of Yahweh based on His written word as we engage in worship. God wants worshipers not to be distracted by the beautiful things of this world but rather see Jesus Christ and all of His splendor as their hearts and minds are sprinkled by Christ's blood and the renewing work of God's word.

A similar concept could have been one of the reasons behind attaching "gold bells… around the hem of the robe… The sound of the bells will be heard when [the priest] enters the Holy Place before [Yahweh]" (Ex 28:33-35). Worshipers in the courtyard could only hear the bells as the priest was ministering inside the Holy Place. The people not being able to see, all ears would have been attentive to hear the sound of the ministering priest.

With modern technological advancement where much has to do with the visual and virtual reality, it seems like just reading alone may not be intriguing enough, even for many Christians; in a world increasingly predominated (and thereby actually limited) by the visual, unless something is visually stimulating, it is not considered "interactive" and exciting. It is interesting to note that even the book of Revelation, mostly composed of images, emphasizes at the very beginning of its first chapter the written word that needs to be read, proclaimed, heard, and taken to heart (Rev 1:3). This is not to say that incorporating creativity and art into the worship service is not worth exploring; of course it should. Yet primarily, worship should be based on hearing what God has to say rather than our response to our needs and perception.

The Visible Manifestation of God's Glory

In the last chapter of Exodus, both the terms "tabernacle" and "Tent of Meeting" are used within the same verse (Ex 40:2, 6, 22, 24, 29, 34, 35). The reason behind this could have been to emphasize the fact that the whole purpose of worship was to experience God's presence, meeting God to have intimate fellowship with Him. When "Moses finished the work" of setting up the tabernacle, "then the cloud covered the Tent of Meeting, and the glory of [Yahweh] filled the tabernacle. Moses could not enter the Tent of Meeting because the cloud had settled upon it, and the glory of [Yahweh] filled the tabernacle" (vv. 33-35). At the most surface level, if the tabernacle was filled with cloud, it made it impossible for anyone to minister before Yahweh. Perhaps the only act of service to Yahweh possible at that point was to bow down in worship. It was an awesome manifestation and reminder of God's presence among his people, foreshadowing the future Holy City in Christ, "the name of the city from that time on will be: the Lord Is There" (Ezek 48:35).

It was the only time the glory cloud ever filled the tabernacle; from that point on, the cloud of Yahweh would continue to be over the tabernacle throughout the wilderness journey (Ex 40:38). The next time the glory cloud filled a sanctuary would be in the newly built temple building by Solomon (1 Kings 8:10-11). But there, just as with the tabernacle, it happened only once. Yet there would still be yet another time, for God made a promise through the prophet Haggai to those who returned to Jerusalem from the exile, "The glory of this present house will be greater than the glory of the former house" (Hag 2:9). It was so since the Son of God would eventually "come to his temple; the messenger of the covenant" (Mal 3:1). And when Christ came, He would cleanse the temple (John 2:13-19), foreshadowing His death on the cross so the people would "bring offerings in righteousness" (Mal 3:3).

Although God filling the tabernacle with His glory cloud happened just once, it was a reminder for the Israelites to place their hope in Yahweh, a sign that one day, God would personally through the Holy Spirit dwell in the midst the community of worshipers under the new covenant in Christ Jesus.

After the golden calf incident in Exodus 32, Moses desperately sought and pleaded for God's ways and presence (vv. 13-15). In response to Moses' plea, God caused all His goodness and glory to pass by Moses (vv. 19-22). From what Moses experienced on Mount Sinai, his face ended up reflecting God's glory (Ex 34:29-30). Although God's glory was only reflected on Moses' face, nevertheless the grace of His indwelling presence among the sinful people was visible over the tabernacle/tent of meeting in the form of the cloud. The cloud of Yahweh continued to be over the tabernacle "in the sight of all the house of Israel during all their travels" (Ex 40:38). Although the Israelites were unfaithful to the covenant, the faithfulness of Yahweh never departed from them. Surely, Yahweh granted Moses' plea on behalf of the Israelites!

Whether the visible manifestation of God that came down in "the pillar of cloud" at the entrance of the tent of meeting (v. 9), or later when the same manifestation of God's glory continued to cover "the tabernacle, the Tent of the Testimony" throughout the Israelites' wilderness journey for forty years (Num 9:15-16), it must have been a spectacular scene. The glory cloud continued to be visible both day and night, and its movement served to signal when the Israelites were to set out or settle in a particular place in the wilderness (Num 9:15-23). More than anyone, Moses knew what it meant to have Yahweh's glory cloud over the tabernacle since that was what he desperately sought (Ex 33:15). Moses sang the following song of prayer "whenever the ark set out... 'Rise up, O [Yahweh]! May your enemies be scattered; may your foes flee before you.' Whenever it came to rest, he said, 'Return, O [Yahweh], to the countless thousands of Israel'" (Num 10:35-36). It must have been just an awesome sight to see the glory cloud actually arise or come down upon the tabernacle.

When the people first witnessed God's glory resting upon Moses' tent of meeting and the tabernacle, it left the Israelites with no choice but to rise and "worship[ed]" (Ex 33:10). If it only happens once or twice, anything, whether miraculous or even just out-of-the-ordinary, could amaze us. But since the manifestation of God's glory was continuously visible on a daily basis for forty years, since people are easily bored with familiarity, did the Israelites continue to respond in awe and worship Yahweh each day?

The cloud over the tabernacle was the visible manifestation of God's glory as a reminder and sign of God's faithfulness and His presence over His people. Every Sunday as we enter into worship, we are reminded of God's faithfulness, even if we have been unfaithful: "If we are faithless, he will remain faithful, for he cannot disown himself" (2 Tim 2:13). The covenant between God the Father and the Son was ultimately fulfilled through Christ's death and resurrection. Although the gospel message may seem repetitious each week, through it, there ought to be a renewed sense in the worshipers' minds that God is faithful. Has the cross of our Lord Jesus Christ become too familiar to us such that it no longer moves us into a state of awe in worship?

PART IV - WORSHIP AT AN ALTAR WITHOUT A TEMPLE BUILDING

After the Israelites settled in the Promised Land, during Joshua's days, they set up the Tent of Meeting at Shiloh (Josh 18:1). Shiloh became the central place for worship since the Tent of Meeting continued to serve as a reminder of God's presence (1 Sam 1:3). Since God had told the Israelites, "Three times a year all the men are to appear before the Sovereign" Yahweh (Ex 23:17), worshiping at the Tabernacle was infrequent. Since the Israelites could only worship at the Tabernacle, and the people eventually lived some distance from Shiloh, it made more sense to appear before Yahweh three times a year, while individuals prayed daily.

The worship at the Tabernacle not only involved worshipers offering sacrifices; prayers were also offered to Yahweh (1 Sam 1:9-10), commitments made, and the priestly assurance and blessing was pronounced (1 Sam 1:9-11, 17).

During the days of Samuel, the Ark of the Covenant became more than just a reminder of God's presence for the Israelites; the people wrongly came to believe that it actually "was" God's presence. Therefore, they believed "it" could save them from their enemies (1 Sam 4:3), and rather than seeking Yahweh, they sought after power and perhaps "fortune" or some type of answer from Yahweh. They had lost touch with the Living God and limited Yahweh to a material thing, the Ark of the Covenant; more than the visible Ark or the Tabernacle, they were supposed "to commit" themselves to Yahweh "and serve him only" (1 Sam 7:3), which they often failed to do.

Once the ark of Yahweh was "recaptured" and placed in Abinadab's house at Kiriath Jearim (1 Sam 7:1), it is likely that gradually, over a period of time, the original tabernacle, which was at Shiloh without the Ark, lost its significance in the religious life of Israel. Because of this, it is also probable that Samuel built altars in various places (v. 9) apart from the Ark of the Covenant. Although Samuel was better known as a prophet, without anyone from the main priestly line of Eli really serving the Lord (1 Sam 2:34-36), and Samuel himself being a descendant of Kohath the Levite (1 Chr 6:22-28), it was most likely that Samuel was the one who mainly offered sacrifices by building altars to Yahweh. Samuel's prophetic ministry, especially intercessory prayer and worship, reminds us of Abraham's prophetic ministry of prayer (Gen 20:7) and building altars wherever he went.

Contrary to Samuel, Saul used worship and the sacrificial act, although he was not authorized to do so, to win God's favor in his desperate situation (1 Sam 13:12). Saul tried to receive some type of answer from God by using "the ark of God" as a means to hear from God; for Saul, worship through sacrifice was just a means to get what he needed in his desperation (1 Sam 14:18-19). Saul's interest was not Yahweh. Yahweh was just a means to what Saul desired. Therefore, towards the end of Saul's tragic life, when Yahweh "did not answer him by dreams or Urim or prophets," Saul even sought out " a woman who [was] a medium" (1 Sam 28:6-7). For Saul, the truth could be sacrificed as long as his curiosity about his own "fate" could be satisfied. Saul would do the act of worship—building an altar to offer sacrifices, as long as he could get an answer from God, or any gods or spirit for that matter.

This skewed belief and deviation from the revealed will of Yahweh regarding worship challenges the modern day worshipers. Has worship become a means to an end, about getting our way by using God? Do we come to worship thinking we can twist God's arm through our religiosity and performance (Matt 6:7)? Has the cross of Jesus become our false security in the same way the Israelites regarded the Ark? Are we in any way guilty of "being spiritual" or "seeking spiritual things" without having any regard for the truth, the written revelation of God? Let us return to the true heart of worship, that through the blood of Christ, worshipers can approach God and seek His presence.

11

WORSHIP AND THE PROPHET'S MINISTRY

Besides Samuel (1 Sam 7:3-4), throughout Israel's history when the nation failed to worship Yahweh and turned to other gods, from time to time, like in the days of Judges, God would raise up prophets to turn the nation back to Yahweh (1 Kings 18:32, 36-37), and the emphasis was on worshiping the true God (v. 24). For the prophets, the issue was the truth. One of the major prophetic ministries was seeing the situation of the society from the vantage point of Yahweh which was defined by God's word, and from this spiritual perspective, confronting the nation(s) or individuals with a message from the Lord. The old covenant prophet's ministry continued on down to John, the son of Zechariah, and often the prophets' experience and ministry played an integral part in establishing the true life of worship in Israel before and after the establishment of the temple building. This could have been the reason that the Samaritan woman brought up the issue of worship after realizing that Jesus was a prophet (John 4:19-20).

Training in Worship and Intercession

Although God's calling on Samuel's life was that of a prophet—"all Israel ... recognized that Samuel was attested as a prophet of [Yahweh]," he grew up in Shiloh where the daily schedule revolved around worship under the ministry of Eli. Therefore, by the time Samuel entered into ministry as a prophet, more than anything, he was well-equipped, unlike Eli's two sons, for doing worship ministry. Samuel's understanding of worship is best revealed in his interactions with Saul. One of the major areas in which Saul continued to spiral downward spiritually was in his understanding of worship and the way he used it towards his own ends rather than actually worshipping Yahweh alone.

Samuel entered the stage as a spiritual leader of Israel when he led people in repentance at Mizpah (1 Sam 7:5-6). The timing was appropriate for Samuel's leadership since the Spirit of God was already working in the hearts of the people—"all the people of Israel mourned and sought after [Yahweh]" (v. 2). Without any further delay, Samuel told the people to get rid of "the foreign gods and Ashtoreths and commit" themselves to Yahweh and "serve him only" (v. 3). It is interesting to note that people can actually seek the Lord while still having idols in their hearts. For those who enter into the house of the Lord to worship, there has to be a self-examination of the heart. It was the case not only for the Israelites at Mizpah but also for the people in Joshua's days (Josh 24:19-23). Worship can become a great opportunity to do a spiritual self-inventory to examine whether there are competing members being allowed in one's heart.

When the Philistines came to attack the people who had gathered at Mizpah, out of fear they asked Samuel to intercede for them (1 Sam 7:7-8). Samuel sacrificed a whole burnt offering and "cried out to [Yahweh] on Israel's behalf" (v. 9). Not only was there a "call[ing] on the name of [Yahweh]" in worship (Gen 4:26), but also a prayer of intercession was offered in worship. For Samuel, the act of worship by sacrificing a burnt offering was not an end itself or just doing things as a part of a religious ritual, but rather, through this worship, he offered the sacrifice of prayer.

Much of a typical evangelical Sunday worship service has to do with a sermon, the singing of hymns and a public prayer. From the text, it is not clear whether the people joined Samuel in prayer or whether just Samuel alone interceded for them and the situation Israel was facing. But one thing that is certain is that while the suckling lamb was being offered, burning up and turning into ashes, Samuel was crying out to the Lord in prayer. There is a place for public or pastoral prayer in the worship service. At the same time, worshipers should be encouraged and given an opportunity to participate in prayer that is not being led by someone else but is a crying out to the Lord in unison corporately in Jesus' name. Otherwise, in the name of having an "orderly worship service," worshipers only get to participate by listening to a sermon, joining in on someone else's prayer, and singing hymns, and they seldom have the opportunity to participate in crying out together in the prayer of intercession.

Samuel's ministry of leading the people back to Yahweh at Mizpah reminds us of the importance of preparing one's heart for worship and having intercession in worship. If worshipers at a church in a city or town dared to look deeply into their hearts and examine themselves before entering into their weekly Sunday worship service, willing to renounce any idols in their hearts, being fully committed to Jesus Christ and serve Him only, who knows, what was said about Samuel's days could become true for our church—"Throughout Samuel's lifetime, the hand of [Yahweh] was against the Philistines" (1 Sam 7:13). May the Lord continue to increase the sphere of influence of His church in the city and beyond; may the Lord protect His church since "the gates of Hades will not overcome" it (Matt 16:18)! May our church continue to receive help from the God of Ebenezer as the worshipers unceasingly offer prayers of intercession for the church and the city, as our prayers rise upward towards the throne of God, just as it was for Samuel's burnt offering, that while the black burning smoke was rising into the sky, Yahweh delivered Israel.

Worship and the Coming of the Spirit, Music and Songs

When the Israelites witnessed Yahweh's mighty act of deliverance by the Red Sea, "the people feared [Yahweh] and put their trust in him... Then Moses and the Israelites sang this song" (Ex 14:31-15:1). It is clear that prior to praise, there has to be faith in God; only those who have experienced God's salvation can truly worship God in praise (Rev 15:2-3).

Miriam the prophetess was the first one to praise Yahweh for Yahweh's mighty act of deliverance and led other women to sing praise unto Yahweh (Ex 15:19-21); in today's language we could say that she was the first "worship leader."

The word "prophetess" (appearing here for the first time in feminine form) is used closely connected with the following verse on praising Yahweh. Here, early on in the history of Israel, one of the prophetic ministries was worshipping Yahweh in praise. Later, the prophetess Deborah, who led Israel as a judge, composed a song of celebrating Yahweh's victory in praise (Judges 5:1).

People like Moses, Miriam, and Deborah, who were known as prophets, led or contributed musical songs of praise in the religious life of Israel. Therefore, it should be no surprise to find a group of prophets prophesying while playing musical instruments (1 Sam 10:5). It was most likely that the music the prophets were playing was spiritual, praising Yahweh, since they were prophesying in the context of the music. In the context of worship, the Spirit of Yahweh came upon Saul in power, and he prophesied with them (vv. 6, 10).

The Bible does not always say what exactly the people were prophesying when the Spirit of Yahweh came upon the individuals, especially in the Old Testament. "Prophesying" carries mainly two meanings: "speaking forth or into" and "foretelling." But one thing that was certain was that the prophetic spirit came upon the people in the context of worship, as they were praising Yahweh.

The New Testament gives us a fuller understanding of the relationship between prophesying and praising. When the Holy Spirit came upon the believers on the day of Pentecost, one of the characteristics marking the arrival of the Last Days, they began to "declare" in different languages "the wonders of God" (Acts 2:1-4, 11, 17). Most likely they were speaking about and proclaiming the accomplishment of God's marvelous redemptive work through the death and resurrection of Christ since Peter used that phenomenon as a platform to proclaim the gospel message in a historical and systematic way in the following section.

If prophesying is associated with "speaking by the Spirit of God," the main crux of the content should be the gospel, proclaiming, "Jesus is Lord"

(1 Cor 12:3). One of the ministries of the Holy Spirit in us is making known to us what is of Christ (John 16:14). This really assures us and helps us with discerning the spirit; the context is always Christ-centered and based on His word. The apostle John in his impulsive response as he was overwhelmed by the grace of God in being invited to "the wedding supper of the Lamb... fell at [the angel's] feet to worship him" (Rev 19:9-10). But the angel reminded John, "Worship God! For the testimony of Jesus is the spirit of prophecy." Notice the spirit of prophecy or proclamation (which is really the gospel of Christ) is associated with worship.

When there is a prophetic word proclaiming Christ, the right response should be worshiping God, and this response often leads the people to worship in praise. When "the Spirit of [Yahweh] came upon Jehaziel," who was a descendant of Asaph, Jehaziel prophesied/proclaimed God's promise to the people who were in fear of the vast armies of Moab and Ammon. In response to the prophetic words, "Jehoshaphat... and all the people of Judah... fell down in worship before [Yahweh]... Jehoshaphat appointed men to sing to [Yahweh] and to praise him for the splendor of his holiness" (2 Chr 20:14, 18, 21).

It is interesting to note how the author gives Jehaziel's background information—connecting him with Asaph, who was mainly known as a Levite who had written many Psalms. Earlier in the First Chronicles are also mentioned the sons of Asaph whom David "set apart" along with others "for the ministry of prophesying accompanied by" various different musical instruments (1 Chr 25:1); the ministry of worship and the ministry of prophecy go hand-in-hand. These two are almost inseparable with the prophetic spirit: prophesying is proclaiming God's gracious promise of salvation, and primarily in the worship context, the prophetic word is released. Therefore, all the more it is imperative that today's worshipers and worship leaders need to be filled with the Holy Spirit like in the past when individuals became prophetic as the Spirit came upon them (Num 11:25).

The whole event of 2 Chronicles 20 is centered on worshiping/ praising Yahweh—"they praised [Yahweh]. This is why it is called the Valley of Berakah to this day" (2 Chr 20:26). The pattern we find in this passage—the coming of the Spirit, the proclamation of God's promise, and the people worshipping Yahweh in praise in response to His word, shows an integral connection between prophetic ministry and worship, specifically praising God.

The apostle Paul in his letter to the Ephesians says, "be filled with the Spirit," and then immediately in the next verses connects being filled with the Spirit with worshiping the Lord in praise. Most commentators have different opinions on what the types of musical songs listed in Ephesians 5:19 actually were, especially regarding "spiritual songs." Historically, many pagan religions, with regard to their spirituality and pagan religious practices, especially in connection with Dionysus, the god of sensual pleasure, believed one of the ways to tap into the spiritual realm and "transcend the drabness and monotony of day-to-day life" was getting intoxicated with wine that led to debauchery (Clinton E. Arnold, *Power of Darkness*, p. 43-45). But true spirituality is being filled with the Holy Spirit that would result in worship in praise of Yahweh.

Christians cannot be presumptuous when it comes to "being filled with the Spirit," assuming they are always in this state because the Holy Spirit resides in them. Those who are musically gifted should not assume musical ability alone qualifies them to serve in the music/worship ministry. A song written for Jesus by someone who is a Christian does not automatically become a spiritual song. When the tabernacle was being built, the skill of the best artisans recruited did not suffice; Yahweh had to fill them with the Spirit for the work to be properly done. Therefore, as repeatedly throughout the bible worship in singing praises was tied together with the coming of the Spirit and becoming a prophetic person, today the worshiping community of faith should seek to be filled with God's Spirit at the Sunday worship service more than at any other meeting of the church.

The Sign of God's Acceptance and Rejection

Because of Saul's prophetic experience amongst the group of prophets worshiping, "Is Saul also among the prophets?" (1 Sam 10:11) became a proverbial saying in Israel. The Spirit of Yahweh not only came upon Saul in his obedience (1 Sam 11:6) but also in his outright disobedience to God (1 Sam 19:19-24). Since the coming of the Spirit is used synonymously with receiving the Spirit's power or being empowered by God especially in the Old Testament, God in His sovereignty could use the prophetic utterance to prophesy regardless of the heart's condition or one's ability.

Another classic example would be the case of the prophet Balaam. While he continued to persist and rush into error "for profit" (Jude 11), going his own way, nevertheless, God's words continued to come upon the wicked prophet (Num 22-24). And why not? If Yahweh "opened the donkey's mouth" to speak to the rebellious Balaam, surely Saul could become a prophetic person. Therefore, it would be inappropriate to assume or try to make a connection between one's salvation or right standing before God with being able to prophesy; we cannot even assume the genuine conversion of a person because of their ability to prophesy (Matt 7:22).

God chose Saul to be the first human king of Israel for forty years before removing him from his position (Acts 13:21). As a sign of the divine acceptance to be God's instrument, Samuel told Saul, "The Spirit of [Yahweh] will come upon you in power... you will be changed into a different person" (1 Sam 10:6). Yet when Saul failed to keep Yahweh's command, God rejected him (1 Sam 13:13-14). We do not know when exactly this first outright disobedience regarding worship took place, but most likely it took place in the very early part of the forty year span of Saul's kingship. From that point onward, Saul's spiritual and political leadership began to spiral downward, and the major flaw of Saul that the author points out was that "the Spirit of [Yahweh] departed from Saul." This happening was related to Saul's mistaken approach to worship, reflecting his problematic attitude towards and troubled relationship with God (1 Sam 14:18-19; 15:7-31).

Music Ministry

David was introduced as someone who could minister to Saul in music to alleviate, perhaps in our terms, his "migraine headache" and would be suitable to be one of Saul's armor-bearers because of David's reputation of being brave and a warrior (1 Sam 16:18, 21). How was it that David's musical skill could alleviate Saul's migraine headache? Does this have any connection with today's music therapy? If it is music ministry, then what does this have to do with and what role does this play in worship?

The major turning point of both David and Saul's lives and their con-trast was not in the physical, intellectual, or psychological, but spiritual aspect. The author clearly describes each one's condition spiritually: "from that day on the Spirit of [Yahweh] came upon David in power... Now the Spirit of [Yahweh] departed from Saul" (1 Sam 16:13-14). Perhaps because David witnessed what it meant for his master Saul to have had the Holy Spirit upon him and afterwards what it was like when the Spirit left him, later in Psalm 51:11, David prayed in his repentance, "Do not cast me from your presence or take your Holy Spirit from me." And the author con-tinues to make the stark contrast based on each one's spiritual condition: "an evil spirit from [Yahweh] tormented [Saul]... [Yahweh] was with [David]" (vv. 14, 18).

Readers are not given enough information regarding what exactly Saul's symptom was, whether he was having a severe migraine headache or simply having the kind of bad day where he could easily snap at any moment. But one thing was certain, the real root of Saul's problem was spi-ritual, in his relationship with Yahweh. And likewise, it is most likely that David's musical skill of playing the harp had the power to bring relief so that "the evil spirit would leave" Saul (v. 23) was because Yahweh "was with him" (v. 18). Therefore, unlike modern music therapy or secular coun-seling, it is never the musical skill alone but the Spirit of Yahweh that brings true spiritual healing through worship in praise.

It is not necessary to spiritualize or moralize the text in order to inter-pret the somewhat difficult passage, 1 Samuel 18:10-11. But since the readers were already familiar with what it meant to be "spiritual" from the beginning of God's calling upon Saul in chapter ten, the passage should be interpreted in the light of such spirituality.

Saul was harboring anger, which was the direct result of jealousy that arose from his own insecurity (vv. 8-9). Because Saul's anger and jealousy were never checked, a spiritual attack had taken its toll (v. 10); Saul's heart was filled with bitterness, which made him vulnerable to an evil spirit (Eph 4:26-27). Some see Saul's action in verse 11 as an anger problem that he just could not shake off. But the text clearly gives the source of Saul's problem—"an evil spirit from God came forcefully upon Saul." This does not make God an author of evil, but rather, the emphasis should be placed on God being the one who has sovereignty over all things, including evil, otherwise evil or the evil spirit would not be checked. It is God in his grace who limits the work of enemies, keeping them within boundaries. For this reason, ultimately the starting point of the solution to all problems in life should be theological rather than psychological or sociological.

In such spiritually vulnerable state, Saul was "prophesying in his house, while David was playing the harp." Most likely David was playing a tune that was spiritual and related to praise, which led Saul to prophesy. One may wonder, "How could someone prophesy in his anger?" More such apparent paradoxes come in the following chapter nineteen where while they were in hot pursuit of David's life, "the Spirit of God came upon" both Saul and his men, keeping them from carrying out Saul's plan (1 Sam 19:19-22).

Based on Saul's life and the spirit of prophecy, it is possible to sing praises and prophesy while harboring anger in one's heart. Again, we are not given the content of Saul's prophetic words, but that should not be our concern. Rather, it should help us to look at our own hearts when we are engaging in worshiping the Lord. Perhaps for Saul, praise and prophesying was just part of a religious duty or ritual. Saul never learned the crucial lesson from Cain and Abel regarding worship in Genesis 4. James has warned us, "Out of the same mouth come praise and cursing. My brothers, this should not be" (Jas 3:10).

Prophesying, Proclaiming, and Musical Praise

Why was prophesying often accompanied with music? The prophet Elisha told the king of Israel to bring him "a harpist... While the harpist was playing, the hand of [Yahweh] came upon Elisha" (2 Kings 3:15). The word "prophesy" (*nava*) in oldest forms, is defined "of religious ecstasy with or without song and music; later, essentially religious instruction, with occasional predictions" (BDB). Besides the popular understanding of prophesying—telling the future, there are at least three more aspects of prophesying that overlap with one another to some degree.

First, there is the aspect of proclaiming what God has said or revealed. In this respect, the apostle Paul's teaching on the different ministries or activities that occur when the community is gathered together to worship helps us to have a better understanding of prophesying—"When you come together, everyone has a hymn, or a word of instruction, a revelation, a tongue or an interpretation" (1 Cor 14:26). Paul's main concern had been prophesying and tongue speaking, which had to be intelligible in order to edify the community of believers. Although the context of verse 26 is a discussion of prophecy and tongues, prophecy is not on the list in verse 26. It is most likely that since prophecy has to do with proclaiming, it encompasses all the elements on the list. Hymns proclaim God's faithfulness and goodness based on God's word and its experience in life through songs. When a person proclaims/preaches or teaches based on the written revelation, the listeners are being instructed. Prophesying is proclaiming based on God's revelation (Amos 3:8). Speaking in tongues is a means through which God reveals or illumines God's word in our hearts; it needs interpretation to become a prophesy/proclamation for the people to hear, understand and be edified (1 Cor 14:19).

Second, prophesy is more than merely speaking or sharing; the emphasis is on speaking "into" and with an expectation that the hearers would respond. However, not all true prophets' words were well-received by the people when they were first prophesied/proclaimed; they were actually more rejected than received. Even in the first century, the prophet John's message of repentance was widely rejected by especially the religious leaders who were respected by the people (Matt 11:18). Nevertheless, since prophesying is based on what God has revealed mainly in His written word, God honors His servants' preaching if it is based on God's word and not just the servants' own conviction or preconceived notion. Just as it was at Creation when "God said, 'Let there be light,' and there was light," (Gen 1:3), God's word (in this case, Isaiah's prophetic words) "will not return to [Yahweh] empty, but will accomplish... and achieve the purpose for which [Yahweh] sent it" (Isa 55:11). For this same reason God commanded another prophet, Ezekiel, in his vision experience to "Prophesy to these bones and say to them" (Ezek 37:4) with the expectation that His word would be fulfilled (v. 7).

Third, prophesying is a person speaking or confessing what he believes to be true based on the conviction in his heart resulting from the Holy Spirit working in this person's heart to reveal and illumine Christ's word (John 16:14). One of the last words of Moses was concerning God's word in our hearts (Deut 30:14). The real reason the Israelites failed to obey God's revealed will, His word, was not because it was difficult or beyond their reach but because they failed to believe God's word in their hearts (vv. 11-14). This gospel message, which is the same gospel message for the people under the new covenant, needs to be believed with our hearts, confessed with our mouths and proclaimed (Rom 10:5-14).

Therefore, when people are called by God to place their faith in His Son Jesus Christ through the preaching of the gospel, they have started their spiritual journey as God's people and have become the prophetic people of God. And this prophesying should not end there as a one-time experience at their conversion but be an ongoing obedience in faith through proclaiming the good news and confessing/proclaiming/prophesying through the songs of praise—"Through Jesus… let us continually offer to God a sacrifice of praise—the fruit of lips that confess his name" (Heb 13:15). In sum, prophesying in relation to the gospel is, "It is written: 'I believed; therefore I have spoken.' With that same spirit of faith we also believe and therefore speak, because we know that the one who raised the Lord Jesus from the dead will also raise us with Jesus" (2 Cor 4:13-14).

Although there are more similarities than differences between prophesying and preaching, nevertheless, preaching is not exactly the same as prophesying as much as teaching is not the same as preaching in a strict sense (although there is a teaching element in preaching). Even though the preaching of God's word seeks to address the listeners' hearts, it is prepared beforehand and using the art of homiletics. In contrast, prophesying is more specific and spontaneous; there is a conviction of one's heart by the Holy Spirit based on God's word, and it speaks to the people. In this sense with preaching, more emphasis is (or should be) on the written word of God, the Bible, while prophesying focuses on the particular moment of conviction. Yet God's written word is always the ultimate and primary source for both preaching and prophesying.

In order to prepare a message, a preacher has to study God's word, apply it and communicate this to the audience. The preacher needs to study God's word based on sound hermeneutical principles after which he ought to communicate it in accordance with the art of homiletics. However, with respect to prophesying, the person does not prepare with the part of the Bible he will be prophesying from in mind beforehand, but rather, from God's word that has already been deposited in the person's heart, on a certain occasion, the person trusts the Holy Spirit to use a certain portion of the word of God in his heart to give conviction in his heart in order to speak/prophesy to others. Therefore, for preaching, God's word serves more as the ground or foundation while for prophesying, it serves as a perimeter, limitation or safeguard.

Since prophesying was done under the influence of the Spirit of Yahweh at a particular moment, often the praise or spiritual music provided a context in which the Holy Spirit worked in the hearts of the worshipers, who submitted themselves on their knees before Yahweh. The musical praise touched and appealed primarily to the worshipers' emotion, while the instruction of God's word appealed to their minds first. And when their hearts were in submission to Yahweh, the Spirit of Yahweh illumined God's word planted in the hearts of the worshipers, which meant that they were having a certain conviction in their hearts; and then, oftentimes prophesying became an inevitable and proper response of the inner conviction of the Holy Spirit. For this reason, prophesying that was practiced by the prophets under the old covenant was often found in the context of musical praise.

Both preaching and musical praise should prepare the hearts of worshipers to engage in worship. In this respect, preaching focuses primarily more on preparing the mind of the listeners—proclaiming the gospel, God's attributes, and His wisdom in life, which should prepare the congregation to enter into worship in praise. Once the congregation enters into worship in praise, the Holy Spirit continues to stir the worshipers' hearts. During the worship in praise, sometimes spontaneous prophetic praise would arise, either led by one person while the others would be in the mode of listening or all the worshipers spontaneously proclaiming the greatness of God, especially for His great act of redemption that He accomplished through His Son Jesus Christ as the Holy Spirit gives the conviction in each one's heart.

Such a worship progression and response in worship can be seen in Revelation 5. There we find a responding to the understanding of the gospel through "preaching" and the proclamation of the gospel through praise. First, the meaning of and insight into the gospel message of Christ is understood in the light of the Son of God being the Lamb of God in relation to God's redemptive work (vv. 1-7). Next, we find the twenty-four elders along with the heavenly creatures, worshiping in prayer and praise in response to knowing the gospel message (vv. 8-10). Then, the countless heavenly angelic beings echo and respond to the previous worship with another praise (vv. 11-12). Then finally, every creature sings a song of praise (v. 13). In response to God's word and its understanding, the heavenly creatures and the twenty four elders worshiped (v. 8). In response to every creature worshiping in praise, the heavenly creatures responded with, "Amen," and the twenty-four elders responded in worship (v. 14).

The congregation responds in worship to the gospel message that has been heard. The congregation further responds while worshiping with prophecy/proclamation either in a musical song of praise or in a non-musical proclamation, both of which can be said to be prophetic words, proclaiming God's wonderful act (Acts 2:11). The result is that it leads the congregation further and deeper into worship. Therefore, prophesying could be in response to musical praise that has its focus on exalting God which most likely was what Saul was doing when "he joined in [the prophets'] prophesying" (1 Sam 10:10).

12

GOD'S HOLY PRESENCE AND BEING MINDFUL OF GOD

As much as David sought and loved Yahweh, a human's best way of relating to the ark of God that represented the very presence of God and of loving God could never be good enough for God. Yahweh has His own particular standard, which is often expressed in His holiness, and only in His prescribed way were His people supposed to approach Him. The prophet Isaiah spoke about Israel's stubbornness and how they insisted on going their own sinful way. Therefore Isaiah said, "all our righteous acts are like filthy rags" (Isa 64:6). Either in one's own zeal apart from being aware of God's precepts or in one's outright rebellion against and disregard for God's ways, what we think is best is often not best at all; as matter of fact, it could be far worse, tragic even.

Because of David's passion for God's presence while Yahweh's prescribed instructions regarding the ark of God were being overlooked, what started as a day full of joy, excitement and anticipation ended with David and others full of fear and wanting to keep a distance from the ark of God, which represented the holy presence of Yahweh (2 Sam 6:1-10). On the other hand, when the ark of God was taken "to the house of Obed-Edom the Gittite" instead, the blessing of Yahweh came upon "him and his entire household" (v. 11).

Worship according to God's Prescription

After David's failed attempt to transport the ark of God from Baalah of Judah to the City of David with the ark ending up in Obed-Edom's house, David probably thought about what it meant to have the closeness of God's holy presence in his life and re-learned why Yahweh had such meticulous prescriptions regarding the offerings and how the sacrifices were to be offered.

Having the closeness of God's holy presence might even cost one's life (2 Sam 6:6-7). Clearly Yahweh had already said, "Among those who approach me I will show myself holy; in the sight of all the people I will be honored" (Lev 10:3). David with the best of intentions was transporting the ark of God "on a new cart" (2 Sam 6:3); after all, not too long ago Israel's neighboring people, the Philistines had done it and it worked (1 Sam 6:7). Uzzah out of his natural response and with pure intention, "took hold of the ark of God" to keep it from the possibility of toppling over, which would have been a disaster, not to mention making a huge scene. But instead of commending Uzzah for his heroic act, Yahweh's "anger burned against Uzzah because of his irreverent act; therefore God struck him down and he died" (v. 7). Yahweh had given specific instruction for all the tabernacle furnishings to be designed in such way that the designated clans of the Levites could carry them in the wilderness, and it was not because there were no suitable carts available.

Although Yahweh did not give the reason He wanted the assigned Levites to carry the ark of God when transporting it, one thing was certain, His people were to simply trust God's given instructions. One does not have to experience something of tragedy or blessing to believe in God's word. Our understanding of God's creation "that the universe was formed at God's command, so that what is seen was not made out of what was visible" (Heb 11:3) did not come from a scientific proof or a theistic evolution of logical, philosophical, or religious compromise; our assurance and certainty of God's word (Heb 11:1) comes from our inner conviction from the Holy Spirit in our hearts. Was there any practical, moral, or scientific way to know why Yahweh required the ark of God to be carried on the designated people's shoulders?

Much time had passed since the wilderness days. Apparently a much more efficient way to transport the ark of God was available, thanks to technological advancement and the Philistines, who had already tested out whether it worked or not. But through the first attempt to transport the ark of God, David learned, not that it was impractical or risky to transport the ark of God with something more efficient and contemporary, but rather that it was about what was "biblical" for he said, "No one but the Levites may carry the ark of God, because [Yahweh] chose them to carry the ark of [Yahweh] and to minister before him forever" (1 Chr 15:2).

The design of the ark only further emphasized the prime importance and sacredness of what worshipers must regard and seek behind what the ark represented, His holy presence—"the ark of God... the Name... the name of [Yahweh] Almighty, who is enthroned between the cherubim that are on the ark" (2 Sam 6:2). Most likely most of the other Canaanite gods were worshiped before their idols or at temples that were of significant grandeur and size. But for Israel, sacrificing and worshiping revolved around the ark of God. The actual physical ark of God was roughly 45 inches long and 27 inches wide and high in size, and having Yahweh "enthroned between the cherubim," it must have been a very small place from which Yahweh ruled. But when visibility, physicality, and technological advancements become more important and replace the invisible presence of the holy God, worshipers would have lost the very essence of worship that is to seek Yahweh—"Seek me and live; do not seek Bethel... Seek [Yahweh] and live" (Amos 5:4-5).

What has been the focus of the typical modern day evangelical Sunday worship service? Ever since the Reformation, if God's word has been one of the main concerns in the worship service, has the preaching highlighted the crucial importance of and created a greater hunger for God's word in the hearts of worshipers? With an orderly worship service format, tightly organized worship schedule, everything is done on the dot, according to the schedule, down to second; there is no room for mistakes or flexibility in the name of excellent worship service done professionally. What is the real outcome of our best and "innocent" intention utilizing the best technology to prepare and plan the worship service for God? Are we seeking the very holy presence of God in worship? Are we just simply impressed with the sermon, music, and other various artistic forms of expressing worship to God but having forgotten the exhortation to wor- shipers under the new covenant in Christ—"Let us... approach the throne of grace with confidence, so that we may receive mercy and find grace to help us in our time of need" (Heb 4:16)? It is worth noting here that at one time under the old covenant, "the throne of grace" that the author of Hebrews was referring to was the invisible throne "between the cherubim that are on the ark" that represented the very presence of God.

It seemed like everything that we would like to see in worship was there when David and thirty thousand men of Israel, who were chosen by David, were transporting the ark of God. Uzzah and Ahio were carefully guiding the new cart. Everyone was celebrating "with all their might before [Yahweh], with songs and with harps, lyres, tambourines, sistrums and cym- bals" (2 Sam 6:5). David's zeal for God's holy presence was expressed in his best intention with a vast number of people, worship as a joyous occasion, and a celebratory spirit before Yahweh. At that time, the ark of God was guided by the people unlike in the past when the glory cloud guided the Israelites during the forty years of the wilderness journey. Surely, Yahweh's instruction on how God's people, the worshipers, were to relate to the ark of God was overlooked.

Being near God as a Spiritual Privilege and Blessing

There is something about God that would make anyone uncomfort- able to have Him near. If God were to be the light that exposes and nothing is hidden but everything is laid bare before His sight (Heb 4:13), then surely attempting to hide from and avoid Him is the natural and instinctive response of a sinful person who lives in darkness—"Everyone who does evil hates the light, and will not come into the light for fear that his deeds will be exposed" (John 3:20).

Asaph once confessed, "as for me, it is good to be near God" (Ps 73:28). Asaph, after having gone through confusion from having a wrong perspective of life in general, gained the eternal perspective when he entered God's sanctuary to worship. But for David, although he desired God's presence, after the tragic judgment from God on Uzzah, having the ark of God near him became a possible liability as fear gripped his soul—"How can the ark of [Yahweh] ever come to me?" (2 Sam 6:9).

Obed-Edom the Gittite, by the order of the king, accepted the ark of God being kept at his place and guarded it. The ark of God was in Obed-Edom's house "for three months, and [Yahweh] blessed him and his entire household" (vv. 10-11). We do not know exactly whether Obed-Edom had a choice, whether he voluntarily brought the ark of God into his house or not, whether or not it was an unexpected joy and honor for Obed-Edom to host it. But one thing was sure, he and his household were experiencing what they had never expected, God's abundant blessing.

God's blessing was not just for the three months while the ark of God was in Obed-Edom's house. They continued to experience Yahweh's favor throughout his and his sons' lifetimes, since their names appear as the ones who served God in relationship to worship. Obed-Edom served God with a musical instrument while the ark of God was being transported the second time to Jerusalem (1 Chr 15:18-20). More permanently, he was appointed as one of the ministers in music "before the ark of [Yahweh]" under Asaph along with other Levites (1 Chr 16:4-5), and also as a gatekeeper (v. 38). He and his descendants and his relatives were reputable people who " were capable men with the strength to do the work" (1 Chr 26:8) related to the house of God.

It is unclear regarding his family background whether he was a Levite (since David had him in charge of the ark of God) or from Gath of the Philistines. Since he was first introduced as a Gittite, it could have been that he was from Gath although this does not mean he was a Philistine any more than residing in Philistine territory for awhile would have made David a Philistine. Later, he could have been one of "the six hundred Gittites who had accompanied [David] from Gath [and] marched before the king" (2 Sam 15:18); Gittites were said to be foreigners according to the following verse 19. Regardless, towards the end of First Chronicles, the author gives the reason Obed-Edom was able to serve a dual role relating to the worship ministry and for the house of God—"For God had blessed Obed-Edom" (1

Chr 26:5). There, not only he but also his sons were mentioned most likely to emphasize that they also served as gatekeepers. Mainly, Obed-Edom was in charge of the South Gate while his sons were in charge of the storehouse (v. 15).

Regardless of whether he was a converted gentile or a Levite, surely God's blessing upon Obed-Edom the Gittite foreshadowed what the Son of David, the Christ, would do through his death—"For through [Christ] we both [Jews and Gentiles] have access to the Father by one Spirit. Consequently, you are no longer foreigners... In [Christ] the whole building is joined together and rises to become a holy temple in the Lord" (Eph 2:18-19, 21).

The psalm of the sons of Korah would be appropriate for Obed-Edom —"Better is one day in your courts than a thousand elsewhere; I would rather be a doorkeeper in the house of my God than dwell in the tents of the wicked" (Ps 84:10). Through Christ's death, we "who once were far away have been brought near " (Eph 2:13) to God and His presence. God "has blessed us in the heavenly realms with every spiritual blessing in Christ" (Eph 1:3). What is the spiritual blessing in Christ in relation to worship? Is it not the "access to the Father" in Christ through worship (Eph 2:18)? Asaph committed himself to the blessing of God's nearness; the sons of Korah desired the nearness of God; Obed-Edom the Gittite experienced the blessing that comes from being near Yahweh; and David had learned the true blessing and privilege of being near God over against any danger.

What would our average Sunday worship service be like if our greatest desire was simply to be near God? What if we were more conscious of and sought out God's presence more than any other thing in worship? Jesus said, "I will build my church" (Matt 16:18); what kind of church is Christ building which is based on the confession that Jesus is "the Christ, the Son of the living God" (Matt 16:16)? The whole purpose of the tabernacle and the temple building was so that His people would worship and seek His presence there. How much more should it be so if we the church are "the temple of the living God" (2 Cor 6:16).

Worship as a Culturally Expressed Action and Beyond

Worship is man's expression in response to God for who He is and what He has done and is doing in our lives. Although worshiping God itself is transcendent, how we express our response to God, who is worthy of our worship, is limited by worshipers' cultures. Since cultures are diverse, the expressions in response to God are diverse, just as different artists express a certain object or the same idea differently through various kinds of music and art. When people limit themselves to their own culture, however, and become rigid, then the worship service order, its form, becomes an end in itself. When this happens, the form and expression take over the life of the worship; a methodology takes over the spirit and emotion of worship dynamics; religious duty and obligation take over submission in faith; we limit ourselves to a system, and there is no relationship and fellowship with the living God.

Unfortunately, Michal, the daughter of Saul who was married to David, "watched... King David leaping and dancing... [and] despised him in her heart" (2 Sam 6:16). Perhaps Michal thought it was inappropriate, culturally, for a king to "distinguish[ed] himself... disrobing... as any vulgar fellow would" (v. 20). But if what David did was culturally unacceptable, then the act of worship, expressing God's love and faithfulness, for David, superseded in importance the cultural acceptance and sensitivities of his days. For David, the form of worship went beyond cultural sensitivity and appropriateness; he "danced before [Yahweh] with all his might... leaping and dancing before [Yahweh]... It was before [Yahweh]... I will celebrate before [Yahweh]. I will become even more undignified" (vv. 14, 16, 21-22).

Sailhamer summarizes the parallel passage about David and the people transporting the ark of God to Jerusalem after learning the hard way how to do it properly, found in 1 Chronicles 15:

"David was following the instruction that God gave to Moses... (Ex. 26:7ff)... The importance of that point is shown by the detail supplied in these verses. To show that his heart was in the right place, David carried out God's will to the letter... All this concern for the exactness of the procedure was not an empty formalism; it was a desire to please God and worship Him in reverence that overflows into action. David had learned the lesson that in worship, as well as in life, actions can speak as loud as words. All the emphasis, however, is not put on David's actions. Worship is more than a prescribed set of activities carried out to the letter; worship is also an expression." (John Sailhamer, *First & Second Chronicles*, p.43)

The Son of David, Who Would Establish the True Worship

Whether in public or in private, David never lost sight of God. Even though Yahweh "had given him rest from all his enemies," for David, that really did not give him rest—"Here I am, living in a palace of cedar, while the ark of God remains in a tent" (2 Sam 7:1-2). The minds of those whose hearts are set in the right place would be filled with God and with worship. That was how it was for David. But as long as Yahweh continued to meet David at the cherubim above the ark of God, why would David need to build a better dwelling place for God? It seems like God was not in need of a better, more permanent place for Himself to dwell in (v. 7). Instead, God would continue to be faithful to what He had started and promised: the promise that God would make Abraham's name great would still be true for David (v. 9). Just as God provided a place for Adam and put him in the Garden, so was God going to "provide a place… and plant" His people there (v. 10). Just as the promise of the woman's offspring was given, God would be establishing David's house/kingdom through David's offspring (vv. 11-12). And, David's offspring would have a special relationship with God the Father (v. 14).

The promises Yahweh made in the Old Testament would ultimately be fulfilled in Christ; all the promises God made pointed toward Christ. A reader would notice that what seemed like an immediate fulfillment of God's promise continued to serve as a mere shadow and further down payment of what was to come and be fulfilled in Christ. When a reader goes back to God's promise to David (the Davidic Covenant) read through the lens of the "promised theology" mentioned above, the reader would notice all the promises could not have made to the nation Israel or David's immediate son, Solomon. There could only be one fulfillment, which is the Son of David, Jesus Christ.

The reason David's name would be made great is that the Son of God, Jesus Christ, would come to be known as the "Son of David." After Solomon, the kingdom was divided into two; the divided kingdom con-

tinued to "be disturbed," taken into exile, and politically, foreigners continued to rule Israel down to the First Century until the coming of David's
offspring to whom the scepter "belongs and the obedience of the nations is
his" (Gen 49:10). Although Solomon did build a house for God's Name (2
Sam 7:13), the promised offspring of David could not be Solomon since the
throne of Solomon's kingdom did not last forever. This means that the fulfillment of the promise of God's house could not be the temple Solomon or
others would build later.

Later, David's son, Solomon, "loved many foreign women," which
inevitably turned his heart from Yahweh. Israel began to experience national
and political instability towards the latter part of Solomon's life (1 Kings
11). Yet, when Solomon did wrong, he was not punished "with the rod of
men, with floggings inflicted by men" as God had said He would to
Solomon's father, David (2 Sam 7:14). But we have the Son of David, Jesus
Christ, who shares a unique relationship with God the Father. Because of
our sin, indeed the Son of God was "stricken by God, smitten by him, and
afflicted. But he was pierced for our transgressions" (Isa 53:4-5).

Jesus' prophetic act of cleansing the physical temple would point ulti-
mately to the fulfillment of God's promise to David—"He is the one who
will build a house for my Name" (2 Sam 7:13). Therefore, Jesus said,
"Destroy this temple, and I will raise it again in three days" (John 2:19).
The temple Christ was referring to was His own body (v. 22); through
Christ's death and resurrection, true worship would be established.
Carson's comment on John 2 in relation to worship is helpful:

Jesus' cleansing of the temple testifies to his concern for pure worship, a
right relationship with God at the place supremely designated to serve as
the focal point of the relationship between God and man. But it is that very
concern that is attracting opposition. For John the manner by which Jesus
will be 'consumed' is doubtless his death." (D. A. Carson, *The Gospel
according to John*, p.180)

What started as David's concern for God's house and worship, God
revealed what He started in the creation, and the promise He made with
Abraham, which would be ultimately fulfilled in Jesus Christ, the Son of
David. Christ through His death would purify worship and worshipers—
"Then [Yahweh] will have men who will bring offerings in righteousness,

and the offerings of Judah and Jerusalem will be acceptable to [Yahweh]" (Mal 3:3-4).

The apparent paradox is that Solomon did wrong but was not punished, while the Son of David, Jesus Christ, was punished although "he had done no violence, nor was any deceit in his mouth" (Isa 53:9). Likewise, it is beyond debate that more than anyone in the Bible, David, who was known as a prophet more so than as a king (Acts 2:30), had so much passion for God and worship, to the point of confessing, "zeal for your house consumes me" (Ps 69:9), and in this, he foreshadowed the Son of David, Jesus Christ.

But as strange as it may seem, David was not given the privilege of building a permanent dwelling place for Yahweh. Because David's years were dominated by being in the wilderness (during which time many psalms were written), going through trials of many kinds, and in his career as a king, he fought many battles, the building of the temple was given to David's immediate son, Solomon (1 Chr 22:7-10) who would have a different kind of reign.

God told David that Solomon, referred to as "a man of peace and rest," would be the one who would build a house for His Name. David and his life's experiences foreshadowed and pointed to the Son of David; his life on this earth anticipated the coming suffering servant of Yahweh, who would prepare and establish true worship through His death and resurrection. David's son, Solomon, a man of peace and rest, also foreshadowed the Son of David, Jesus Christ, but in a different way: Christ, who in His body would be destroyed but in three days, rise in His bodily resurrection, would become the true temple (John 2:19-22). Despite Solomon's accomplishment of building God's temple, however, because of his shortcomings as a king, the kingdom was divided into two, and both kingdoms would constantly be under attack. Eventually, Solomon's temple was burned down and destroyed. Therefore, ultimately, Solomon's temple building was not the building Yahweh had in mind, but rather, His Son becoming man, Jesus' body, would be the true temple.

During Abraham's lifetime, "God gave him no inheritance… not even a foot of ground" even though God called him to the promised Land (Acts 7:5). Instead, he and others "were longing for a better country—a heavenly one" (Heb 11:16). Moses was told to build the tabernacle "exactly like the pattern" that Yahweh would show him (Ex 25:8). Therefore, Moses knew that human hands could not build the real sanctuary on this earth; the tabernacle was a copy of the true heavenly sanctuary. David, who had written many psalms relating to worship and the temple in which the worship would take place, was never given the privilege to build a temple building. Could it be that what David was to seek was not a manmade temple building but the heavenly sanctuary? His son Solomon prayed concerning the temple he had built—"But will God really dwell on earth? The heavens, even the highest heaven, cannot contain you. How much less this temple I have built" (1 Kings 8:27).

For David, the God who "daily bears our burdens" was Yahweh; the One who "ascended on high" was the One who chose to dwell in the assembly of the worshipers in praise (Ps 68:19, 24, 26). For David, no matter how magnificent the temple building would be, it held no attraction in comparison to God's sanctuary since God was "awesome... in [His] sanctuary" (v. 35) in the assembly of worshipers.

Because of David's zeal for God's house, he went through hardship in life; his hardship in life foreshadowed Christ and what He would go through (Ps 69: 9). In order to establish true worship, Christ faced various trials and temptations, "tempted in every way, just as we are—yet was without sin," and through His death, He paved the way so that worshipers may "approach the throne of grace with confidence... [to] receive mercy and find grace to help us in our time of need" (Heb 4:15-16).

One follower of Christ in the early church years, Stephen, directed listeners of the gospel message to seek Christ, worship the Son of God, as he preached what Yahweh said through Isaiah, "Heaven is my throne, and the earth is my footstool. Where is the house you will build for me? Where will my resting place be?" (Isa 66:1-2). Worshiping and proclaiming Christ would end up costing Stephen his very own life, yet he did not depart without experiencing what his heart had been longing for—"full of the Holy Spirit, looked up to heaven and saw the glory of God, and Jesus standing at the right hand of God... 'Look... I see heaven open'... While they were stoning him... he fell on his knees and cried out" (Acts 7:55, 59-60). Stephen experienced a glimpse of what he would experience in heaven, worshiping the glorious Christ; perhaps, he died just the way he lived, in the presence of God, in worship, on his knees.

That was how it was for some people; they lived and died, worshiping God—"By faith Jacob, when he was dying, blessed each of Joseph's sons, and worshiped as he leaned on the top of his staff" (Heb 11:21). Towards the end of David's life, "old and well advanced in years... could not keep warm even when they put covers over him" (1 Kings 1:1). If it were not for God's sovereign intervention, David would again have become victim to the conspiracy of yet another one of his sons, Adonijah (v. 5). But David, most likely bedridden and although every strength and desire within his body was slowly dissipating, after placing his son Solomon on his throne and probably rallying every ounce of energy within him, the Bible says, "the king [David] bowed in worship on his bed" (v. 47).

David is introduced in the Bible as the one after God's own heart who would "do everything [Yahweh] wanted him to do" (Acts 13:22). Under Saul, David's profession was being one of the king's armor-bearers, but his ministry was as a harpist and prophet, ministering to his master. In David's first public appearance as an inexperienced young man who faced Goliath because of his faith in God's promise to Abraham—"whoever curses you I will curse" (Gen 12:31, compare with 1 Sam 17:43), God defeated the Philistines through David. But his enjoyment of the popularity that came as a result of this success was short-lived because of Saul's jealousy arising from his insecurity. From that point on, David faced persecution and was on the run from Saul until the day Saul died.

Surely, David portrayed the coming Messiah, "a man of sorrows, and familiar with sufferings" (Isa 53:3). And those painful experiences in life made David's life foreshadow Christ's more than almost any other person's in the Bible. Nevertheless, the author of the book of 2 Samuel concludes with David as a worshiper and his understanding of sacrifice which paved the way for a deeper understanding of worship and greater appreciation of Christ's crucifixion in relation to worship—"I will not sacrifice to [Yahweh] my God burnt offerings that cost me nothing" (2 Sam 24:24).

Every Sunday we are given the privilege to worship. Worship is costly because it cost the life of God's Son. Yet for some, the longer they have been Christians, the less excitement and gratitude they have for the fact that

Jesus Christ paid the price for our sins. We as worshipers stand before God, not as sinners, but righteous; it is because the Second Person of the Trinity became "a merciful and faithful high priest" so "that he might make atonement for the sins of the people" (Heb 2:17). Jesus "is not ashamed to call [us] brothers" since He is the one who makes the worshipers holy (v. 11). It is mind-boggling that in every Sunday worship service, the Son of God, Jesus Christ, is "in the presence of the congregation" and leads the congregation into worship (v. 12).

Probably David's passion in life was best portrayed in his prayer, "One thing I ask of [Yahweh], this is what I seek: that I may dwell in the house of {Yahweh] all the days of my life, to gaze upon the beauty of [Yahweh] and to seek him in his temple" (Ps 27:4). Yet the price David had to pay because of his zeal for God and His sanctuary makes us examine our own hearts. The Son of David had to die in order to purify the worshipers, in order for there to be right worship so that Yahweh God might dwell in the assembly of the worshipping community.

In light of all these, what should be our attitude towards pure and right worship? We, as Jesus' disciples, what is it really costing us, because of our passion for God's dwelling place? What is it that has really been sought out in our worship service? A better message, praise songs that are culturally more relevant, more prayers, and sacrificial offerings are definitely needed, but more than anything, the "sacrifices of God are a broken spirit; a broken and contrite heart... [God] will not despise" (Ps 51:17). It is because our God is a God who lives "in a high and holy place, but also with him who is contrite and lowly in spirit" (Isa 57:15, and also in 66:1-2).

PART V - WORSHIP AT THE ALTAR AND THE TEMPLE BUILDING

Why could they not just have the ark of God to worship, the way it had been for the past four hundred eighty years since the Israelites first came out of Egypt (1 Kings 6:1)? It reminds the reader of God's faithfulness; Yahweh would not rest until God established His people in the Promised Land. Yahweh, who took the first man and "put him in the Garden" (Gen 2:15), is the same God who called Abraham to the Land that God would show him (Gen 12:1). Yahweh repeatedly confirmed His promise to Abraham that He would make his descendants "as numerous… as the sand on the seashore" (Gen 22:17). In line with what God did for Adam by placing him in the Garden and promised to Abraham regarding the Land (Gen 15:16), Yahweh Almighty promised David, "I will provide a place for my people Israel and will plant them" (2 Sam 7:10). Prior to the temple construction, the stability and blessings that Israel enjoyed under Solomon in the areas of the nation's general life and her political relationship with the surrounding nations served as a reminder of the fulfillment of God's faithful promise to Israel (1 Kings 4:20-34). The building of the temple was one of the expressions and representations of Yahweh's faithfulness to His promise and love for His people.

13

THE TEMPLE BUILDING

The main focus of the evangelical worship service can be noticed in the layout and design of the church interior where the main Sunday worship service is being held. It reflects much influence received from the Reformation days when worship was "rediscovered," redefined and reformed according to God's word. A liturgical worship took dominance for a more God's word-centered and orderly worship; the preaching of God's word, mainly the gospel, became the primary focus in the worship service, and God-centered hymns were written and used in worship.

Today, not much has changed other than an increased awareness of our ever-evolving culture by fitting the style of worship music to the art and music of the cultural mainstream in order to be more relevant to the masses. Since preaching and music have been the focus, church main "sanctuary" has been replaced by more of an auditorium, theater, or stadium-style space for multipurpose usage. It is obvious that the main focus of the worship is listening to a sermon and engaging in worship by singing praises. Therefore, the lecture or seminar style of preaching has been more appealing to and sought out by many of the Sunday worshipers. To them, hearing God's word through preaching should take up the major portion and be the highlight of worship service.

For others, the worship service that focuses more on "spiritual" and emotional experiences through music is more appealing since they are able to engage and participate rather than just listening and being taught. Along that line, to some, the line between worship and a musical worship concert is almost indistinguishable.

When the interior is designed more functionally as an auditorium, the center of the interior architectural design has a stage for various performances relating to art and music that express worship of who God is and what He does. The multimedia, sound, acoustics, and lighting are all for one purpose, to help the audience to listen and engage in worship. In that sense, a typical medieval cathedral design of the interior would not meet today's worshipers' preferences. Rather, an ancient Greek amphitheater, where various plays were performed, would be a better fit for our purpose of what we call "worship service."

When the Muslims took over the Hagia Sophia in Istanbul in the year 1453 to be used as mosque, they destroyed and plastered over all of the images until it was used as a museum in 1935. To them, having images of any sort in relation to their religion, especially in their mosque, was a form of idolatry and sacrilege; there could only be the Arabic language or patterns if there were to be any artwork in the mosque.

Likewise, some Protestant evangelicals may take certain artwork or statutes in a cathedral as a form of idolatry. They are not totally off since some people do actually pray before the statutes. The artwork continued to flourish in the Roman Empire soon after Christianity became the only official religion allowed by the Roman government. One of the main reasons for its development was that a large number of illiterate people, in addition to others, were streaming into the church since by default everyone was supposed to be a "Christian," and one of the ways to communicate the biblical stories to illiterate people was by using artwork.

To give a clear sense of the separation between the sanctuary and the outside world and to give the experience of being the closest to the heavenly realm, stained glass was developed. In order to maximize bringing the outside light into the sanctuary, the Gothic pointed arch and its supporting flying buttresses were developed. Therefore, when we understand the architectural rationale behind the design, we come to appreciate its artwork more.

The Temple Building's Extravagance as a Reflection and Expression of Yahweh's Beauty

When the new covenant community of believers came together in the New Testament, it was often called the temple of God (2 Cor 6:16). The early church did not meet in an official building that was dedicated for gathering and worship but rather wherever was appropriate and suitable, often one of the believers' houses. Therefore, our understanding of the Old Testament temple building need not hold any interest to modern day readers of the Bible; the people under the old covenant worship in the temple building has now been replaced with the New Testament temple, which is God's people.

But if the Bible uses the temple to refer to God's people gathering mainly to worship, then we need to have a better understanding of the temple from the Old Testament in order to understand biblical worship and the church. Otherwise, our understanding of worship and the purpose of church gathering would be defined by and limited to our own experiences rather than be biblical.

The average person reading about the preparation and temple construction in 1 Kings 5-7 may find it quite boring—another instance of detailed instructions and account of construction like that of the tabernacle (predominantly from Exodus 25 to 40). But a couple of things should be noted before we dismiss the importance of detailed information regarding the temple construction: the contrast to Solomon's palace construction which was probably more exotic and of greater grandeur in scale, and the giving of the "overly" detailed information regarding the temple's materials and decorative design.

The details are given, not because the author wanted the readers to find some type of deep spiritual and symbolic meaning behind every detail and item. Rather, it was just the best human expression of the beauty of Yahweh's glory. God, who is invisible, who does not have any form, and if there were any visible manifestation of Yahweh, which was very rare during the kingdom of Israel, then it would have been in a fire, cloud, or miracles - with what and how could God's glory be expressed? If one were to use imagination, then it would be another attempt closer to idolatry. Though man has been created in God's image, we do not imagine God's image or picture God based on man's image.

The passage on the building of Solomon's palace that took thirteen years (1 Kings 7:1-12) is sandwiched by the temple construction and its furnishings that took seven years to complete (1 Kings 5-6 and 7:13-51). In other words, nothing is more important than worshiping God and its related matters, not even Solomon's grand palace. Including a relatively brief mention of Solomon's palace right in the middle of the temple construction passage only further highlights the primary importance of worship; worship is more important than politics and human affairs.

The author of Kings spared no ink in describing in detail the place of worship, the temple building, where most of the religious life of Israel would take place until "suddenly [Yahweh] [they were] seeking [would] come to his temple; the messenger of the covenant" (Mal 3:1), and the physical temple would be replaced by the incarnate Son of God.

Most likely, especially from the outside, Solomon's palace just in sheer size alone would have put the temple structure to shame. Yet spending more time describing the temple in all of its tedious details makes us wonder, "What is more important and beautiful in God's sight?" And also, "What makes the temple so uniquely special compared to all other buildings?"

In God's economy, the true value is in what God considers as sacred. And if the temple was going to be where God has chosen to dwell in the midst of His people, then every small, mundane detail would be important as well as beautiful in God's sight, although maybe far from perfect. The materials that would be used to decorate the interior and temple furnishings would be the best, most costly metal, gold. For this reason, shamelessly, everything in the temple interior and its furnishings were overlaid with gold (1 Kings 6:20-7:50). Surely, the "gold of that land is good" since it was used to reflect, if even just an infinitely tiny glimpse of, God's glory!

Was it not Yahweh who was the One who gave all the details for the tabernacle and its furnishings to Moses in the wilderness so that he could make them "exactly like the pattern" that he witnessed (Exod 25:9)? In the case of Solomon's temple design, neither Solomon nor his father David went up to a mountain and received God's instruction as in the case of Moses. Yet David "gave his son Solomon the plans... of all that the Spirit had put in his mind... [David] gave him instructions for the divisions of the priests and Levites" (1 Chr 28:11-13). God spoke to Moses directly regarding the design of the tabernacle, but when it came to the actual making of the tabernacle, Yahweh "filled [Bezalel] with the Spirit of God, with skill, ability and knowledge in all kinds of crafts" (Exod 31:2-3). With David, most likely the Holy Spirit was working, giving conviction, and illumining God's word in David's heart, so he could come up with a blueprint that his Solomon would get to build.

Until God would speak "by his Son" in the last days and His completed written word, the Bible, God would continue to speak "through the prophets... in various ways" (Heb 1:1-2). Therefore, in a way, one could say that the temple was the Holy Spirit's design using David the prophet to come up with a blueprint that came from what was in his mind that was put there by the Holy Spirit.

It is interesting to contemplate, as we pause for a moment, the irony between David and his son Solomon in relation to the temple and worship. David, who would never get to build the temple, planned for it, including the design, materials, and designating the Levites' ministry at the temple. Many of David's psalms were written about God's dwelling place, Yahweh's sanctuary, even though he would never have the chance to build or see the actual temple.

His son Solomon, on the other hand, had everything prepared for him; all he had to do was to follow the plan his father David had given him. Yet even after building the temple for worship and prayer, shortly afterwards, his passion was directed toward physical beauty rather than the beauty of Yahweh, regardless of whether they were spiritually compatible to him or not. In taking wives from foreign nations, Solomon disregarded the *Torah*, the Pentateuch, the written word of Yahweh (1 Kings 11:1-2).

Through such irony, we are reminded and warned: what do we really love? Who or what is the object of our passion (Mark 12:30-31)? We may find the reading of 1 Kings 5-7 quite boring. But like Moses who really did not mind rehearsing everything Yahweh had told him about the tabernacle to the Israelites and found it no trouble at all to write again how God's word concerning the tabernacle was executed and followed by the Israelites (Exod 35-40) (let us remember this was the same Moses who desperately sought seeing Yahweh's glory in Exodus 33:18), for the author of Kings, it would have been a privilege, honor and pure joy to record the temple design and all of its details.

The closest (if I dare to say, since Yahweh is beyond comparison according to Isaiah 46:6—"To whom, then, will you compare God? What image will you compare him to?") to the beauty of God's glory on this earth for Moses was the tabernacle, and for Solomon and the people of Israel in Solomon's days, it was the temple. It was so, not because the tabernacle and temple were decorated with all the precious jewels and gold, but because God chose to dwell there in the midst of His people. Therefore, nothing was "overly" decorated, nor were the most expensive materials used too lavishly or "wastefully," nor was it an excess to give all the details in writing the description of the temple, since anything in this world would come short in comparison to the beauty of Yahweh as worshipers experience in worship.

Moses never entered the Promised Land, but his passion in life and goal was not Canaan but seeing Yahweh's glory. Although Moses never entered the Promised Land on this side of the glory, God did give Moses the opportunity to stand on the Land with Christ and foresee that the only way the exodus would be completed/fulfilled was through the death and resurrection of Christ whom "Moses wrote about in the Law" (John 1:45). There on the mountaintop, Moses and Elijah stood with Jesus and "spoke about [Christ's] departure [=exodus], which he was about to bring to fulfillment at Jerusalem" (Luke 9:30-31).

Like Moses, in some way, David had the same passion for beholding the beauty of Yahweh's glory in His sanctuary. For that reason, David passionately made all the preparations for the temple construction although he would never get to see, enjoy or be in the temple to worship. One would never understand what David did unless he also had the same type of passion as David for experiencing God's dwelling place in worship.

All this is to show and make us slow down to get a glimpse of the beauty of God's glory in worship. More than the music, sermon, or being impressed with a beautiful building or worshipers, whatever it takes, worshipers need to redirect their passion, focus, and seek the beauty of God's holiness with all of His splendor in worship. The temple construction narrative section expresses nothing is too overly or meticulously done in comparison to the beauty of Yahweh.

Davis' comments and illustration shed light on our understanding of the temple's intricate description written in these chapters:

"Does *the writer* [the author of the Kings] find it laborious and tedious? ... And the answer is, Not likely, or he wouldn't have gone into such detail. Item by item he sees science and art in the service of Israel's God... a European craftsman who traveled to America to give his life to some of the most intricate work in one of its grandest places of worship. A tourist was viewing the edifice one day and noticed this craftsman doing meticulous work high up near the ceiling, focusing his skill on some symbol all but invisible from the floor. In fact, he was occupied with a detail that faced the ceiling, out of view of any worshiper. So the sightseer asked, 'Why are you being so exact; no one can even see the detail you are creating from this distance?' The busy artist shot back, 'God can!' Is that not the position of the writer of 1 Kings 7? Is he not suggesting that intricate, carefully wrought *beauty* is most fitting for the God the Bible? Is he not implying that nothing can be too good, too lavish, too well done for such a marvelous God? We must never offer slop to him. Who would have thought that the Holy Spirit might use 1 Kings 7 to convict us of the flippant and casual procedures we sometimes call 'worship'?" (Dale Ralph Davis, *The Wisdom and the Folly*, pp.76-77)

Obedience Surpasses the Temple Building's Extravagance

Besides the contrast with Solomon's palace, there is another interruption by the author that breaks the flow of the temple construction narrative. Perhaps God's word came to Solomon while the temple was still undergoing construction. Yahweh tells Solomon that the Israelites would continue to experience the blessing of having Yahweh as their God with His presence dwelling among them, if Solomon carries out God's commands (1 Kings 6:11-13). Yahweh had to remind Solomon of God's covenant with his father, David; otherwise, Solomon could be tempted to forget the main purpose behind the temple construction.

From the very first worship of making sacrifices to God offered by Cain and Abel, Yahweh established a worship mandate that took priority over the act of worship. As worshipers approached God, faith in Yahweh and doing what was right in his sight was prerequisite and imperative—"if you do what is right, will you not be accepted" (Gen 4:7).

Worship and obedience to God are inseparable, both prior to and after worship. Just the completing the act of worship alone or saying a sinful act was actually done for the purpose of worship (as Saul did when he said the reason he did not destroy all the animals as God had commanded him was because he wanted to use them for sacrifice to God) cannot justify one's disobedience or cover up one's rebellion. David's prophetic mentor Samuel once said to David's master "Does [Yahweh] delight in burnt offerings... as much as in obeying the voice of [Yahweh]" (1 Sam 15:22).

Saul the first king of Israel failed in the area of worship. He was able to justify dichotomizing the ritual of worship and the heart of obedience to the revealed will of God. There was no reason for Saul to think otherwise since most of the surrounding religions did not have a moral obligation to their gods as long as the worshipers knew how to offer sacrifices in a particular way. Their religious rituals were a separate issue, able to be performed regardless of how they lived and what they did. It took a kick in the teeth by the prophet Samuel to remind Saul, "to obey is better than sacrifice" (1 Sam 15:22), but sadly, even that did not seem to make any real impact on his soul. To Saul, approaching Yahweh to sacrifice was a way to save his own face and fulfill his religious obligation (v. 30); in this way, his attitude towards worship was not unlike that of the first murderer, Cain.

Some religious people believe that as long as they carry out their temple regulations regarding sacrifices and prayers, they are pretty much safe to do whatever they want to do. That was how it was in the days of the prophet Jeremiah. The people of Judah made a separation between their daily life and the religious practices in the temple; the integral connection that should have existed between the two was rather ignored or minimized. They felt secure as long as they could come to the temple regularly, pray and carry out their rituals. As long as the temple of Yahweh, His dwelling place, stood in Jerusalem, they believed that God would never bring judgment upon Judah (the southern kingdom) as He had on the northern kingdom Israel.

Against such deception, Yahweh said that because of their dichotomizing of the two, their separation of life and worship, the temple that bore God's Name had become "a den of robbers" (Jer 7:11). In those times, this denoted a place, perhaps a cave, where a group of robbers would hide themselves at daybreak after committing all kinds of crimes in the night. God also reminded Judah of what had happened to Shiloh where God had "made a dwelling for [His] Name" in the past (Jer 7:12). Shiloh became a historical proof that no place, town, or city could be secure once Yahweh had decided to withdraw His glory.

Later, Judah was taken into exile, and the temple was burned down and destroyed. But even after seventy years of captivity, down to the time of Jesus, the lives of the people were in general still separated from their worship rituals. Therefore, Jesus said that although God originally planned for His house to "be called as a house of prayer for all nations," sadly as a nation, Israel forfeited this grace and made the temple "a den of robbers" (Mark 11:17) instead. So God had to judge Israel's apostasy.

In response to the disciples being impressed with the size of the temple building, Jesus said, "Do you see all these great buildings?... Not one stone here will be left on another; every one will be thrown down" (Mark 13:2). God would not tolerate His temple to be desecrated. Yet what God considered desecration was not so much that not all the right components of the ritual were there; it was that the worshipers' lives had become separated from their acts of worship – there was no consistency between the two.

The question the people in Micah's days were supposed to ask and be concerned with was, "With what shall I come before [Yahweh] and bow down before the exalted God?", to which God answered, "To act justly and to love mercy and to walk humbly with your God" (Micah 6:6, 8)—coming to Yahweh with more than burnt offerings. Worshipers were to come to God, not just with offerings or rituals alone but remembering that with their whole being, who they were and how they lived, they were offering themselves to the Living God.

For this reason, serving/worshiping God goes beyond just the worship ritual act; the new covenant people in Christ must live in obedience to God daily, offering our "bodies as living sacrifices... this is [their] spiritual act of worship [or service]" (Rom 12:1). Our obeying and serving God with God-given capacity does not replace the very act of worship to God on Sunday. But our obedience to God in our daily lives and serving according to "the measure of faith God has given" (Rom 12:3) must flow out from the act of worship and a worshipful heart. Apart from worship, perhaps our efforts to live a life of obedience without our hearts being sprinkled with the blood of Christ as we "draw near to God" (Heb 10:22) would only be legalism or a humanitarianism rising out of man's standard of moral goodness.

People everywhere "came to listen to Solomon's wisdom" (1 Kings 4:34). Alluding to such desire and enthusiasm of all nations, Jesus in His days rebuked those who refused to accept His teaching and warned that they would be condemned since Jesus was the one "greater than Solomon" (Matt 12:42).

Every Sunday worship service the Word of Christ is (should be) preached. The worshipers are given an opportunity to hear and apply it to their life—God's word demands of us that we make our life right if it is not in line with God's revealed will. In our busyness and diligence, God interrupts us. In order to get our attention, He speaks to us of where we need to place our first priority: in worship. When we obey, we have taken worship to God seriously.

The Temple Court and Longing for the Inner Sanctuary

God should never be sought out merely in order to satisfy our curiosity to know about the future since what is behind such seeking is really an inner desire to control the future or outcome. A classic case would be Saul who had entered into the political arena as the first prophetic king of Israel. But ironically, unlike David, he both forfeited and eliminated what could have been God's provision of the means of prophetic grace, being able to know God's will and receive His guidance in his life: his relationship with the prophet Samuel was severed (1 Sam 15:35), and he killed off eighty-five priests (1 Sam 22:18-19).

Saul was never interested in knowing God's will in order to obey but instead was trying to know the outcome of his future like many of those who seek palm readers or fortunetellers in our days. People seek out such spiritual prostitution trying to avoid impending problems in life; in so doing, they are trying to get a better control of their future, "luck" or "fortune" rather than placing their faith in the Living God.

The only time Saul desperately sought Yahweh was when his heart was filled with terror before the Philistine army (1 Sam 28:5). This was the man whom "the Spirit of God [had come] upon," and as a result, there was a proverbial saying going around in Israel, "Is Saul among the prophets" (1 Sam 10:10-12), yet this time when Saul "inquired of [Yahweh] ... [Yahweh] did not answer him by dreams or Urim or prophets." Prior to that event, Saul had consistently rejected the revealed will of God that was graciously given to him. Because of this, God at this time withdrew His prophetic grace from Saul, like back in the days of Eli—"In those days the word of [Yahweh] was rare; there were not many visions" (1 Sam 3:1). In Saul's life, God's word and visions were completely absent.

Some people desperately seek certain types of "words" from God for their lives, but sadly at the same time, they are less interested in the written revealed will of God, God's word, the Bible. To them, the Bible is just too "generic." Out of their personal interest or curiosity, they rely on other "spiritual" people to get some information they are hoping could help them, they themselves not seeking God on their own in order to obey.

For Saul, Yahweh God was no more than a god who could tell Saul the outcome of the future. What was really in Saul's heart and his motive for "seeking" God all along finally came to the surface in his actions. Once Saul learned that God was no longer revealing His will to one who was not interested in obeying God's will, ironically, Saul sought out a medium though he himself "had expelled the mediums and spiritists from the land" earlier (1 Sam 28:3, 6-7).

No one other than the designated "Kohathite branch of the Levites" could transport the ark and the tabernacle furnishings. Before they were transported, Aaron and his sons were to cover them with hides of sea cows (Num 4:1-12). During the forty years, no one other than Aaron and his sons saw the ark or the tabernacle furnishings.

No one could ever enter into the inner sanctuary other than the high priest once a year, and only the priests were allowed to be in the outer sanctuary to minister. Since no one is righteous before the Holy God, even the high priest had to "offer sacrifices for his own sins, as well as for the sins of the people" (Heb 5:3). In a way, the temple served not only as a reminder of God's dwelling place but also of the worshipers' sin—"sacrifices are an annual reminder of sins."

Now after four hundred eighty years, once the temple was built and the ark and the temple furnishings were set in their places, no one other than the priests would ever get to see them, not even the covered ark of the Covenant. Therefore, one could just imagine the curiosity that could have been built up in the minds of the people. That was how it was in the earlier days of Samuel when the ark was returned by the Philistines and set "in the field of Beth Shemesh." Seventy men died when they looked into the ark of Yahweh out of their curiosity (1 Sam 6:18-19).

Since worshipers in general would never get to be beyond the bronze altar in the sanctuary, it was necessary to describe every detail of the inner and outer sanctuaries since the worshipers would never get to see them while serving Yahweh at the temple court where the corporate worship took place. Giving such detailed description of the inner and outer sanctuaries was another means of God's grace for His people; otherwise, worshipers would always be more concerned and occupied with curiosity about the sanctuary than seeking the invisible Yahweh God.

The author of Kings made it very clear that "there was nothing in the ark except the two stone tablets that Moses had placed in it... where [Yahweh] made a covenant with the Israelites" (1 Kings 8:9). In other words, the worshipers should seek Yahweh and His revealed written word, their covenant relationship with Yahweh and His holy presence.

Not much has changed since then. Rather than seeking God's word, His presence, and relationship with God, people find it more exciting to have their curiosity met, seeking music or an intellectually challenging sermon in worship. God's word was very clear to the Israelites. The full version of the old covenant stipulation written on the two stone tablets was clearly revealed in *Torah*. There was no need for speculating, guessing or seeking something more "spiritually deep." Until they were taken into exile to Babylon, to the point of hearing "foreign tongues," they continued to reject God's word spoken through the prophets God had been sending; in Israel, especially by the religious and political leaders, even the simple word of God was rejected—"Who is it he is trying to teach... children weaned from their milk?" (Isa 28:9).

The worshipers, as they entered the temple court, were to seek God's face, to hear God's will clearly revealed in His written word, and live in obedience. In the temple court, the worshipers (and we also) were to renounce all temptations to live apart from God's sovereign control and try to control their own destiny, seeking instead to find satisfaction and meaning in this life by the written revealed will of God spoken in the worship service.

The worshipers at the temple court may not have had the privilege like the priests in the temple being closer to the "throne of grace," but if they sought Yahweh and His presence, hearing God's word would have truly satisfied their spiritual hunger like in the days of Nehemiah—"all the people [who] had been weeping as they listened to the words of the Law... [then went] to celebrate with great joy, because they now understood the words that had been made known to them" (Neh 8:9, 12).

Unlike the worship under the old covenant, the new covenant worship in Christ takes us beyond the altar, allowing us to "enter[s] the inner sanctuary behind the curtain" (Heb 6:19). By "the blood of Jesus, by a new and living way opened for us through the curtain, that is, his body," the new covenant worshipers "have confidence to enter the Most Holy Place" (Heb 10:19-20). We do not engage in worship in order to be reminded of our sins but rather to be overwhelmed with the grace of God's forgiveness through His Son, Jesus Christ.

What are we seeking in our Sunday worship service? Do we seek to hear God's voice from His written word or do we try to find an answer to satisfy our curiosity? Are we only sensing a hopeless chasm between God and us, or are we confident in Christ to leave the temple court and enter the inner sanctuary for the intimate relationship and fellowship with the Father that we have been longing for? In worship, worshipers' hearts and motives must be cross-examined.

14

YAHWEH'S GLORY CLOUD AND FIRE

After all the tedious, detailed instruction and the extraneous, meticulous work on the tabernacle was completed, in the wilderness, "the cloud covered the Tent of Meeting, and the glory of [Yahweh] filled the tabernacle." This made it impossible for Moses to dwell there (Exod 40:34-35), but because of God's dwelling presence manifested in His glory cloud, it made it all worth it.

We also see a similar pattern with the completion of the temple built by Solomon. When the temple construction was completed and the glory cloud of Yahweh filled the temple of God, it made it impossible for the priests to "perform their service because of the cloud" (2 Chr 5:7, 13-14), not because the area was cloudy and visibility was poor but because again, as they faced the very presence of holy Yahweh, there was something that made them incompatible with and therefore not able to be in the same place as God's holy presence.

But to be honest and more practical, in reality, if cloud and fire were all there were to the manifestations of God's glory, then I am not sure there would have been all that much to it other than the unusual and spectacular sight that would have brought awe for a short period of time and no more. After all, "we fix our eyes not on what is seen, but on what is unseen, since what is seen is temporary but what is unseen is eternal" (2 Cor 4:18). But the cloud and fire manifestations of Yahweh's glory did bring the people of Israel to worship.

In the presence of this glory cloud of Yahweh, what else could mortal men do, even if the "blood of goats and bulls... who [were] ceremonially unclean [sanctified] them so that they [were] outwardly clean" (Heb 9:13), but respond in worship—"they raised their voices in praise to [Yahweh] and sang: 'He is good; his love endures forever'" (2 Chr 5:13).

The Chronicler lays out the whole procedure of the worship that took place upon the completion of the temple construction, describing each activity in sequence. First, the people who were responsible for the ministry in the temple—the priests and Levites, who were musicians and singers, responded in musical worship once the ark of Yahweh's covenant was placed in the inner sanctuary (2 Chr 5:7-14).

Second, Solomon prayed in response to God's filling of the temple with His glory cloud (2 Chr 6:1-42). Although God was mysterious and could not be fully known (v. 1), and the "heavens, even the highest heaven, [could not] contain [Yahweh]" (v. 18), Solomon prayed that the temple would be God's dwelling place just as Yahweh had promised (vv. 20-21). The whole prayer focused on God's dwelling place that was represented by the temple and the prayers of both the people of Israel (v. 24) and foreigners (v. 32).

One of the main activities that would take place in the temple would be prayer. Not only did God promise that He would put His Name there, but many years later through Isaiah, God would promise that His "house [would] be called a house of prayer for all nations" (Isa 56:7). Ultimately, this promise would be fulfilled when Christ cleaned and sanctified the temple that is the church, the gathering of His people under the new covenant through His blood on the cross.

Based on what has been discussed so far, worship is the main activity, service to God by recognizing the assembly of God's people as God's dwelling place in faith, and respond to God's presence in singing praise and prayer. We sing and praise because we are in the very presence of God.

And all these would not have been possible if it were not for "the blood of Christ, who himself unblemished to God, cleanse[d] our consciences from acts that lead to death, so that we may serve the living God" (Heb 9:14).

Third, when "Solomon finished praying, fire came down from heaven and consumed the burnt offering and the sacrifices, and the glory of [Yahweh] filled the temple." Again, just as before, the "priests could not enter the temple" even though they were the only ones authorized to go in (2 Chr 7:1-2). And this time, "all the Israelites" witnessed "the fire coming down and the glory of [Yahweh] about the temple," and worshiped in thanksgiving with the musical song that was sung by the Levites earlier saying, "He is good; his love endures forever" (v. 3). Here, the congregation's confession is more emphasized than the musical praise. Worship took place in response to witnessing the fire consuming the sacrifices and God's glory cloud above the temple.

How are we to worship? When do we respond to God in worship? These two questions may be too broad to answer in one chapter. But if we were to limit the scope to a study of the fire consuming the sacrifices and the filling of the temple with God's glory cloud, then these two questions could be more specifically answered, these two miraculous activities being the two major works of Yahweh in the context of worship.

God's Consuming Fire

Although prior to Abraham, the most popular type of sacrifice was burnt offering, the word fire (*esh*) does not appear for the first time until Genesis 15:17. The blazing torch, which was a manifestation of God that "passed between the pieces," gave Abraham the assurance that Yahweh would keep His promise. Yet, perhaps because of the nature of the covenant ceremony, the blazing torch just "passed between the pieces" rather than consume them.

It was almost as though the author of the Pentateuch, Moses, was saving the word until the connection was made with the manifestation of Yahweh. When Yahweh "appeared" to Moses for the first time at Horeb, the mountain of God, God drew his attention, interrupting his daily duty as a shepherd, by appearing "in flames of fire from within a bush" though the bush itself, strangely, was not consumed (Exod 3:2-3). And this manifestation of God's glory in the form of fire continued to be visible throughout the Israelites' wilderness journey for forty years every evening although the tabernacle was not consumed while the fire was on the tabernacle (Exod 40:38; Num 9:15-16).

But when the manifestation of Yahweh was connected with the burnt offering, the fire actually consumed the offering; the fire "came out from the presence of [Yahweh] and consumed the burnt offering... all the people saw it, they shouted for joy and fell facedown" (Lev 9:24). This took place shortly after the completion of the Tent of Meeting when Aaron and his sons were carrying out the priestly ministry for the first time.

And the next time we see fire from Yahweh consuming the offerings would be at the completion of the temple. Upon the completion of the temple, the glory cloud filled the temple (1 Kings 8:10) just as it had the tabernacle (Exod 40:34). And just as the fire came out from Yahweh's presence and consumed the first offering of Aaron and his sons at the tabernacle, later at the temple "fire came down from heaven and consumed the burnt offering and the sacrifices... When all the Israelites saw the fires coming down... they knelt on the pavement with their faces to the ground... worshiped" (2 Chr 7:1, 3).

Fire from God's presence consuming the offerings happened only once each time (i.e., it was not a regular occurrence at either tabernacle or temple) at the very beginnings of the priestly ministry with the newly built tabernacle and at the temple. It was God's miraculous sign of assurance that Yahweh would accept the priestly ministry and offering sacrifices in worship. Therefore, whenever the people of Israel entered the temple court to worship, they were to have faith in Yahweh that their God would accept worship from them.

To which god or gods would Israel offer worship? The only true living God would be the One who would accept offerings. But just as it was in the beginning with Cain and Abel, the true living Yahweh either accepted or rejected depending on the individual worshiper, whether he had faith in God or not.

Many years later in the days of the prophet Elijah, the question that hung on receiving an answer by fire was twofold: 1) which god(s) was the true God, and 2) what type of worshiper's faith would God answer by fire.

Based on the acceptance of the offerings, Israel and the four hundred and fifty prophets of Baal would have to decide which god(s) to follow—"the god who answers by fire—he is God" (1 Kings 18:24). There on Mount Carmel, Yahweh consumed the sacrifice that was offered to Him by Elijah (v. 38) to show Israel that 1) Yahweh was God (v. 39) and 2) it was the sacrifice offered in faith like Elijah's, faith in no other god but Yahweh that would be accepted.

Roughly over eight hundred years later, the Son of God Himself made an offering on Mount Calvary. On the cross, Jesus took the wrath of God that was supposed to come upon us. There, on Mount Calvary, God the Father demonstrated "his own love for us… while we were still sinners, Christ died for us" (Rom 5:8).

Therefore, when the new covenant community gathers to worship, we have confidence in Christ to approach the throne of grace. We need to have faith, not in our own good merits, or ourselves but in Christ who offered the perfect sacrifice to God.

In worship, our minds need to be cleansed through Christ and His body as the offering that was accepted by God the Father. We should never be presumptuous; just having a well-organized worship service format—the responsive reading from a biblical text, singing Christian songs, hearing a message about God, and putting offerings in the plate, does not make or guarantee that service to be acceptable worship to God. In the light of what God accomplished through His Son Jesus on the cross, we are called to "be thankful… and worship God acceptably with reverence and awe, for our 'God is a consuming fire'" (Heb 12:28-29).

When fire from Yahweh was connected with sacrifices and consumption, it meant the divine acceptance of not only the sacrifices, but also those who ministered in the tabernacle as well as the temple. One of the most importance aspects of worship and the ministries during the worship service is the fact that God accepts our worship and service before Him because of Christ. Based on the acceptable sacrificial work on the cross, the believers are called to make themselves available as "living sacrifices" (Rom 12:1).

When Yahweh first appeared to Moses "in flames of fire" although the bush did not burn up, despite Moses' lack of self-confidence to serve God, especially when he felt like he failed forty years go, God was commissioning

Moses to bring God's people out from Egypt. Similarly, the disciples of Christ were commissioned to "go and make disciples of all nations" (Matt 28:19) but not until they were baptized with the Holy Spirit (Acts 1:5), which the last prophet under the old covenant John had already testified— "[Christ] will baptize you with the Holy Spirit and with fire" (Luke 3:16). And on the day of Pentecost, "what seemed to be tongues of fire... came to rest on each of them " (Acts 2:3). Although fire came to rest on them, the hundred twenty disciples were not consumed.

The day of Pentecost phenomenon took place only once, but the phenomenon was another signpost of the Last Days (Acts 2:17). Living in the Last Days, the new covenant worshipers are called to renew their commitment to Christ and participate in reaping the spiritual harvest as they recall what took place on Pentecost. As they engage in worship, seek to be filled with the Holy Spirit and declare "the wonders of God" in praise, like the prophet Isaiah who, once he saw "the Lord seated on a throne, high and exalted" became committed to God's call (Isa 6:1, 8), the conclusion of worship should be the worshipers' commitment "to offer [their] bodies as living sacrifices, holy and pleasing to God" (Rom 12:1).

God's Glory Cloud

Yahweh does not have a physical image since God is spirit and invisible, and "what is seen was not made out of what was visible," but God, who is invisible, created all things by His command (Heb 11:3). The visible manifestation of the glory cloud was a sign of God's holy presence, yet at the same time it was another reminder to His people that God does not have an image.

Solomon knew the tension between who and what God is like and the limitation of human effort. Solomon had never seen what it meant to have God's dwelling place in their midst. Just as when Moses approached the ark of God to offer sacrifices it required faith in God's promise that God would meet Moses there (Exod 25:22), and just as the covenant Yahweh made with his father David that Solomon would be the one to build God's house (2 Sam 7:13) was based on a promise for David to believe in, so now Solomon also could only trust in Yahweh's promise.

When David, out of his own passion for God's dwelling place, brought the ark to the City of David and "set it in its place inside the tent that David had pitched for it" (2 Sam 6:17), there was no glory cloud that filled the tent. Yet in the case of Solomon, when the ark of Yahweh's covenant was brought "to its place in the inner sanctuary of the temple... the cloud filled the temple of [Yahweh]" (1 Kings 8:6, 10). The visible manifestation of God's glory cloud was absent in the case of David, not because the tent was far less glorious than the magnificent temple building, but because of what the temple stood for. In contrast to the temporary, movable tent that signified the Israelites' wilderness journey, the stable and relatively permanent structure of a temple building showed that God had finally settled His people in the Promised Land.

Upon the temple's completion, Solomon witnessed for the first time the glory cloud filling the temple. In that awesome moment, Solomon recalled that the same glory cloud filled the tabernacle in the past (Exod 40:34), and Yahweh had said that he "would dwell in a dark cloud" (1 Kings 8:12). The filling of the temple with God's glory was the means of God's grace, giving assurance to Solomon and the people of Israel that God would dwell in the newly-built temple just as He had promised He would. Therefore, God's filling of the temple with His glory cloud was a sign of God's promise of His presence, to dwell among His people and in the midst of their praises.

The glory cloud was one of various forms in which the invisible God manifested Himself. Why a cloud? What could the form of a cloud convey about the divine nature? Natural clouds being found in the sky, the chosen form of a glory cloud could have been meant to remind people that God was in heaven (Ecc 5:2). Like a cloud, physically God could not be touched or felt although His manifestation was visible (like the work of the Holy Spirit, who is invisible, and yet His work and manifestation is undeniable, John 3:8; 1 Cor 12:7). Or, it could simply have been meant to convey that Yahweh was mysterious and that man in his natural mind could not fully comprehend Him.

Solomon knew the fact that what he had built for God, who was invisible, was a contradiction in itself since Solomon confessed, "Will God really dwell on earth? The heaven, even the highest heaven, cannot contain you.

How much less this temple I have built" (1 Kings 8:27). Solomon knew man's best effort would still come short of preparing an adequate dwelling place for God. This knowledge humbled Solomon and made him appreciate all the more Yahweh's choosing to manifesting Himself in the glory cloud to assure His people that He would be there. More than anything, Yahweh's glory cloud gave the worshipers assurance of His presence. After all, Yahweh who is holy is enthroned on His people's praise (Ps 22:3).

We, the new covenant worshipers, should sense the same type of tension as Solomon had. We need to sense the holy tension between 1) what we are able to do and accomplish never possibly being good enough for God and 2) nevertheless, at the same time, seeking and expecting in faith, based on God's redemptive work accomplished through Christ, that all the activities performed by the worshipers of the new covenant community would be in the very presence of God. There, in the midst of His people worshiping, God's holy presence would come to have fellowship with His people just as He said He would—"I will put my dwelling place among you... I will walk among you and be your God, and you will be my people" (Lev 26:11-12).

In 1 Kings 8, there were two things in relation to God's presence: the ark of Yahweh's covenant (v. 6) and the glory cloud (v. 10) in which God would dwell (v. 12). The author said, "there was nothing in the ark except the two stone tablets" (v. 9). The emphasis was on the simplicity of God's written revealed word which was objective, while the glory of Yahweh in the cloud was mysterious - as Solomon said, Yahweh would dwell in a "dark" cloud (v. 12) which suggests obscurity, i.e., that God's nature is not clear or simple or straightforward but rather beyond the grasp of human nature to understand.

In other words, the glory cloud in which Yahweh revealed Himself in a mysterious manifestation that was incomprehensible and indescribable could be properly and objectively experienced through Yahweh's written revelation. The presence of Yahweh could be mainly discerned through the objective truth of God's word.

The cloud and God's word also appear together in a similar relationship in the Gospels. On one occasion during the earthly ministry days of Jesus, he took three of His disciples and "led them up a high mountain."

There, the three disciples eye-witnessed the glorious Christ. They also experienced what Moses and the priests had experienced in the newly-erected tabernacle and temple respectively, i.e., the glory cloud—"a cloud appeared and enveloped them." It must have been a spectacular scene and experience. Yet nothing was supposed to hold more attraction than what God the Father said from the cloud, "This is my Son, whom I love. Listen to him" (Mark 9:1-8).

The person, Jesus Christ, accompanied by the glory cloud was none other than Yahweh, God Himself incarnated. In the Old Testament, Yahweh was seen as a cloud rider (Ps 18:9; 97:2; 104:3). The presence and coming of Yahweh was often associated with clouds—"Sing to God, sing praise to his name, extol him who rides on the clouds—his name is [Yahweh]" (Ps 68:4). Therefore, what Daniel saw in his vision, a "son of man, coming with the clouds of heaven" (Dan 7:13), was Jesus Christ in all of His glory when He comes for the second time (Mark 14:62)—"[Jesus] was taken up... a cloud hid him from their sight... This same Jesus, who has been taken from you into heaven, will come back in the same way you have seen him go into heaven" (Acts 1:9, 11).

Peter, one of the three, wrote about what he and the others witnessed on the mountaintop which he refers to as "the sacred mountain" in 2 Peter 1:16-18. Although they were literally "eyewitnesses of his majesty," of Christ's coming, nothing was more certain than God's written word (v. 19); whatever we subjectively experience in life cannot be more certain than God's written word. No matter what we experience, even if they are "miraculous signs and great wonders" from Yahweh, unless God gives us "a mind that understands or eyes that see or ears that hear" (Deut 29:3-4), they are just experiences that have no lasting effect in our lives because we miss the greater significance (i.e., like it was with many people of Jesus' time who experienced his miracles but failed to see who he truly was).

Peter and the others did experience the second coming of Christ that belonged to the distant future. At the beginning of Jesus' ministry, although Jesus clearly said that His time had not yet come, He still performed the miracle, changing water into wine at the wedding of Cana, thus revealing His glory (John 2:1-11). As Jesus was eagerly awaiting and anticipating "the wedding of the Lamb" (Rev 19:7, 9) with His church at His second coming, though it was not quite yet time, in his excitement He let His disciples have a foretaste of what was to come; perhaps in that way, they would also have the same longing as their Lord Jesus.

Therefore, the glory cloud that God's people witnessed at the tabernacle and the temple was not only a manifestation of God's glory giving assurance of God's presence in the worship context, but it was also a sign pointing towards the future fulfillment that "the messenger of the covenant" would come to His temple (Mal 3:1) and finally that Christ would come for the second time with all of His glory—"Look, he is coming with the clouds, and every eye will see him" (Rev 1:7). Each of God's miracles served as a down payment that would lead up to the final fulfillment in Christ.

Regardless of one's eschatology, whether one believes the Book of Revelation is about the future or mostly about the present, the Lord God "who is, and who was, and who is to come" (Rev 1:8) constantly brings what belongs to the future fulfillment to the present now so that His people living in the last days could experience and "press on to take hold of that for which Christ Jesus took hold of [them]" (Phil 3:12).

Since the new covenant worship and ministry incomparably and far outweighs the old covenant—"we, who with unveiled faces all reflect the Lord's glory" (2 Cor 3:18), in our days do not expect the visible manifestation of God's glory cloud to fill our meeting place if we understand its purpose from tracing the glory cloud from the Old Testament to the fulfillment in Christ of the New Testament. The manifestation of Yahweh's glory cloud in the Old Testament was a shadow of what would be better to come. For the glory cloud was not only the manifestation of God's presence but also the foreshadowing of the glorious coming King, Christ Jesus. For this reason, even the second temple built by the remnant that came back to Israel from the exile would be filled with much greater glory (Hag 2:9).

The construction of the second temple was resumed under the prophetic ministry of Haggai, yet due to its size, building materials, and decorations, compared to the first temple built by Solomon, the second temple seemed "like nothing" (Hag 2:3) to the returned exiles. For that reason, Yahweh encouraged the people of the land not to be dissuaded by the external look of the temple building but rather to resume the construction that was interrupted for a time because Yahweh Almighty promised His presence among them (v. 4).

Please note that while all the other pagan gods needed a temple to dwell in, Yahweh God mandated the building of His temple because He was already with the people. This helps us to understand Yahweh and the purpose of building His temple better. God is not in need of a temple building to dwell in since He has said through his prophet Isaiah, "Heaven is my throne, and the earth is my footstool. Where is the house you will build for me?" (Isa 66:1). Just as God is not in need of our offering for He said, "I have no need of a bull from your stall or of goats from your pens, for every animal of the forest is mine, and the cattle on a thousand hills" (Ps 50:9-10) but offering is a form of expression of the worshipers' gratitude, so the temple building should be an expression of worshipers' desire to be near Yahweh as they firmly believe and take hold of in faith His promise that He would put His Name there (1 Kings 9:3).

Yahweh promised that David's son Solomon would be the one to build the house for God, and He fulfilled this promise in Solomon's lifetime. However, at another level, the covenant with David went far beyond his son Solomon and the temple, ultimately being about the Son of David, Jesus Christ. Likewise, God's word concerning the second temple (Hag 2:6-9) was not just about the second temple itself but beyond; ultimately, it was fulfilled in Christ when He entered and cleansed the temple, a prophetic act indicating that through His death on the cross, the true temple cleansing would take place. And now, the true temple, the church as Christ's body, is the fulfillment of what had been said about the second temple.

While there was no visible manifestation of Yahweh's glory cloud upon the completion of the second temple construction, from Haggai 2 it is clear that Yahweh is the One who would be making the manmade temple glorious (vv. 3, 7, 9). In what way(s) would God make the temple more glorious? If it was not going to be the manifestation of God's glory cloud this time, then what would make this second temple outshine "the glory of the former house?"

Prior to the building of the tabernacle or the ark of the covenant, the visible manifestation of Yahweh in the form of the "pillar of cloud" was already with the Israelites when they came out of Egypt in the wilderness (Exod 14:19-20; 33:9-10). And shortly after the golden calf incident, God told Moses He would "send an angel before" them but that He Himself would not be going with the Israelites (Exod 33:2-3). Dismayed at the thought, Moses declares their absolute need for God's presence and then asks to see God's glory (v. 18). Surely Moses was not referring to the visible manifestation of Yahweh's glory cloud since that had already and always been visible ever since the exodus. What Moses desperately sought was a greater and deeper knowledge of 1) God's ways (perhaps how He does things, His deeds) (v. 13) and 2) who God is.

Moses was about to "experience" God's goodness and "hear" God's name, but since no one can perceive or comprehend beyond what one can handle, Moses was allowed to experience only the aftereffect of Yahweh (vv. 19-23). For Moses, seeing the glory of God was to know and get a closer look at how Yahweh sovereignly works behind the scenes in the visible world. It also meant to experience Yahweh's goodness, compassion, grace, abounding love and faithfulness (Exod 34:5-7).

God's glory was revealed not fixed in a particular moment but in motion (passing by) lest Moses experience something beyond what he could handle. Two people, Moses and Elijah in the Old Testament, were given the privilege of experiencing God's glory "pass by." It was a time of discouragement and uncertainty for the Israelites because of their guilt from their idolatry of the golden calf. What Moses really needed was not some type of guarantee of their safe arrival and conquering of the Promised Land (which the angel would have provided) but more of Yahweh Himself.

Even after Yahweh showed Himself in the standoff between Elijah and the prophets of Baal that Yahweh was the only true living God, the northern kingdom of Israel failed to turn back to Yahweh, and Jezebel went after Elijah's life because of the killing of all the Baal prophets (1 Kings 19:1-2). The word of Yahweh came to Elijah who was filled with fear and discouragement to the point of wanting to die and invited Elijah to "Horeb, the mountain of God" (v. 8). And there, Elijah was about to experience what Moses had on the mountain of God—"Go out and stand on the mountain in the presence of [Yahweh], for [Yahweh] is about to pass by" (v. 11). Yahweh was not in the powerful wind, earthquake, or fire, but He was in the "gentle whisper" (v. 12). For Elijah, being a prophet, hearing Yahweh's voice was not something unusual, but in the moment, as Yahweh was "passing by," the "gentle whisper" was more than enough for Elijah to pull "his cloak over his face" (v. 13); Elijah was gripped with a holy fear because he had just encountered Yahweh in a way he had never experienced Him before.

Only two people, Moses and Elijah, witnessed God's glory ("Yahweh is about to pass by") in that unique sense; especially in Moses' case, his unique intimate relationship with Yahweh is summarized in Numbers 12:7, "With him I speak face to face, clearly and not in riddles; he sees the form of [Yahweh]." And those same two people later in the New Testament witnessed the full manifestation of God incarnate in His glory when Jesus "was transfigured... His face shone like the sun, and his clothes became as white as the light" (Matt 17:2).

Perhaps what the two men witnessed on their own separate occasions in the Old Testament foreshadowed on a tiny, miniature scale what they would be witnessing in the glorious Christ. For this reason, John in the very beginning of his Gospel wrote, "The Word became flesh and [pitched a tabernacle] among us. We have seen his glory, the glory of the One and Only... No one has ever seen God, but God the One and Only, who is at the Father's side, has made him known" (John 1:14, 18).

One time when Jesus' disciples were in a boat "straining at the oars, because the wind was against them... [Jesus] went out to them, walking on the lake... He was about to pass by them" (Mark 6:48). They had just witnessed Yahweh's glory in human flesh although "their hearts were hardened" and they were not able to connect what they had witnessed—something of the divinity of Christ, Jesus' walking on water— with their teacher being God Himself—"[God] alone stretches out the heavens and treads on the waves of the sea" (Job 9:8).

Every Sunday, a new covenant community in Christ has an opportunity to witness His divinity, the fulfillment of the manifestation of God's glory that Moses and Elijah witnessed, far deeper and more glorious, in worship. And when the worshipers encounter the glorious Christ, the only natural and impulsive response would be to be gripped with holy reverence, with either Yahweh having to cover our faces as He did for Moses or we cover our own as Elijah did. Then, just as Moses "bowed to the ground at once and worshiped" (Exod 34:8), like the disciples, we bow down in worship and say, "Truly you are the Son of God" (Matt 14:33)!

Therefore, if this generation wants to truly worship God, it is imperative that what is being preached at the regular Sunday morning worship service must be not only be the humanity of Christ but also the glorious risen Christ just as the apostle John witnessed in his vision experience on the Lord's Day when he was in the Spirit in Revelation 1:12-16. The praise songs should proclaim Christ's glory, something of the divinity of Christ. Through prayer, the congregation should seek the apparent paradox of experiencing intimacy with the Lord, being gripped with holy reverence at the same time having the nearness of Christ—"Serve [Yahweh] with fear and rejoice with trembling. Kiss the Son... Blessed are all who take refuge in him" (Ps 2:11-12).

15

THE TEMPLE COURTS, WHERE AND HOW THE WORSHIP TOOK PLACE

Much of our energy tends to be spent on studying the priestly ministry in the Holy Place. Although the primary priestly duty was to approach God on behalf of the people, the corporate worship of Israel took place in the temple court since the rest of the worshipers were forbidden to be in the temple. Since the new covenant people in Christ are now "a chosen people, a royal priesthood, a holy nation, a people belonging to God, that [they] may declare the praises of him" (1 Peter 2:9), a church as a whole, and not individually, is to fulfill God's calling for his people and carry out what the nation Israel failed to do by breaking the covenant (Exod 19:5-6). As a church, corporately and on behalf of all nations, we need to intercede and "proclaim [Christ], admonishing and teaching everyone with all wisdom, so that [we] may present everyone perfect in Christ" (Col 1:28) in order to be the salt and the light of the world (Matt 5:13-16).

Unlike the non-priest worshipers of Israel, we have Christ as our Great High Priest "who has gone through the heavens" and can therefore "approach the throne of grace with confidence" (Heb 4:14, 16). The worshipers under the old covenant served Yahweh at the temple court and relied on their high priest to enter the Most Holy Place on their behalf, having faith in God's promise that their God would meet the high priest between the two cherubim.

Like the worshipers under the old covenant, the new covenant worshipers also come together as a church and serve God with their Great High Priest leading them. But unlike with the high priest and the ceremonial regulations under the old covenant, because of the Great High Priest Jesus Christ, new covenant worshipers are all invited to enter into God's Most Holy Presence, directly approaching the throne of grace in faith. While the Old Testament worshipers could only envision from the *Torah* what it would be like to be in the inner sanctuary, the worshipers in Christ approach the very presence of God for intimacy and to "receive mercy and find grace to help" them in their "time of need" (Heb 4:16).

There was only one designated place for corporate worship in all land of Israel. Just as there was One God, there was one altar and one temple for the place of corporate worship. For biblical and perhaps also practical reasons, Yahweh only made it mandatory for the people of Israel "to celebrate a festival to [Him]" (Exod 23:14) three times a year since it would be difficult for those who lived a distance from Jerusalem to travel to the designated place more often. Making the long distance to travel an excuse, after the kingdom was divided into two, Jeroboam, the new king of the northern kingdom, Israel, set up two golden calves, one "in Bethel and the other in Dan" to keep the people from going down to Jerusalem to worship (1 Kings 12:25-30).

Although it might have been very inconvenient to have only one temple for the place of corporate worship, God most likely set it up this way because the people would always be tempted to serve Him on their own terms and out of their own convenience. I wonder how modern Christians feel about this. In our days, being committed to a local church, committed to worship with the same congregation each and every week, is not that popular among some evangelical Christians.

For some, it all depends on the message or worship or music ministry style. A person may enjoy going to one church for the music in worship while attending another church for the message or teaching, and on top of that, they regularly give to some Christian mission or humanitarian organizations without being first committed to giving to their local church. Perhaps to some degree such low commitment to the local church on the part of some Christians does reflect our modern day American culture—desiring and longing for a meaningful relationship but not willing to be committed.

While we expect God to be committed to meet His end of the bargain, we shy away from committing to one particular church. We want to serve God in our own way, on our own terms. Such was the case in the book of Judges, with different groups of people ignoring the worship mandate given by Yahweh in the *Torah*—"There the Danites set up for themselves the idols... They continued to use the idols... [while] all the time the house of God was in Shiloh" (Judges 18:30-31). The corporate worship was supposed to happen in only one place, Shiloh, since that was where the ark of the covenant was, but various groups of Israelites set up other places and ended up worshiping other gods there.

Knowing how the people of Israel worshiped in the Old Testament and also what was being taught to them about offering the worship that took place in the temple court should help us to have the biblical foundation of worship. While not much is written on corporate worship in the biblical narrative, the book of Psalms is filled with the corporate worship that is related to the temple courts. The largest percentage of the worship Psalms were taught to the people of Israel and used in their corporate worship setting.

The Life of Worshipers from Psalm 50

Yahweh was the one who prescribed the worship mandate and its rituals, mainly sacrifices. In the same way that miracles would lose their significance if they happened on a regular, routine basis, if offering sacrifices, which made up the main portion of the act of worship, became mere routine, it could easily have become a religious system that worshipers went through without having any connection to their lives outside of worship.

For this reason Psalm 50:1 says that the "Mighty One, God, [Yahweh]" spoke, not to those who do not know Yahweh, but His "consecrated ones" who were in the covenant relationship with Yahweh (v. 5). Yahweh did not simply give prescriptions about worship and then let the system run its course without speaking any further to the people. But rather, when there was a discrepancy between the act of worship (v. 8) and the way the worshipers were living their lives (vv. 17-20), Yahweh, as the righteous judge (v. 6), would not be "silent" but "testify against" them (vv. 3, 7).

There was a wrong assumption made by the worshipers, thinking it was as though God was in need of their service (vv. 9-13). The apostle Paul told the Athenians in the New Testament that God "is not served by human hands, as if he needed anything" (Acts 17:25). For some, when worshiping God became a regular routine, it stopped being the expression of their hearts' desire for God but rather became giving and doing something for God who seemed to be in need of the people's service. But the Creator Yahweh has the sole ownership of every area of His creation (Ps 50:10-11), and rather than God being in need of man, man is in need of God, "For in him we live and move and have our being" (Acts 17:28).

Sacrificing "thank offerings," fulfilling "vows," and calling upon God in Psalm 50:14-15 have to do with our attitude and acknowledging God in our everyday life, making commitment to Yahweh, and desperately seeking God in our time of need. At times, finding a reason to thank God could be difficult for some people. One of the reasons for this could be from failing to see God or acknowledging God's presence in their lives. At the same time, when worshipers give the sacrifice of praise of thanksgiving, they begin to see the sovereign God who is in control and actively involved in their lives. Having our spiritual eyes opened, we are able to see and know beyond what we can perceive with the naked eye. For this reason, the apostle Paul continued to give thanks for the church in Ephesus because of God's blessing "in the heavenly realms with every spiritual blessing in Christ" (Eph 1:3, 15-16).

If fulfilling vows is the act of worship, then the worshiper must have acknowledged God or sought help from Yahweh in his life prior to worship. In that sense, worship should be the direct result and expression of how we have lived during the week by looking forward to worship to finish or fulfill what we have started or committed.

But sadly, God was absent in the minds of many people in Israel in the days of Asaph. They were religious only when they were worshiping God; apart from worship, they lived as though God did not exist. Therefore, "in the day of trouble," rather than seeking and relying on God, they took matters into their own hands. They were supposed to "call upon" God in worship at the temple court, but the people of Israel failed to live up to Solomon's prayer (1 Kings 8:31-51); eventually they continued to spiral downward and ended up in Jesus' days turning the temple that would "be called a house of prayer for all nations" into a "den of robbers" (Mark 11:17).

At the temple court, they recited God's word (Ps 50:16). The purpose of reading and teaching God's word in the worship context was not only to magnify God also to remind and exhort the worshipers to put it into practice; sadly, that they had no desire to do so (v. 17) was proven in the way they lived (vv. 17-20). For this reason, the preaching of God's word should not only encourage worshipers, but also teach, rebuke, correct and train them in righteousness (2 Tim 3:16).

It is possible for the worshipers of God to forget about God (v. 22). Worship could be about God and at the same time be non-God-centered. The words of the praises the people sang and the psalms they recited could have been about God, but just as the prophet Isaiah would prophesy, "These people come near to me with their mouth and honor me with their lips, but their hearts are far from me" (Isa 29:13).

In order to avoid such grave error, we need to "guard [our] steps when [we] go to the house of God. Go near to listen rather than to offer the sacrifice of fools" (Ecc 5:1). Not only do we approach God in worship with offering and formalities but also with the heart to hear what God has to say about the way we have lived prior to worship. Have we acknowledged Him? Is our life currently in line with what we are singing and confessing to the Lord? Jesus said, "Why do you call me, 'Lord, Lord,' and do not do what I say?" (Luke 6:46)

Worship as Witnessing God's Power from Psalm 68

The background of Psalm 68 is the coming of Yahweh and His victory over His enemies, which resulted in God's provision for His people (vv. 10, 18). Out of this great salvation of Yahweh, the author David prayed and expected that the "God of Israel [would give] power and strength to his people" in His sanctuary as His people in worship "proclaim the power of God... whose power is in the skies" (vv. 34-35).

Solomon was the one who actually built the temple building, yet David, who wrote Psalm 68, mentioned God's "temple at Jerusalem" (v. 29). If the temple David was referring to was wherever God chose "to reign... dwell" (v. 16), then David, as a prophet seeing what was ahead, could have been prophesying about the coming of the Son of David and about Christ's death and resurrection that resulted in God's provision for His new covenant people who would be "clothed with power from on high" (Luke 24:49).

Since Psalm 68 becomes one of the primary prophetic psalms regarding worship and the gospel ministry for the new covenant community, we will revisit it in more depth in the section on the New Testament worship under the new covenant in Christ. But for now, looking at the psalm in the original context, we see David telling what worshipers in his days could expect Yahweh to do based on God's great saving work of the past.

Yahweh God is the One "who rides on the clouds" (vv. 4, 33), dwells "in his holy dwelling" (v. 5), and came to the Mount "Sinai" (v. 8) to "reign" and "dwell" (v. 16). Yet God came down "from Sinai into his sanctuary" (v. 17) that Yahweh would "dwell there" (v. 18).

David rehearsed God coming down from Sinai and the visible manifestation of Yahweh's glory cloud over the tabernacle that was with the Israelites throughout the wilderness journey for forty years and continued to save His people in the days of the judges. Based on the great saving work of Yahweh in history, David expected the same God to come and dwell in the sanctuary where His people come together to worship, whether before the ark of the covenant, or the future temple that his son Solomon would build, or the final fulfillment in the worshiping community of believers in Christ.

Earlier, there was a procession of worshipers led by David while the ark of Yahweh was transported to the city of David (2 Sam 6:12-15). Now in the sanctuary, the procession of the worshiping congregation, which was made up of all classes of God's people, should worship God with the same type of reverence, joy, and excitement (Ps 68:24-27).

David said, "your [God's] procession has come into view" (v. 24), referring in the following verses to the worshipers perhaps as they were making their ways into the temple court. Previously the procession of God's people took place when the ark of Yahweh was being transported. Now, although the ark of Yahweh was already "set... in its place inside the tent that David had pitched for it" (2 Sam 6:17), David still spoke about God's procession "into the sanctuary" (Ps 68:24). It means that worshipers should not only praise Yahweh for His salvation but also for God's presence coming into the sanctuary in the midst of the worshiping community.

From the coming of Yahweh into His sanctuary in the context of His people congregating together to worship, David moves on to focus on corporate prayer. The worshipers should expect and pray for the manifestation of God's power "as [God has] done before" (v. 28). One way of witnessing a manifestation of God's strength would be worshipers seeing all nations come to the temple, honoring the God of Israel and "submit[ting]... to God" (vv. 29-33). Along with other prophets, Isaiah prophesied what God would do in the Last Days for the new covenant community—"The products of Egypt... will be yours... They will bow down before you... saying, 'Surely God is with you, and there is no other" (Isa 45:14).

The apostle Paul spoke about the new covenant people's gathering in worship in 1 Corinthians 12. He taught that if the new covenant community (which in this letter was the church in Corinth primarily) would properly practice in an orderly fashion the speaking-related gifts—prophecy and tongues with interpretation, which were the manifestations of the Spirit (1 Cor 12:7), the church would be experiencing what was said about the new covenant community in Isaiah 45:14 that would be fulfilled in the Last Days (1 Cor 14:25).

Just as Yahweh came from Sinai and scattered His enemies before His people in the wilderness (Ps 68:1), which was the prayer/song of Moses "whenever the ark set out" (Num 10:35), the Son of God came down from heaven, was crucified on Calvary, and defeated the last enemy, death, through His resurrection (1 Cor 15:26). Therefore, the new covenant community in Christ should sing the song of David, Psalm 68, as the congregation looking back and meditating on the implications of Christ's crucifixion and resurrection for the victory Christ had won for His people.

Surely, we give the Son of God praise, for Christ indeed is our Savior and Lord. It is He who bore our eternal burden of sin in His body (Ps 68:19-20; 1 Peter 2:24). As we "proclaim the power of God" (Ps 68:34) in His sanctuary that was accomplished on the cross and resurrection, may the church witness and confess, "You are awesome, O God, in your sanctuary" (v. 35) as the new covenant community is being "clothed with power from on high" (Luke 24:49).

Experiencing God's Goodness in the Sanctuary from Psalm 73

Asaph, the author of Psalm 73, was most likely a Levite but not a priest, if 1 Chronicles 6:39 refers to the same Asaph. If Asaph was not a priest, then he most likely would never have gone into the sanctuary since only priests were allowed to be in the sanctuary. As a Levite, like any other worshiper, the closest Asaph could get to the ark of Yahweh that represented the very presence of God which was in the inner sanctuary, was the temple court. Therefore, the eternal perspective that was refreshed in Asaph's mind—"till I entered the sanctuary of God; then I understood their final destiny" (v. 17), happened at the temple court, mostly likely when he was engaging in worship.

The prosperity of the "arrogant" (v. 3) who did not regard God at all (v. 11) was unstable and could turn into poverty overnight (v. 18). In order for a person to avoid becoming envious of the health and wealth of those who are influential and proud of living in the absence of God (vv. 3-12), the person needs to live with an eternal perspective—"[God] has also set eternity in the hearts of men" (Ecc 3:11). Having the proper eternal perspective helps the person to realize that any prosperity that comes apart from the eternal God would be utterly short-lived (vv. 19-20).

Even though spiritually and emotionally Asaph was in no condition to worship God (vv. 21-22), through worship, Asaph nevertheless gained the eternal perspective that helped him to see that God was never separated from him. God was guiding Asaph with His word (vv. 23-24).

For Asaph, being "near God" (v. 28) was being faithful to God even when what he experienced in life seemed unjust, i.e., the prosperity of "those who [were] far from [God]" (v.27); in our days, such people are sometimes called "happy pagans." Rather than seeking worldly things according to the worldly standard of comfort and "prosperity" in life (v. 3), Asaph recommitted himself to make "the Sovereign [Yahweh his] refuge" (v. 28).

The influence of the secular culture that both overtly and plainly proposes and propagates through the media what it means to be happy, satisfied, and fulfilled, and that all these can be gained from having more wealth, health and external beauty, should never be underestimated by the worshipers of God. Jesus said that in order for us to keep ourselves from attempting to "serve two masters... both God and Money," the aim of our life needs to be focused on heaven (Matt 6:19-24).

Therefore, it is crucial that what is being preached and sung in worship service should draw the worshipers closer to God who is in heaven and lead them to confess, "Whom have I in heaven but you? And earth has nothing I desire besides you" (Ps 73:25).

The real issue in life is not about the prosperity of the arrogant and their apparent freedom "from the burdens common to man... not plagued by human ills" (v. 5). The question we need to ask before such perception of prosperity is, "Are we going to trust and rely on what we are able to feel in our flesh, and perceive and evaluate according the worldly standard of successful living? Or are we going to ask God to strengthen our hearts to have the eternal perspective and have "God [be] the strength of [our hearts]" (vv. 26-27).

Worship should never be separated from how worshipers live; through worship, God speaks into how worshipers should properly perceive what they face in life. Although believers' work and careers are ultimately (or should be) for God's glory, most Christians spend most of their time working in a "secular environment" where, without being aware and without even having to make an effort, we are subtly being influenced by the secular culture or at the very least tempted to redefine happiness apart from God and eternity.

Compared to how much time we spend in this world, the time we spend worshiping God is minimal. For this reason, what is being preached and sung in the worship service is absolutely crucial for the believers; otherwise, the line between worldly and godly, secular and the gospel, humanistic and biblical, and man-centered value as opposed to God-centered, becomes indistinguishable. And it is through worship that the worshipers' hearts are strengthened with God's word by the guidance of the Holy Spirit.

Through worship, we make the Sovereign Yahweh our refuge and proclaim that presently God is working out things in life according to His eternal purpose (v. 28). When the gospel is being preached and praise songs are centered on God and His sovereignty, what seems so unfair to the point of asking, "Where is God in the midst of happiness without God?" The worshipers regain their spiritual foothold and place their trust in God who never ceases to "guide... with [His] counsel" (v. 24).

The Heart's Desire of Worshipers from Psalm 84

Those who lived a distance away from Jerusalem where the temple was would have to take a one to three day trip at least three times annually. Psalm 84 was most likely written to celebrate the pilgrimage as those "who have set their hearts" (v. 5) made their way to the temple in Jerusalem "before God in Zion" (v. 7) to worship.

First, the psalmist expresses his inner desire for God's "dwelling place" (vv. 1-2). Again, we can assume the psalmist was one of the Korahites, one who was not in the priestly line; the nearest he could come to God's presence was the altar at the temple courts (v. 10). God's dwelling place was seen as non-threatening and inviting, even as seemingly non-significant a creature as a "sparrow" or "swallow" could make her home, a place for herself, "near [Yahweh's] altar" (v. 3). If even a sparrow could make her home near the altar, then how much more could people, who have been created in God's image, find the true security of life in God's presence as they worship. Are people not "worth more than many sparrows" (Matt 10:31)?

It would be helpful to raise a number of questions in order to apply Psalm 84 in worship. What makes God's dwelling place so attractive (v. 1)? Why does the psalmist have a yearning desire for the courts of Yahweh (v. 2)? How does one find true security in life in worshiping God

(v. 3)? In what way(s) are those "who have set their hearts on pilgrimage" blessed (v. 5)? Why is the only prayer in this psalm about God's "anointed one" (v. 9)? Why is being in God's courts better than being elsewhere (v. 10)?

The psalmist found God's courts to be the object of his affection since that was where He chose to dwell and place His Name (v. 1). Unlike other pagan deities of that time, Yahweh God was omnipresent and not limited to a particular place. But when it came to worship, He chose one particular place, Jerusalem, to be site where the ark of the covenant resided and His temple stood. Only at the temple were God's people expected to congregate to engage in corporate worship in the way David and other spiritual leaders prescribed based on God's word; again, how they worshipped was never left to the worshiping individuals.

From the very beginning, God revealed Himself as a God of community, a Triune God as we have seen earlier in Genesis 1:26-27 and 2:18. Once the establishment of God's people was made at Mount Sinai, God also prescribed how people should worship, as one people, in one place, to reflect who God is: one God in three Persons in perfect unity. Therefore, worship was always corporate in the religious life of Israel.

The concept of corporate community may not settle well in the hearts of modern day Christians, especially city dwellers. For people living in a city, the meaning of "community" takes on a completely different nuance, especially since most people rarely even get to talk to the person living next door. They could just as well be asking the same question of Jesus as the "expert in the law" who "wanted to justify himself... [and so] asked... And who is my neighbor" (Luke 10:25, 29).

A typical, modern day, evangelical worship service attendee's concern is the sermon, music and a good worship environment. They do not have to know who is sitting next to them since that would not be a main concern. They are oblivious to the biblical teaching on the importance of the corporate worship. Their concern is not the dwelling place of God where His presence is when the worshiping community comes together in unity. There is only one dimension in worship—my God and me, while "let us" (Ps 95:1) or "speak to one another" (Eph 5:19) is ignored. Though in everyday life we may spend so much time front of our own personal computer monitors or on our smart phones, these ways of life we have become so accustomed to must not carry over into our worship, translating into an indifferent attitude towards other worshipers and the spiritual fellowship with one another that could take place in worship.

The psalmist's "soul yearns... for the courts of [Yahweh]," not because there would be a good preaching from a teacher of the Law, but because in the place of the corporate gathering to worship, the living God promised he would meet them there. I wonder if some modern day worshipers could relate to another psalm written by one of the Korahites, "As the deer pants for streams of water, so my soul pants for you, O God... These things I remember as I pour out my soul: how I used to go with the multitude, leading the procession to the house of God, with shouts of joy and thanks-giving" (Ps 42:1, 4).

Perhaps an "innocent" sparrow that knows no fear built "a nest for her-self" (Ps 84:3) at the temple court since the temple court was an open space. Likewise for the psalmist, out of all places, God's dwelling place, the temple court, was the place where he felt most secure and the place where he belonged. The reason for such security is elaborated on in verses 10 and 11.

The only prayer we find in Psalm 84 is in verses 8-9. The psal-mist's prayer seems somewhat incongruent with his desire for God's dwelling place and his belief in Yahweh's blessing for those who have such a desire, being about asking God to "look with favor on [His] anointed one" (v. 9). In the book of Psalms, an "anointed one" could be referring either to a king (Ps 18:50) or a prophet (Ps 105:15).

Since the anointed one is connected with the concept of a "shield" earlier, here it most likely refers to a king. Although ten out of twelve times in the book of Psalms the word "shield" directly refers to Yahweh God, here in Psalm 84:9—"Look upon our shield... look with favor on your anointed one" and in Psalm 89:18—"our shield belongs to [Yahweh], our king to the Holy One of Israel," the metaphor clearly refers to a regent king.

Why did the psalmist petition on behalf of the political leader? We find in the book of First and Second Kings that often one man, the king, and his relationship with Yahweh could determine the spiritual condition of the entire nation. One bad king would set up idols or pagan altars in the temple court. Under King Hezekiah of Judah (some scholars believe Psalm 84 was written during Hezekiah's reign), not only Judah but also the people from the northern kingdom of Israel came to Jerusalem to celebrate the Feast of Unleavened Bread. King Hezekiah also reinstituted the priests and Levites for the ministry in the temple (2 Chr 30-31).

Just as the psalmist was desperately interceding for their "shield," God's "anointed one," that Yahweh would show His favor so that God's dwelling place would continue to be the object of the psalmist's and other worshipers' affection and passion, we are also under a Christ and King, Jesus, God's own Son. But unlike all the other kings who succeeded King David, Jesus Christ, the Son of David, is "full of grace and truth" and made His dwelling among us (John 1:14). Rather than us interceding for Him as our king, our Great King is interceding for us (Heb 7:25), and this amazing reality leads us to "worship the Father in spirit and truth" (John 4:23), causing to true worship to arise among us (Ps 22:22).

In the New Testament, Paul urged the church to intercede "for everyone—for kings and all those in authority, that we may live peaceful and quiet lives" (1 Tim 2:1-2). We need to pray for our political leaders, not only for their saving faith in Christ but also for the decisions that they make so that we may practice our godliness in this secular world and so that our worship of God would not be interrupted by political laws and ideologies.

To "dwell in the tents of the wicked" (v. 10) does not necessarily mean to live with the wicked, but rather, just as the one who is truly blessed by Yahweh is the one "who does not walk in the counsel of the wicked or... sit in the seat of mockers" (Ps 1:1), the psalmist here in Psalm 84 is expressing that rather than keeping company with the wicked, he would rather be in the company of those who trust in Yahweh (Ps 84:12) as they worship God together in one spirit.

As a Korahite, being "a [gatekeeper] in the house of [his] God" (v. 11) was no small matter for the psalmist. It was his family clan's responsibility as Levites—"the Korahites were responsible for guarding the thresholds of the Tent just as their fathers had been responsible for guarding the entrance to the dwelling of [Yahweh]" (1 Chr 9:19), which continued on even after Israel's return from exile. For the psalmist, being a doorkeeper was a privilege since it meant that he was that much closer to God's dwelling place where the corporate worship took place regularly.

Whether we are aware of it or not, living and working in a city, there is a subtle secular cultural influence that we cannot deny. Unlike the psalmist whose daily responsibility (career) was guarding the temple as a gatekeeper, for most people, most of our time each day is spent in the secular world. What we hear and witness certainly is not God-centered. Living in such an environment, can we truly say with the psalmist, "better is one day in [God's] courts than a thousand elsewhere" (v. 10)? Do we really believe that it is a blessing and privilege from the Lord that we are given the opportunity to worship the Lord at least one day out of the week? How else are we going to receive godly influence if it is not from the worshiping community?

The psalmist saw, "no good thing does [God] withhold from him whose walk is blameless" (v. 11). Because of the sinful nature of human beings, it is utterly impossible to live blamelessly; as Solomon stated in his temple dedication prayer—"for there is no one who does not sin" (1 Kings 8:46). But what David wrote in one of his psalms sheds light on our understanding. David wrote concerning the true worshipers—"He who has clean hands and a pure heart, who does not lift up his soul to an idol or swear by what is false" (Ps 24:4). In other words, a true worshiper is the one whose heart is pure; in a sense, he renounces all competing members that dare to take a place in his heart alongside Yahweh. When a worshiper like Asaph truly confesses, "Whom have I in heaven but you? And earth has nothing I desire besides you" (Ps 73:25), would not Yahweh not withhold any good thing from the worshiper (Ps 84:11)? Could it be that the reason some of today's worshipers feel God is withholding good things from them is because other things are cherished in their hearts besides God?

Psalm 84 deals with our heart's desire (vv. 1-2): what are we really longing for? The ones who are truly blessed are the worshipers worshiping at the place where God dwells (v. 4). Despite the inconvenience and perhaps difficulty of travel, they make every effort to "[appear] before God in Zion" (vv. 5-7) while they place their trust in God regarding all the unseen things that could come their way and discourage them on their journey (vv. 5-7). Their effort reflects their heart's desire. Since their hearts are set in the right place, God sees and blesses every step of their travel, even the places they pass through on their journey (v. 6).

The concept of the pilgrimage is a challenge to the hearts of those who might be serving God out of their own convenience. It is not about encouraging modern day worshipers to drive two, three hours just to experience something spiritual, whether miracles, a musical worship "concert," or going from one conference to another. The people under the new covenant in Christ are not called to appear before Yahweh three times a year, but they are called to come together in worship every Lord's Day, the day our Lord Jesus rose from the dead. For city people, there are many churches nearby; therefore, traveling a long distance is not an issue. Yet when people choose a church based on convenience rather than on seeking God's dwelling place, even though this commitment will mean their attending a meeting there only once or twice at the most weekly, it is something to think about. What are we really seeking when it comes to a worshiping community? What has been the first priority in deciding on committing to a particular local church?

Tender-Hearted Worshipers from Psalm 95

Psalm 95 can be divided into three parts. The first two give the reasons why the people needed to worship Yahweh. The third part has to do with what actually took place in worship, which will be our main focus.

The God of Israel did not leave it up to individuals themselves to decide how they should worship, and it is clear in this psalm that worship is not done individually or in private but corporately—"let us sing" (v. 1). Worship is also the submission of our will, expressed here in the act of kneeling down (v. 6). In sum, worship is the corporate submission of our will to His revealed will.

This psalm contains various different elements of worship including: singing (vv. 1-2), approaching God with thanksgiving (v. 2), acknowledging who Yahweh is in contrast to other gods (v. 3) and in relation to creation (vv. 4-5).

The second section is more focused on who Yahweh is in relation to His people (vv. 6-7). Out of one man, Abraham, God created the nation Israel. Likewise, the Son of God, Jesus Christ has created "in himself one new man, out of the two" (Eph 2:15), which is the church. Yahweh is also Israel's shepherd (v. 7). We worship God because Jesus Christ is our "good shepherd" who laid down his life for us (John 10:11).

In the beginning, Yahweh is called "the Rock of our salvation" (v. 1). God is referred to as "the Rock" in various psalms and other songs—"He is the Rock, his works are perfect, and all his ways are just" (Deut 32:4). Yet, the third section of Psalm 95 focuses on the event that took place in Massah and Meribah (v. 8). Therefore, we need to consider why God is referred to as "the Rock" in connection to Massah and Meribah.

Yahweh had been proving through His manifestations, signs and wonders that the gods of Egypt were no match for Yahweh, the Great Warrior. After the miraculous crossing and final judgment on Pharaoh and his army, Yahweh healed the bitter water to become sweet and provided manna in the desert. Yet even after all the miraculous works, when there was no water at Rephidim, "they quarreled with Moses" and then turned to even dare to "put [Yahweh] to the test " (Exod 17:2). But Yahweh, who had always been and would never fail to be gracious and compassionate, told Moses, "take… the staff with which you struck the Nile… I will stand there… [on] the rock… Strike the rock, and water will come out of it" (vv. 5-6).

In a way, Moses' staff that had struck the Nile and turned the water into blood represented God's judgment upon Egypt's disobedience as represented by Pharaoh. With that same staff, God told Moses to strike the rock upon which God Himself would be standing. In other words, the staff of God's judgment, instead of coming down on the grumbling and disobedient Israelites, came down upon God; as strange as it would seem, Yahweh took the hit instead.

What took place at Rephidim foreshadowed what Jesus of Nazareth, about whom Moses and the prophets wrote (John 1:45), would do. The rod of God's judgment that should have come down upon us came down upon Jesus Christ on the cross—"[the Israelites] all… drank from the spiritual rock that accompanied them and that rock was Christ. Nevertheless, God was not pleased with most of them; their bodies were scattered over the desert" (1 Cor 10:3-5). It is through Christ's death and resurrection that our weary souls are refreshed.

Rephidim took on two new names, "Massah and Meribah because the Israelites quarreled and ... tested [Yahweh]" (v. 7). The real issue behind their complaint was not the lack of water but the lack of faith. Even after Yahweh had proven Himself again and again through the miraculous signs, when facing hardship, they doubted—"Is [Yahweh] among us or not," the promise of God's presence among them. Exactly like Pharaoh, after witnessing signs and wonders (Exod 8:15), the Israelites hardened their hearts and doubted Yahweh's integrity.

Using Massah and Meribah as a backdrop, the psalmist warned how worshipers could enter into worship with the condition of their hearts being hard (Ps 95:8). It was expected that Yahweh would speak, and the worshipers were called to heed His voice. Yahweh did not just speak once by giving the Torah to the Israelites in the wilderness through Moses, but God continued to speak to the people who came to draw near to Him in worship. It was expected that worshipers, through the reading of the text, or prophesying by a prophet based on His written word, or singing psalms, would hear God's word.

The same warning should be taken to heart by new covenant worshipers (1 Cor 10:6, 9). God had promised through the prophet Jeremiah that He would write His law on people's hearts (Jer 31:33). God's promise for the people under the new covenant was that God would "remove... [the] heart of stone and give... a heart of flesh" (Ezek 36:26).

As we go through life's struggles and hardships, we might be tempted to question God's presence in our lives, putting "God to the test." As we enter into worship, we need to trust that God will speak to us, whether through the preaching of His word, the Holy Spirit illuminating God's word that has been planted in our hearts, or through praise and worship. And when God speaks in worship, we want to listen rather than doubt His promise and harden our hearts.

When the Israelites continued to harden their hearts after all the miracles they had experienced, they ended up wandering in the desert, unable to enter God's rest, the Promised Land, for forty years (Ps 95:11). The Israelites were called to enter God's rest but failed "because those who heard did not combine it with faith" (Heb 4:2). In a similar manner, God's people under the new covenant in Christ are called to His rest but can fail to experience it unless they make "every effort to enter that rest" (v. 11) through faith.

Living in the city with its subtle influences of secularism and hedonism, sometimes what we experience in life can be confusing, and what we come to value in life and our understanding of happiness can become distorted. As a result, we have become restless wanderers, not knowing what it means to truly experience rest that only Jesus Christ can give— "Come to me... I will give you rest... you will find rest for your souls" (Matt 11:28-29).

Coming off from the tyranny of the busyness of the weekdays, on Sunday we enter into worship. Through worship, God has called the worshipers to "make every effort to enter that rest." And the true rest begins when we heed and place our faith in God's word and not in the world or ourselves.

If we harden our hearts when we hear God's word in worship, where else will we experience rest? After all, "the word of God is living and active... it penetrates even to dividing soul and spirit... judges the thoughts and attitudes of the heart" (Heb 4:12).

Worshipers, the People Belonging to God from Psalm 100

Different types of songs are used in worship—"Speak to one another with psalms, hymns and spiritual songs" (Eph 5:19). Different songs and musical styles help the congregation to engage in worship. Some songs are more celebratory or reflective of God's great redemptive work in history, while other songs may simply magnify God, exalting Him for who He is (in this case, the focus is on the various attributes of God). Still other songs bring worshipers into intimacy with God.

Psalm 100 begins, "Shout... to [Yahweh]" (v. 1). The worshipers were expected to worship Yahweh with a burst of emotion, not because of the music but rather knowing "that [Yahweh] is God" (v. 3). The psalm gives "how" we ought to worship (vv. 1-2, 4) based on "who" Yahweh is and who we are in the light of our relationship with Him (vv. 3, 5). Basically, our emotion is stirred up, not by the type of music played in worship but based on our knowledge and acknowledgement of how Yahweh revealed Himself in His written revelation. A sermon illustration or certain type of music may help the congregation to engage in worship emotionally, but it should not be the basis for their emotion.

In worship, the congregation is being reminded of her relationship with God. There should be emotional gladness (v. 2) because Yahweh God "made us, and we are his" (v. 3). There is a tension between desiring to live our own lives, setting up our own goals, and surrendering and acknowledging the sole Lordship of Christ. Some of us are not really happy with life, especially with what we are going through or may have gone through in the past week, and we can tend to bring this same emotion and attitude into worship. Under such a condition, people may often find themselves disconnected from the message or songs in worship.

Therefore, the first and foremost important aspect of worship is getting the congregation to know "who God is." Out of such knowledge, the worshipers' emotions are stirred up together with musical praise. Through the preaching of God's word where God's word is explained, expressed, taught, and applied, the connection is made between God's word, the congregation, and the world or situation she is in. Psalms, hymns, and spiritual songs are other means of communicating God's word, expressed in an artistic form. But regardless of the specific form of expression, most important is that God's word be clearly communicated to the audience in a particular culture.

The goal of any communication of God's word is understanding and reminding the congregation of who God is and who she is in relationship to God the Creator. From a right understanding of this relationship, through worship, one is reminded of one's true purpose and goal in life as values which have subtly become more influenced by the world get redefined and properly realigned. As the apostle Paul told the church in Corinth why the members needed to "flee from sexual immorality," today's worshipers need to hear and be reminded that we are not our own; we "were bought at a price" (1 Cor 6:18-20). All of us are tempted to set up our own goals and experience a meaningful life apart from the lordship of Christ, our main concern being: as long as it serves our need and satisfies our fleshly desires. It is through worship that we surrender and lay aside the control that we want to have, as though we belong to ourselves, and recommit to Christ's sole ownership of our life.

Although the emphasis is placed on God as the One who was pastoring the flock as "his people" are referred to as "the sheep of his pasture" (v. 3), the imagery of the sheep entering "his gates… courts" (v. 4) is a further reminder of with what purpose we are entering the courts to worship.

The sheep entering the gates had only one purpose: to be slaughtered and offered to God as sacrifices. It might be a bit of a stretch to apply it in this way, but similarly, in worship, we do not just bring songs of praise or offerings to God, but we bring ourselves in surrender to the altar. Our personal agendas, the emotional and volitional conditions we may be in, all become secondary. Just as the sheep's life was denied at the altar, so should our plans, wills, emotions – our very selves, be denied as we offer ourselves to the Living God. The image of God in which we have been created, though marred because of sin, through Christ, is restored in us. Therefore, as we imitate the Father "as dearly loved children," and just as Christ, the Lamb of God "gave himself up for us a fragrant offering and sacrifice to God," (Eph 5:1-2), we surrender our life to Him who has called us to worship.

The praise of thanksgiving flows out from a recognition of Yahweh's goodness, love and faithfulness (v. 5). All the attributes of Yahweh that had been revealed in His word were not meant to remain as a memory of the past but to continue to be experienced as a reality on down to the psalmist's days and beyond. God's "faithfulness" was not limited to one particular past generation but "continues through all generations."

It is through worship that the worshiping community experiences these attributes of God. At times we may feel so overwhelmed with what we face in life. We may be tempted to question, like the psalmist, "Will you forget me forever? How long will you hide your face from me" (Ps 13:1)? But as we enter into worship, the attributes of God—goodness, love, and faithfulness—become our strength, a sure anchor to our weary and uncertain souls. The worshipers' confession should be like Moses, the man of God, "[Yahweh, you have been our dwelling place throughout all generations… from everlasting to everlasting you are God" (Ps 90:1-2). Surely, our Lord "Jesus Christ is the same yesterday and today and forever" (Heb 13:8).

Fulfilling One's Commitment to Worship from Psalm 116

Life is unpredictable. Often in our human perception, good and evil, wealth and poverty, or health and sickness do not seem to discriminate between the righteous and the unrighteous. When bad things happen to "good" people (or "the righteous" in our context), one of the privileges and advantages believers have is that they can look up to the Lord in prayer for His mercy and deliverance (vv. 1-6).

In the case of Psalm 116, the psalmist was able to experience God's answer to his prayer, "Be at rest once more, O my soul, for [Yahweh] has been good to you" (v. 7). Why does God answer our prayers and deliver us from evil when we cry out to God, confessing, "I am greatly afflicted" (v. 10)? In his suffering, the psalmist cried out to God and realized no human should be relied upon (v. 11); Yahweh should be the only One to be trusted.

There is a divine purpose when His people go through "trials of many kinds" (Jas 1:2). God delivers us so that we "may walk before [Yahweh]" (Ps 116:9). Suffering helps us to become more mature in our faith by enabling us to gain a heart of wisdom for spiritual discernment and live according to His will (Jas 1:4-5).

Psalm 116 foreshadows what believers under the new covenant would go through because of Christ according to 2 Corinthians 4. Often, suffering does remind us that "all-surpassing power is from God and not from us" (v. 7). God's purpose for His children to go through suffering is "for Jesus' sake, so that his life may be revealed in our mortal body" (v. 11). Just as the psalmist in his suffering confessed that men cannot be relied upon and only God is trustworthy, so did the apostle Paul say, "with that same spirit of faith we also believe and therefore speak" (v. 13). Just as the psalmist committed himself to "sacrifice a thank offering" (Ps 116:17), so did the apostle Paul foresee "that grace that is reaching more and more people may cause thanksgiving to overflow to the glory of God " (2 Cor 4:15).

The psalmist first describes the suffering he went through and then shares how in the midst of his suffering, he "called on the name of [Yahweh]" and his prayer was heard. Calling on the name of Yahweh is mentioned three times in this psalm (vv. 4, 13, 17). The first instance has to do with the psalmist's prayer for Yahweh's mercy in his perilous situation while the other two have to do with calling on God's name in the context of worship.

As a person cries out to God in a desperate situation in his private life of prayer, he should be able to foresee calling on God's name in public worship. Walking before Yahweh in a secular world certainly does not exempt us from facing hardship in life. Often it is the complete opposite; believers "are hard pressed on every side... always being given over to death for Jesus' sake" (2 Cor 4:8, 11). Here we see how in this instance, God does not wait for His children to come to worship to deliver them. Just as Yahweh delivered and protected the psalmist while he was still in the middle of his suffering, so does God deliver his children—"hard pressed... but not crushed; perplexed, but not in despair; persecuted, but not abandoned; struck down, but not destroyed" (vv. 8-9).

In the same way that the Bible does not give the reason Jabez's request was granted as he cried out to the God of Israel (1 Chr 4:9-10), so does Psalm 116 not give any reason for God's deliverance of the psalmist other than Yahweh's grace, righteousness, and compassion (v. 5). When the psalmist called on God's name in his suffering, he experienced God's deliverance which then became the source from which the psalmist's worship flowed. Because he had experienced the deliverance of God, the psalmist had something to offer to God in worship.

In this way, worship is how we "repay" God for His goodness to those who are "simple-hearted" (v. 6) enough to simply trusting Yahweh in prayer (vv. 12-14). Through suffering and God's deliverance, the psalmist gains a renewed perspective of his own life and its security, that Yahweh would not hand him over to death because his life, even when he was going through suffering, was "precious in the sight of [Yahweh]" (v. 15). As a result of experiencing God's deliverance and gaining renewed perspective, in the end, the psalmist recommits himself to Yahweh's lordship (v. 16).

Worship in Psalm 116 is fulfilling one's vows to Yahweh in sacrificing a thank offering to Yahweh (vv. 12-14, 17-19). Although it is God's will for believers to "give thanks in all circumstances" (1 Thes 5:18), specifically and primarily the psalmist was committed to give a thank offering because he had experienced God's mercy and deliverance in his real life situation.

In a way, we can say that worship is the end goal or fulfillment of experiencing who God is in our daily lives. Psalm 116 is a challenge to today's worshipers. Why do we often find worship to be not exciting but rather boring; is it because of the sermon or music? God has called His children to walk before Him, being conscious of God in their daily lives. Now and then, His children will face "trials of many kinds." If the worshipper has not been calling on Jesus' name in prayer for deliverance and experiencing God coming through for him in his daily life, Sunday worship could very well end up being frustrating and irrelevant since worship completes what God's children have experienced of God's grace, righteousness, and compassion in life during the weekdays.

Rejoicing in Worship on the Lord's Day from Psalm 118

In Psalm 118, what starts with the psalmist's own personal experience (vv. 5-21) leads into the very reason and ground for worship for a whole community of believers (vv. 25-27) because of what Yahweh did for one person (vv. 22-24). The psalmist first calls the congregation to give thanks for Yahweh's love (vv. 1-4). Next, he gives his own testimony of how He answered his prayer (vv. 5-14). Through Yahweh's deliverance, his faith and confidence in God was renewed with him for the ongoing future (vv. 6-9, 14).

The psalmist anticipates how the mighty things that Yahweh has done would impact the dwellings of the righteous in verses 15 to 23. Yahweh's mighty works are: 1) that there was suffering but it did not end in death (v. 18), and 2) that "the stone" that was rejected by "the builders has become the capstone" (v. 22).

Like many other psalms, Psalm 118 is not just limited to the psalmist's personal experience or just related to his immediate future. Instead, similar to when Yahweh established his covenant with David in 2 Samuel 7:11-16, Psalm 118 speaks prophetically and anticipates God's mighty works through the Son of David which would be far greater than the real-life situation of and Yahweh's deliverance for this one, individual psalmist.

Whatever the reason, the psalmist had been chastised by Yahweh but not given over to death, and this brought him proclaiming "what [Yahweh had] done" (vv. 17-18). This act of Yahweh's deliverance foreshadowed

Christ's death and resurrection. Christ "was despised and rejected," not for His own sin but because "he took up our infirmities... [was] pierced for our transgressions... crushed for our iniquities," punished by God with death (Isa 53:3-5). Unlike the psalmist, Christ was "given over to death," though as we all know, this was not the end. As David was praying for his own safety, prophetic words came to him concerning the Son of David as he prophesied, "my body also will rest secure because you will not abandon me to the grave, nor will you let your Holy One see decay" (Ps 16:9-10).

Therefore, Psalm 118:22, "The stone the builders rejected has become the capstone," was not about the psalmist's own experience but prophesying Christ's death and resurrection as the Gospel writers wrote (Matt 21:42) and the apostles testified (Acts 4:11; 1 Peter 2:7). Just as "the righteous" of Psalm 118:19-21 were the psalmist who had committed himself to Yahweh for salvation and all others who would do the same, and these righteous were called to enter "the gate of Yahweh," the new covenant people are called to enter worship based on the death and resurrection of Christ on "the day [Yahweh] has made" (v. 24). For this reason, from the very beginning of the early church, Christians gathered on the first day of the week, Sunday, celebrating it as the Lord's Day by remembering Christ's death through the Lord's Supper and rejoicing in His resurrection.

Once the psalmist and other worshipers entered the temple courts, there was a prayer for Yahweh's deliverance (v. 25), praise for the one "who comes in the name of [Yahweh]" (v. 26), declaration and confession that Yahweh is God (vv. 27-28), and the receiving of God's grace (v. 27) which was the fulfillment of the priestly blessing from Numbers 6:25. The psalmist concludes the same way he began, calling the people to give thanks to Yahweh for His goodness and everlasting love (v. 29).

Based on Yahweh's mighty acts (vv. 5-24), the worshipers of verse 25 found confidence to pray, "O [Yahweh], save us." "Hosanna," a Hebrew phrase, became a typical phrase of praise or acclamation which Israel would later come to sing at certain religious festivals.

The large crowds in Jerusalem were shouting, "Hosanna to the Son of David" as Jesus was entering Jerusalem riding on a colt (Matt 21:6-9). They believed Jesus was a political Messiah, coming to be the king of the Jews, and the crowds were shouting, "Hosanna!" expecting Jesus "to restore the kingdom to Israel" (Acts 1:6), bringing Israel out from being under the Roman Empire.

Yet if the people had only had eyes to see and ears to hear, their acclamation could have been prophetic in the way Psalm 118 intended. But the people in Jesus' days were so wrapped up in their desire to be liberated from foreign political tyranny, the unceasing foreign rule under which they had been ever since they had been taken into the Babylonian captivity, Jesus' followers placed all of their hope in Him, hoping with all their hearts "that he was the one who was going to redeem Israel" (Luke 24:21).

We, like the people in Jesus' days, may sing a right song of praise biblically, but what are we expecting God to do in our worship? On the Lord's Day, when we gather to worship, if we do not have faith in the death and resurrection of Christ as the foundation for our praise, we may have a right doctrine but wrong motive and expectation from God in worship.

It was very clear to the New Testament writers that Christ had become the capstone of Psalm 118:22 through His death and resurrection. Therefore, all those who "come to... the living Stone—rejected by men but chosen by God and precious to him," need to make and build their lives in line with Christ in order to be built together "into a spiritual house to be a holy priesthood, offering spiritual sacrifices acceptable to God through Jesus Christ" (1 Peter 2:4-5).

We need to praise and pray, shouting, "Hosanna" (Ps 118:25), that God, who "exerted [incomparably great power] in Christ when he raised him from the dead," would also enlighten "the eyes of [our] heart in order that [we] may know the hope to which he has called [us]" and the power of Christ's resurrection (Eph 1:18-20). Out of all places, it is where the new covenant community gathers on the Lord's Day that we should primarily be offering the praise—"we bless you" Jesus (Ps 118:26-27) and "confess[ing] that Jesus Christ is Lord" (Phil 2:11).

Just as the psalmist and others experienced the priestly blessing— "[may Yahweh] make his face shine upon you" (Num 6:25) in Psalm 118:27, may the risen Christ, whose "face [is] like the sun shining in all its brilliance" (Rev 1:16) shine upon the new covenant people as they gather to worship. May every person in the congregation confess and exalt Jesus Christ, saying, "you are my God, and I will give you thanks" (Ps 118:28).

Why Serve and Worship the Living Yahweh from Psalm 135

The reference to the "servants of [Yahweh]... who [stand] in the house of [Yahweh]" at the beginning of Psalm 135 (vv. 1-2) suggests that it, like Psalm 134 just prior, could have been meant to be primarily addressed to the Levites who ministered in the temple courts. But regardless of whether the psalm was addressed to a general congregation or specifically Levites or priests, their act of worship is described as being done by servants of Yahweh, standing in the house of Yahweh.

The concept of standing in God's house as His servants may not be familiar to modern day evangelical worshipers since other than when they are singing hymns, when the sermon, which takes up an especially large and main portion of the worship service, is given, the worshipers are in the sitting position. But before anything, to worship God is to give our service to God or serve God as His servants.

There were no chairs in the courtyard, temple, or the Most Holy Place, but there was a throne. Although "heaven is God's throne" (Isa 66:1) and there was no physical temple that could contain Him, the inner sanctuary was the place where Yahweh chose to allow His invisible throne to reside "between the two cherubim that are over the ark of the Testimony" (Exod 25:22), also referred to as the "throne of grace" in Hebrews 4:16.

David regarded worship as approaching "the thrones for judgment" (Ps 122:5). Basically, while Yahweh the Great King was sitting on His throne, all His servants including the priests, Levites, and the rest of the congregation would stand before the King and be ready to serve. The prophet Ezekiel prophesied concerning the priestly ministry of the new covenant community in the Last Days —"the priests... are to come near to minister before me; they are to stand before me to offer sacrifices of fat and blood... they alone are to come near my table to minister before me and perform my service" (Ezek 44:15-16).

The rest of Psalm 135 elaborates the reasons Yahweh can be called "good" and why it is pleasant to "sing praise to his name" (v. 3). Yahweh is good because of His election love for Israel as "his treasured possession" (v. 4). Yahweh is incomparably superior to the gods of the world (v. 5) as demonstrated by the following: unlike the Canaanite gods, Yahweh is sovereign over nature (vv. 6-7); Yahweh delivered His people by judging the Egyptian gods and their worshipers (vv. 8-9); and, in order to settle His people in the Promised Land, God drove out all the warriors previously living in the land who had been serving other gods (vv. 10-12).

Although the foreign gods are not mentioned specifically in verses 6-12, throughout the history of Israel, Yahweh proved Himself countless times as the Mighty Warrior who fought for His people. Before Moses' departure in the wilderness, he "recited the words of this song" (Deut 31:30). In his song, Moses said, "How could one man chase a thousand... unless their Rock had sold them... For their rock is not like our Rock as even our enemies concede" (Deut 21:30-31). Every battle the Israelites fought was a spiritual one; for that reason, they were not supposed to initiate any battle in order to conquer more territory. Every battle had to be initiated by Yahweh, and most of the time, the people dedicated the spoils and plunder to Yahweh by burning them up completely.

Yahweh is the God of all generations (Psalm 135:13) and therefore "will vindicate... and have compassion on his servants" (v. 14). But sadly, from the very beginning when the Israelites first entered into a covenant relationship with Yahweh and God established them as a nation in Mount Sinai, they broke the covenant almost immediately by worshiping the golden calf. Again in Moses' song he said, "Is this the way you replay [Yahweh], O foolish and unwise people" (Deut 32:6). When the next generation grew up, they quickly "forsook [Yahweh]... followed various gods of the peoples around them" (Judges 2:12).

The history of Israel bears witness to the fact that they had never been completely satisfied with serving Yahweh alone but needed to worship other gods as well. Israel continued to practice such spiritual prostitution until she was taken into exile—"all the leaders... following all the detestable practices of the nations and defiling the temple of [Yahweh]... [Yahweh]... sent word to them through his messengers again and again... But they mocked God's messengers" (2 Chr 36:14-16).

The prophet Isaiah prophesied not only concerning the exile but also regarding God's judgment upon Israel's spiritual condition as the consequence of her idolatry —"Be ever hearing, but never understanding; be ever seeing, but never perceiving" (Isa 6:9). This spiritual condition of blindness and deafness would continue unless they turned to Christ—"[Israel's] minds were made dull, for to this day the same veil remains when the old covenant is read. It has not been removed, because only in Christ is it taken away" (2 Cor 3:14).

Therefore, Psalm 135 not only spoke of how no gods of this world could dare compare to Yahweh, but also of what would happen to idolaters as a result of God's judgment—"The idols of the nations are silver and gold... They have... eyes, but they cannot see; they have ears, but cannot hear... Those who make them will be like them, and so will all who trust in them" (vv. 15-18). During the earthly ministry of Jesus, His disciples asked why he spoke to the people in parables to which Jesus replied, "In them is fulfilled the prophecy of Isaiah" and quoted Isaiah 6:9-10 in Matthew 13:10-15.

Participating in worship is also standing before God to serve Him. One of the issues for the Christians in Corinth was ministering in the congregational worship setting by wrongly exercising the spiritual gift of tongue speaking without interpretation. Earlier in his letter to the Corinthians, the apostle Paul spoke of a "message of wisdom" (1 Cor 2:6) which was the gospel that had been revealed to Paul and others by God's Spirit (v. 10), and they were given the mind of Christ (v. 16) to understand "God's secret wisdom" (v. 7). Since Christians have turned to Christ, their spiritual eyes have been opened, so they are able to perceive the work of God. Their ears are opened spiritually, so as a church, "He who has an ear, let him hear what the Spirit sys to the churches" (Rev 2:7). But if there is unbelief amongst the believers as was the case in the Corinthian church, they will be wrongly practicing the spiritual gifts and experience spiritual deafness themselves (1 Cor 14:21-22).

For this reason, the new covenant worshipers must not take the possible idolatry in their hearts lightly. It is through worship that God reveals Himself and speaks by illuminating His word deposited in our regenerated hearts—"I will put my law in their minds and write it on their hearts" (Jer 31:33). If we allow competing members in our hearts and idolatry unchecked, our spiritual sensitivity could become dull and we could miss the opportunity to see and hear "what God has prepared for those who love him" (1 Cor 2:9).

Rhetorically David once asked, "Who may ascend the hill of [Yahweh]? Who may stand in his holy place? He who has clean hands and a pure heart, who does not lift up his soul to an idol" (Ps 24:3-4). As the new covenant worshipers, may we seek Him in worship with "clean hands and a pure heart" so that we may "receive blessing from [Yahweh] and vindication from [Jesus Christ our] Savior (v. 5).

16

THE PROPHETIC MINISTRY

If a priest's main role was to approach Yahweh on behalf of God's people, a prophet was to speak to God's people on behalf of God. Priests were to regulate worship and teach worshipers according to Yahweh's prescriptive words—"For the lips of a priest ought to preserve knowledge, and from his mouth men should seek instruction" (Mal 2:7). Yet all the way down to the last written prophet Malachi's days, the most of the priests failed to honor Yahweh by what had been revealed in the *Torah*. The Levites who ministered in the temple courts and the priests in the sanctuary were supposed to: 1) have reverence for God, and 2) teach God's word and put it into practice (Mal 2:5-6).

Just as God raised up the prophet Malachi and other prophets in order to put worship in order before the coming of "the messenger of the covenant" Jesus Christ (Mal 3:1), throughout Israel's history, whenever there was a breach between God's word and the priestly ministry in the temple, from time to time God would raise up prophets to speak out against what was happening and turn the religious leaders back to worship the way it was prescribed by Yahweh. The people's attitude toward God could be best revealed by the way they worshipped God—"Cursed is the cheat who has an acceptable male in his flock and vows to give it, but then sacrifices a blemished animal... my name is to be feared among the nations (Mal 1:14).

Proclaiming and Teaching the Right Way of Worship

Although there were prophets prior to the days of Samuel, in a way, he was the first recognized by "all Israel from Dan to Beersheba" to be "attested as a prophet of [Yahweh]" (1 Sam 3:20). Just as the "man of God came to Eli" and pointed out Eli's coming short of meeting the worship regulations earlier (1 Sam 2:27-36), the prophet Samuel led the Israelites back to "commit... to [Yahweh] and serve him only" (1 Sam 7:3), and his entire ministry mainly centered around correcting and establishing the right worship order in Israel, best revealed in Samuel's interactions with the first king, Saul. Saul, not only as a political leader but also a servant of Yahweh, was responsible for maintaining the right worship order through the priests as prescribed in the *Torah*. Sadly, perhaps Saul's main failure was in this very area of worship.

Saul was grossly mistaken in thinking that the act of worship was a means to win Yahweh's favor. Out of his desperation due to the Philistines when "[his] men began to scatter," he "felt compelled to offer the burnt offering" in hopes that as a result, Yahweh would somehow change the situation (1 Sam 13:8-12). Samuel had told Saul earlier to "wait seven days" at Gilgal to receive instruction from him. Samuel was to meet Saul at Gilgal to "sacrifice burnt offerings and fellowship offerings," but for Saul, taking matters into his own hands was more urgent than waiting upon Yahweh in obedience (1 Sam 10:8 and 13:8-10).

If God says, "Wait," we need to wait even if the situation seems like it is becoming worse; otherwise, we will be tempted to coerce God by means of the act of worship. In such a case, worship is no longer submission but rather performance to win God's favor to make Him do what we want Him to do, making Him submit to and obey our desire and will.

Saul, as a king who had received the authority to oversee and lead God's people in the way of Yahweh, may have been tempted to assume authority over God's revealed written word and become the law unto himself. Yahweh had already warned of this through Moses, His servant—"a copy of this law... is to be with [the king], and he is to read... follow carefully... and not consider himself better than his brothers" (Deut 17:18-20).

Samuel's prophetic words of instruction to Saul were mainly about how God's word would be fulfilled in Saul's life. The only part that had to do with obedience was waiting for the authorized person Samuel to come to Gilgal to make sacrifices (1 Sam 10:8).

Interestingly, the major test of the first king's faith was not in the area of military strategy or leadership but rather obedience and respecting the proper authority in the context of worship, and this was precisely the area in which Saul was found to be majorly flawed. His failure to listen to God's voice over against false worship was decisive enough for the prophet Samuel to sever their relationship on account of it. Samuel's last words and instruction to Saul were regarding worship—"To obey is better than sacrifice," and "Until the day Samuel died, he did not go to see Saul again" (1 Sam 15:22, 35).

What is the real reason we worship God? Often, what is in our hearts will be tested through worship. Have we forgotten how worship is described in God's word—as kneeling before Yahweh in submission? Have we undermined Christ's lordship and sovereignty over the circumstances we face in life? Are we doubting His promise and in our desperate situation trying to use worship to win favor from God?

Some Christians attend worship service on Sundays without being aware of the fact that worship is the only spiritual and religious thing they do throughout the week. They do not pray, obey God's word or honor God other than by attending the weekly service; how is this any different from Saul who uses "doing worship" to earn God's favor?

Seeking the Lord in prayer, reading and meditating on God's word daily to hear and obey, walking in the Spirit and living out the gospel in the workplace or wherever God has put us should be a way of life, and worship, its culmination. Worship should not be something we owe God because we have not been living in obedience during the week, yet to some, the Sunday worship service has become something they need to check off of a list of things to do if they are going to be "blessed" by God. This kind of disconnect is in stark contrast to right worship which should be a continuation, an outflow, of our daily walk with God.

Signs and Wonders at the True Altar

Elijah knew there was one true altar, and it was in Jerusalem, in the southern kingdom of Judah. Although Judah was no better, the northern kingdom of Israel had two main religious centers—Bethel and Dan, each with a golden calf set up by Jeroboam out of his own political insecurity— "It is too much for you to go up to Jerusalem. Here are your gods, O Israel, who brought you up out of Egypt" (1 Kings 12:28).

By the days of King Ahab's reign, Israel had lost their commitment to Yahweh as the true living God, and the situation was not made any better as Ahab's wife, Jezebel, continued to promote the worship of Baal, a Canaanite god. Although the Israelites had entered into a covenant relationship with Yahweh at Mount Sinai, they had always served idols or foreign gods along with Yahweh (Josh 24:19-23). Whether they needed to have a visible, man-made god in the form of a golden calf to satisfy their visible sensibility (Exod 32:4), or whether they assimilated into the existing Canaanite culture that inevitably came with its gods, they always had other gods alongside of Yahweh.

Times have not changed much since then. We are a nation that takes great pride in upholding religious freedom, believing that state and religion should be separated. There is no reason to argue against this political view since America is not a theocratic nation. As a matter of fact, no nation in this world (other than Israel) until the coming of the Messiah is under a theocratic government since no nation is under a covenant relationship with Yahweh.

Some Christians are not much different from the general public in being guilty of pluralism when they cannot just be satisfied with the invisible God. Like the Israelites, Christians do not deny God's existence or Jesus Christ being the Savior and Lord. But have we been serving God and Him alone and no other? With the inevitable draw of materialism and never-ending latest technology, especially living in one of the most popular cities of the world, possessions and wealth have become coequal with our God the Creator.

Into a world of religious plurality, Yahweh sent His prophet Elijah to confront the people of Israel to make a choice—"How long will you waver between two opinions? If [Yahweh] is God, follow him; but if Baal is God, follow him" (1 Kings 18:21). But sadly "the people said nothing," which meant that either they did not or could not see the need to choose just one; after all, do not all religions lead to one god?

It was clearly written in God's word, the *Torah*, "Hear O Israel: [Yahweh] our God, [Yahweh] is one" (Deut 6:4). Since there was only one God, the Israelites' hearts were not to be divided or shared with other gods or things. The object of Israel's affection was to be the One that deserves the devotion of every aspect of our being—"Love [Yahweh] your God with all your heart and with all your soul and with all your strength" (v. 5).

Although a copy of the *Torah* was always available to the people of Israel, they still became used to having a pluralistic religious belief. They had probably justified the pluralism in their own minds with the skewed belief that for practical purposes, it was wiser to serve various gods according to their different needs. As long as they did not abandon Yahweh but continued to acknowledge and include Him in their own invented religious system which they did not think was offensive to Yahweh, without shame or guilt, they thought they were being loyal to the God of their fathers.

After all, the Yahweh God was needed when their ancestors were liberated from Egyptian slavery. It was just that now, they were too occupied with more important matters in life—being surrounded and constantly threatened by the neighboring nations and the unusually severe famine that had been going on for three and a half years (1 Kings 18:1). They needed all the help they could get, both religiously and politically. They just could not afford to be committed to one God, Yahweh, and serve Him only, especially when Yahweh only allowed for one place of worship, Jerusalem, in the southern kingdom of Judah.

Without doubt, life in Canaan had become more complex than when they were in the wilderness. But while the times and situation may have changed, Yahweh was still unchanging and everlasting as Moses, the man of God, testified long ago—"[Yahweh], you have been our dwelling place throughout all generations... from everlasting to everlasting you are God" (Ps 90:1-2). In a world of pragmatism, the truth of there being only one true God was at stake.

Unlike what deism suggests, Yahweh was still actively involved in the lives of His people and the world as Elijah desperately prayed—"so these people will know that you, O [Yahweh], are God, and that you are turning their hearts back again" (1 Kings 18:37). Yahweh was still gracious to the people who just could not see the reason why they should serve only one God. The people of Israel just wanted to serve Yahweh whenever and however they wanted, out of their own convenience, yet despite this kind of flawed attitude of service to God, Yahweh still graciously manifested Himself to them, showing that He was God and there was no other.

Elijah, the man of God, was the one who initiated the challenge to the Baal prophets by placing a sacrifice on each one's altar and saying, "The god who answers by fire—he is God" (1 Kings 18:24). In the past, after the first high priest, Aaron, and his sons were consecrated for the priestly duty, when Moses and Aaron "came out [from the Tent of Meeting], they blessed the people; and the glory of [Yahweh] appeared to all the people. Fire came out from the presence of [Yahweh] and consumed the burnt offering... on the altar" (Lev 9:23-24). It was Yahweh's way of vindicating the priestly ministry and the tabernacle.

In the same way, at the completion of the temple and its dedication, when "Solomon finished praying, fire came down from heaven and consumed the burnt offering... and the glory of [Yahweh] filled the temple" (2 Chr 7:1). The manifestation of God's glory and fire was His way of answering Solomon's prayer of dedication of the new temple—"I [Yahweh] have heard your prayer and have chosen this place for myself as a temple for sacrifice" (v. 12).

Therefore, fire from God consuming the sacrifice on the altar was a sign of vindication for the God of Elijah, that He was the only true God and no other. In response to witnessing the miraculous sign from heaven, the people, as expected, "fell prostrate and cried, '[Yahweh]—he is God! [Yahweh]—he is God!'" (1 Kings 18:39).

In the case of sending rain, it was Yahweh who promised Elijah, "Go and present yourself to Ahab, and I will send rain on the land" (1 Kings 18:1). On Elijah's part, faith was needed to present himself to Ahab, especially after three and a half years of no rain, and the rain came only after

Elijah's prayer after offering the sacrifice to Yahweh (vv. 42-44). Elijah continued to act in faith based on God's promise (Jas 5:17-18)

But regarding the fire coming down from heaven, the text does not give us who was responsible for initiating the challenge—whether it was Yahweh who initiated or His servant Elijah. We also do not know exactly whether Elijah was prompted by the Holy Spirit to challenge the Baal prophets for the vindication of God's name or whether Elijah placed his faith in Yahweh based on the *Torah* and the historical events recorded therein, asking for His mercy to answer his prayer. But the real issue is not so much how the challenge was initiated but that regardless of Israel's faithfulness, God in His general grace did provide rain for the rebellious and unfaithful people of Israel.

God's judgment of the three and a half years of drought was about to be lifted, not because the people of Israel were willing to turn back to Yahweh but because Yahweh was gracious. Elijah might have felt he was the only remaining servant of God "while Jezebel was killing off [Yahweh's] prophets," but Yahweh in His grace had reserved a remnant of the "hundred prophets" hidden by His faithful servant Obadiah (v. 4). Later God assured Elijah that He had "reserve[d] seven thousand in Israel—all whose knees [had] not bowed down to Baal and all whose mouths [had] not kissed him" (1 Kings 19:18).

Living in a city with its diverse culture, at times we wonder whether the gospel message would even make a dent in the people's souls. From the early in the morning to late at night in "the city that never sleeps," the people are occupied with so many things in the fast pace of life. How are we ever going to be assured that the city people would come to know that Jesus Christ is Lord and the Savior of the world? Is there any sign of hope that God is "turning their hearts back" to God again, especially those who have left church long ago?

Just as it is true for ethnic Israel—"So too, at the present time there is a remnant chosen by grace... no longer by works" (Romans 11:5-6), so it is true for the rest of the people in the world. Just as it was true for the city of Corinth back in Paul's days—"the Lord spoke to Paul in a vision... I have many people in this city" (Acts 18:9), so there is a remnant of God's people in the city today. Not all Israel, but knowing that there is a remnant of the

Jewish people is good enough to encourage us to share the gospel both to the small pockets of Jewish people here and there as well as to the rest of the diverse groups of gentile people living in the city. To the remnant of Israel, we have the privilege of saying that the long-awaited Messiah whose coming they have been anticipating for thousands of years, did come, as Yahweh was faithful to His promise by sending His Son, Jesus Christ.

What did the coming down of fire from Yahweh prove and accomplish? The four hundred and fifty prophets of Baal were executed (1 Kings 18:40). Perhaps slaughtering religious people who meant no harm and just had a different religion might not settle well with the modern day moralist. But if it is accepted that there was a severe punishment in the court of law for false witnesses, it may not be counted as unfair or cruel when the land of Israel was under the rule of the King Yahweh but the prophets of Baal bore false witness against the true God (v. 24)—"When you enter the land [Yahweh] your God is giving you… a prophet who speaks in the name of others gods, must be put to death" (Deut 18:9, 20, see also 13:1-3).

When "the fire of [Yahweh] fell and burned up the sacrifice," all the people who witnessed it did acknowledge that Yahweh was God and even slaughtered the four hundred Baal prophets (1 Kings 18:38-40), but we cannot say this was a sign of true repentance from the people. The reasons for the lack of genuine repentance could have been many: the fear of Jezebel rather than Yahweh; utilitarianism and the belief in Baal as the chief god who provided rain being more important than the truth that Yahweh was the only true God; resistance to a changing of the popular culture of pluralistic beliefs. When Elijah realized that the people had not repented, even after the fire, he was so discouraged and said, "I have had enough, [Yahweh] … take my life; I am no better than may ancestors" (1 Kings 19:4).

God's word spoken through His prophets was often accompanied by signs and wonders, especially at an altar where sacrifices were made. The king, Ahab, was not the only one who was given a proof that Yahweh was the only true God. After the kingdom was first divided into two, God sent a prophet to Jeroboam, the first king of the northern kingdom and the progenitor of false worship to Yahweh. God, in His grace, sent a man of God from Judah to prophesy against the altar, and it "was split apart and its ashes poured out" (I Kings 13:3). God was judging the false worship that Jeroboam had instituted. The object of worship was a visible gold calf rather than the invisible Yahweh. Although the form of worship was there, the priesthood and the altar was unauthorized by Yahweh (1 Kings 12:32-33).

Yet even after this miraculous sign, Jeroboam did not repent of his sin. As a matter of fact, the only time he ever sought the prophet of Yahweh was when his son, Abijah, became ill—just wanting to know the outcome of his son's illness. Miracles from God do not guarantee anyone's faith or repentance.

It has been proven time and again that signs and wonders from God do not guarantee a genuine faith. It is interesting to note that in Jesus' days, some of the religious leaders requested, even after all the miracles Jesus had already performed, "Teacher, we want to see a miraculous sign from you," to which Jesus responded, "A wicked and adulterous generation asks for a miraculous sign! But none will be given it except the sign of the prophet Jonah" (Matt 12:38-39). In other words, the people of Nineveh did not repent because of the miraculous signs they witnessed from Jonah, but rather, they humbled themselves before Yahweh from the preaching of Jonah's simple message; the Ninevites did not even know the prophet Jonah was in the belly of a fish for three days.

But unlike Jonah, Jesus Christ was crucified, died and was buried for three days but came back to life, which is the very core of the gospel message. Surely, "now one [Christ] greater than Jonah is here" (Matt 12:41). Yet sadly, even long after Christ had come, "the message of the cross" was not miraculous enough for the Jews since they continued to "demand miraculous signs" and the crucifixion was "a stumbling block to Jews" (1 Cor 1:18, 22-23).

In the apostle Paul's days, Athens was the center of learning for their known world. The conclusion of Paul's gospel message to the wise, intellectuals, and philosophers was, "[God] has set a day when he will judge the world with justice by the man he has appointed. He has given proof of this to all men by raising him from the dead" (Acts 17:31).

If God's vindication came in fire, consuming the sacrifice on the true altar to Yahweh on three different occasions for those who were under the old covenant, then what vindication is there for the people under the new covenant in Christ? What greater sign or wonder can there be than Christ's resurrection as the proof that He is the One whom God has appointed to judge both the living and the dead?

How does anyone know that Christ's crucifixion was the presentation from God "as a sacrifice of atonement... to demonstrate his justice" (Romans 3:25-26)? Every Sunday as the new covenant people gather together to worship the true living God, the risen Christ, the gospel message is proclaimed, and God-centered worship songs are offered by those who have faith in Jesus Christ.

In a way, the whole worship service is a way of God vindicating Jesus as Lord and Savior. The Holy Spirit works and convicts even those who may be ignorant of the gospel, and unbelievers attending the worship service could "fall down and worship God, exclaiming, 'God is really among you'" (1 Cor 14:25).

Was there a need to choose a particular god? What was wrong with believing and allowing different gods in their hearts and minds? Why did Jesus say that no one could serve two masters (Matt 6:24)? If God is the Creator and Lord, then every aspect of our being must be gathered to worship Him. If we are called to "love the Lord [our] God with all [our] heart... soul... mind... strength" (Mark 12:30) then it is true that we cannot serve/worship two masters or two gods; as human beings, we are not capable of serving two masters since they are in conflict with one another (Romans 8:5-8; Gal 5:17). And when God vindicates Jesus as Lord in worship, worshipers and spectators must recommit and choose the only true God, Jesus Christ, God Incarnate.

Prophesying and Music

One of the first instances of "prophetic" ministry recorded came after the Israelites had witnessed Yahweh's mighty act of final judgment on Pharaoh and his army by the Red Sea, when "Miriam the prophetess... took a tambourine in her hand" and led others to worship (Exod 15:19-21). There, the prophetic ministry was associated with music praising Yahweh. At times, prophets would just praise Yahweh in worship or prophesy accompanied by music (1 Sam 10:5; 18:10).

On certain occasions, we find that the Holy Spirit came upon individual leaders, especially in the days of Judges. But prior to the book of

Judges, one time, as a sign, the Spirit of Yahweh came and rested on the seventy elders in the wilderness (Num 11:25). At this event, it is possible that the only evidence of the coming of the Spirit was that the seventy elders "prophesied."

Why did the coming of the Holy Spirit and prophesying happen only once in the case of the seventy elders? A couple of things should be noted from this particular event. The whole event was a way God reminded Moses that shepherding and serving God's people was in the Spirit's anointing and spiritual, not simply meeting the physical need per se. Another reason behind this unusual act of Yahweh can be understood by how Moses responded and what he prophetically said, "I wish that all [Yahweh's] people were prophets and that [Yahweh] would put his Spirit on them" (Num 11:30).

The whole event foreshadowed what God's new Israel under the new covenant in Christ would experience, not just once but continually as the Holy Spirit would indwell in God's people permanently. What Moses prophetically longed for was fulfilled in the Last Days when the first group of a hundred and twenty "were filled with the Holy Spirit and began to speak in other tongues" (Acts 2:4).

The meaning of what happened on that day tends to be missed by some people since they focus too much on what kinds of languages the disciples were speaking. But what is important is that the prophetic events of the Old Testament were being fulfilled in the Last Days (Acts 2:17-18). Just as the seventy elders prophesied when the Spirit came on them, the hundred and twenty disciples of Christ were filled with the Holy Spirit and began to speak, proclaim, and declare "the wonders of God" (v. 11).

In a similar manner, when Saul was met by the procession of prophets who were musically praising, "the Spirit of God came upon [Saul] in power... he joined in [the prophets'] prophesying" (1 Sam 10:10). This event connects the coming of the Spirit with not only prophesying/proclaiming like in Numbers 11 but also prophesying in the context of worship/praise (v. 5).

We find this prophesying being associated with music with Elisha, David and Jahaziel. The first two examples are more explicit while the third is less so. In the case of the prophet Elisha, a "company of the prophets" witnessed that the Spirit of Yahweh was resting on Elisha when he miraculously divided the Jordan River (2 Kings 2:13-15). As a prophet under the old covenant, we can safely assume that when Elisha made a pronouncement in Yahweh's name (vv. 21-22, 24), it came to pass just as it had in the case of his master Elijah (2 Kings 1:10); it was a sign of the Spirit having come upon God's chosen prophets.

One time, Elisha had a harpist brought in in order to prophesy—"While the harpist was playing, the hand of [Yahweh] came upon Elisha," and he spoke prophetically to the king of Israel (2 Kings 3:15-16). Now we cannot take this one particular event as prescriptive or a norm, but placing this event of prophesying in association with music can give us a better understanding of the prophetic ministry in the worship context of the new covenant community in the New Testament.

Since music ministry has always played a vital role in worship and some prophets ministered in the context of music, it would be worthwhile to understand the role of music and prophetic ministry in worship. The prophetic ministry under the old covenant foreshadowed the ministry of Christ and the people under the new covenant. In the Last Days, all God's people would become prophetic as was prophesied by the prophet Joel and fulfilled on the day of Pentecost (Joel 2:28-29; Acts 2:17-18).

In his last words, David referred to himself as "the man anointed by the God of Jacob, Israel's singer of songs... The Spirit of [Yahweh] spoke through me; his word was on my tongue" (2 Sam 23:1-2). The same David assigned some of "the sons of Asaph ... for the ministry of prophesying, accompanied by harps, lyres and cymbals... The sons of Asaph were under the supervision of Asaph who prophesied under the king's supervision" (1 Chr 25:1-2). Not only was David known as "Israel's singer of songs" but Asaph and those associated with him were also known as ones who led worship and prophesied.

Another reminder to readers of the connection between prophesying and music, though in this case somewhat more subtle, appears in one particular event in 2 Chronicles 20. After Jehoshaphat prayed "at the temple of [Yahweh] in the front of the new courtyard" and everyone "stood there before [Yahweh]... the Spirit of [Yahweh] came upon Jahaziel" (vv. 5, 13-14). The Ammonites and Moabites and the men of Mount Seir were defeated by Yahweh, as strange it may seem, as the people of Judah "began to sing and praise." As a reminder that Yahweh fought the battle for Judah in the context of worship in singing praise, they renamed the place, and what was once named the Desert of Tekoa became the "Valley of Beracah" (vv. 21, 26). And most likely, the author of Chronicles traced Jahaziel, on whom the Spirit of Yahweh had come and prophesied through earlier, all the way up to Asaph in order to give us, the readers, another connection between the coming of the Spirit, prophetic words, and praise.

Now not all musicians were prophetic people—there should be no mistake about this, but some of the prophesying was done in the context of worship in musical praise. This was so since at times when a prophetic word came, it came not when the person was in a blank state of mind, as some popular Eastern religions encourage meditation by emptying one's mind in our days, or when a person was in a frenzied state which was the case for the Baal prophets (1 Kings 18:28), but when the person's heart was in a state of submission to God in faith and worship and when the mind was filled with God's word.

Unlike with some other religions, biblical meditation is meditating on God's word rather than focusing on a certain concept or making efforts to empty one's mind (Ps 1:2). In the case of the prophet Jonah, some people have a hard time accepting the fact that he was actually able to pray such a prayer under the horrific conditions of being in the belly of a fish (Jonah 2:1-9), not to mention that he was in there for three days. But it is no wonder when as we read the Prophets' writings in the Bible we note that the prophets were prophesying based on the already written revelation. Similarly, Jonah's prayer can be referenced to a number of Psalms. One can say that under such terrible conditions, God's word in Jonah served as the basis for Jonah's prayer.

Whether prophets were praying or proclaiming, the true prophets were dispensers of the truth, seeing the situation or condition of the society of their days through the biblical lens, understanding the old covenant stipulations, and they had a message for the people. Their minds did not go into a blank stage – if they did, the mode of receiving God's word would have been more like dictation. But rather, it was that the prophet's heart was in submission to Yahweh's will and his mind was filled with God's written word.

For this reason when we come to the New Testament, the apostle Paul wrote to the church in Colosse concerning God's word in the hearts of believers in a worship context—"Let the word of Christ dwell in you richly as you teach and admonish one another with all wisdom, and as you sing psalms, hymns and spiritual songs" (Col 3:16). A similar teaching was written to the church in Ephesus concerning them as worshipers, that they should "be filled with the Spirit. Speak to one another with psalms, hymns and spiritual songs… Submit to one another out of reverence for Christ" (Eph 5:18-19, 21).

If we were to put both Colossians 3:16 and Ephesians 5:18-21 together as a fulfillment of the ministries of prophesying and music under the old covenant, then the difference is in the completeness of God's written word and the Spirit's indwelling as opposed to the temporary coming of the Spirit on God's people under the old covenant. At times, the prophets under the old covenant prophesied when the Spirit came upon them in the context of worship. Worshipers under the new covenant are called to let the word of Christ dwell in them richly and to seek to be filled with the Spirit during worship. As they worship by signing "psalms, hymns and spiritual songs," the Spirit takes God's word and illumines it in the worshipers' hearts to "teach and admonish" in Christ.

Endless debate has been made regarding what exactly prophecy and speaking in tongues are and their place in today's church ministry in 1 Corinthians 14. Regardless of the different theological presuppositions that influence their exegesis, the two speaking gifts should be understood in the context of worship since the apostle Paul said in his conclusion, "What then shall we say, brothers? When you come together, everyone has a hymn, or a word of instruction, a revelation, a tongue or an interpretation" (1 Cor 14:26). When the two gifts are understood as speaking gifts based on the Holy Spirit's illumination of God's written word in the hearts of those who ministered in prophesying or tongue speaking as a revelatory gifts, then there is a continuation from the Old Testament prophesying in the context of worship to the New Testament prophesying in the worshiping community, but main difference is in the greater depth and degree because of God's complete written revelation, the Bible.

Although what took place in the church of Antioch can be understood as being unique in its setting "apart [of] Barnabas and Saul," both prophetic and teaching ministries are mentioned especially in a worship setting in Acts 13:1-2. The author was not specific about identifying each one's role as either prophet or teacher, but rather Luke said, "In the church at Antioch there were prophets and teachers."

It seems that the author, Luke, was not so much interested in identifying whether each of the five leaders assumed the two functions together or just one. What was important was rather that both prophetic and teaching ministries were part of the life of the Antioch church, especially when the believers came together to worship and fast, seeking the Lord in the worship context. Before any gathering, out of all the meetings, it is primarily in the worship gathering that God's word needs to be taught; at the same time, there is a great need for the Spirit of God to be enlightening the hearts with His word—"And we have the word of the prophets made more certain, and you will do well to pay attention to it, as to a light shining in a dark place, until the day dawns and the morning star rises in your hearts" (2 Peter 1:19).

Experiencing God in His Sanctuary

Although a majority of the writing prophets wrote concerning the temple and worship, the prophet Isaiah along with a few others also had vision experiences in connection with the temple and worship. It is not clear whether the prophet Isaiah was actually in the temple to pray when his prophetic vision opened, or whether, like the apostle John many years later experienced at the Island of Patmos (Rev 4:2, 8), Isaiah simply saw in his vision "the Lord [sitting] on a throne... and... the temple" (Isa 6:1-7).

But what is clear is that prior to Isaiah's commitment to proclaim God's word, in his vision, Isaiah experienced God being present in His holy temple—"But [Yahweh] was in his holy temple; let all the earth be silent before him" (Hab 2:20). The first thing Isaiah saw in his vision was that God was still sovereignly ruling over the whole earth while the earthly king Uzziah ruled temporarily (v. 1). Second, in Isaiah's perception, the very place God was ruling from was the temple while at the same time the distinction between the earthly and heavenly temple was "indistinguishable" or unclear. Third, the temple was filled with the train of Yahweh's robe. On two separate occasions in the past, God's glory in the manifestation of a cloud filled the tabernacle (Exod 40:34-35) and the temple (1 Kings 8:10-11). Fourth, Isaiah saw, not the two cherubim "[facing] each other, [looking] toward the cover [of the ark]" (Exod 25:20), but above the Lord seated on his throne, "seraphs... flying... calling to one another: 'Holy, holy, holy is [Yahweh] Almighty'" (Isa 6:2-3).

The new covenant community from the early church days had always had problems, from within amongst the believers themselves, and from the outside in the forms of false teaching and persecution. The apostle John was invited, "Come up here," and the first thing or activity he witnessed was God was sitting in His throne (Rev 4:1-2). After hearing Jesus' verdict on each of the seven churches in Asia Minor where the churches were facing persecutions, false doctrine and the accompanying false practice, it makes us wonder whether there is any hope for church in this anti-God world. In worship, we, like the apostle John, must experience our sovereign Lord still reigns. When we feel like the world around us is disintegrating, what can really hold us together? We, like David, must see the immutable God on His throne—"When the foundations are being destroyed, what can the righteous do? [Yahweh] is in his holy temple; [Yahweh] is on his heavenly throne" (Ps 11:3-4).

The uncertainty of whether the temple was heavenly or earthly in Isaiah 6 further foreshadowed what the worshipers under the new covenant in Christ would experience. Through the coming of the Lord Jesus Christ who would make His redeemed people a temple for God to dwell in, worship would become not so much about being at a certain locale as about the moment when true worship takes place—"Yet a time is coming when you will worship the Father neither on this mountain nor in Jerusalem... and has now come when the true worshipers will worship the Father in spirit and truth" (John 4:21, 23); now believers truly worship God in the heavenly realm on this earth.

Ever since Eternity stepped into time, the incarnation of Christ made possible God Himself being present in the midst of the worshiping com-

munity. God's redemptive work, accomplished through the cross and resurrection of Christ, made this the reality: that while God's throne is in heaven,
at the same time, God is on His throne in the heart of every new covenant
worshiper. When the new covenant community gathers together to worship, it becomes the very temple of God—"But you have come to Mount
Zion, to the heavenly Jerusalem, the city of the living God. You have come
to thousands upon thousands of angels in joyful assembly, to the church of
the firstborn, whose names are written in heaven" (Heb 12:22-23).

Solomon once prayed, "The heavens, even the highest heaven, cannot
contain you" (1 Kings 8:27). There was no area that God's glory presence
had left untouched or uncovered in the temple—"the train of his robe filled
the temple" (Isa 6:1). In fact, just as the six-winged-seraphs were "calling to
one another …the whole earth is full of his glory" (v. 3), God had also fore-
told through the prophet Malachi, "My name will be great among the
nations, from the rising to the setting of the sun. In every place incense and
pure offerings will be brought to my name" (Mal 1:11).

In the same way that Isaiah heard through his vision experience that
the whole earth is full of God's glory, new covenant worshipers must hear
and see the world from a heavenly perspective and remember the promise
given in the Last Days for those who have forsaken idolatry and turned to
the living God—"For the earth will be filled with knowledge of the glory of
[Yahweh], as the waters cover the sea" (Hab 2:14). Just as our Sovereign
Lord has determined that the end will come, so it is that the "gospel of the
kingdom will be preached in the whole world as a testimony to all nations"
(Matt 24:14); what was proclaimed and praised by the angelic beings and
prophets will be fulfilled through the proclamation of the gospel.

While the high priest had the opportunity to see the images of the two
cherubim on the ark cover once a year, the prophet Isaiah witnessed the real
throne of God in heaven and the seraphs ministering before the throne,
calling to one another—"Holy, holy, holy is [Yahweh] Almighty; the whole
earth is full of his glory" (Isa 6:2-3). In the very presence of Yahweh, the
seraphs proclaimed, acknowledged, praised and declared "to one another"
who Yahweh was and His omnipresence throughout the whole earth.

In the same way, some of the activities in the worship context,
whether singing or declaring or speaking about God, do not have to be

directed to God, but before His presence, the community of faith can speak to "one another" or "themselves" in their hearts concerning who God is (Eph 5:19; Col 3:16). There is much of "the communion of saints" taking place during worship as the worshipers reflect and speak to themselves and to one another—"Praise [Yahweh], O my soul; all my inmost being, praise his holy name" (Ps 103:1, and also in Ps 104:1; 116:7; 146:1).

Isaiah witnessed in his vision experience what would have been impossible for him to perceive with the naked eye: the heavenly activities centered around the throne of God. It would be awesome and a great privilege to experience a vision such as that of Isaiah. But the heavenly vision, with its activities and ministries, should be reflected on this earth. Moses under the old covenant was called to worship Yahweh by making the earthly tabernacle according to a heavenly blueprint, i.e., the way God had revealed it on the mountain (Exod 25:9; 26:30; 27:8).

In the same way, the people under the new covenant in Christ should reflect heavenly activities taking place on this earth, seeking this in their prayer—"your will be done earth as it is in heaven" (Matt 6:10), as well as pursuing it in their worship. For this is what we see in the book of Revelation. Just as the apostle John was taken into his vision experience to witness what was actually taking place in heaven and heard what the prophet Isaiah heard (Rev 4:1-2, 8), the believers are called to "[read], hear… and take to heart what is written in it" (Rev 1:3). In this way, we are letting "the word of Christ dwell in [us] richly" as we engage in worship (Col 3:16).

God's people under the new covenant have received the same calling from God to worship Him. But unlike the people under the old covenant, the Christian community worships and ministers, not "at a sanctuary that is a copy and shadow of what is in heaven" (Heb 8:5), but in the very presence of God—"Therefore… since we have confidence to enter the Most Holy Place by the blood of Jesus, by a new and living way… let us draw near to God with a sincere heart in full assurance of faith… Let us not give up meeting together" (Heb 10:19-25).

Make no mistake about it. There is no place in His entire creation that could contain God and claim to be the house of God as the prophet Isaiah proclaimed, "Heaven is my throne, and the earth is my footstool. Where is the house you will build for me" (Isa 66:1)?

Isaiah witnessed heavenly activities, but only through his vision experience. For the community of believers in Christ, worship and the experience of heaven goes beyond having a vision. What is so amazing about God's grace in Christ Jesus is that God, the Holy Spirit, dwells in the regenerate people of God. And as they set apart Christ in their hearts as Lord (1 Peter 3:15), Jesus reigns and makes the believers' hearts His throne. When those believers come together as a church, then that church, which is organic rather than organization, continues to grow "to become a holy temple in the Lord... a dwelling in which God lives by his Spirit" (Eph 2:21-22).

What can be more incredible than experiencing what the prophet Isaiah prophesied concerning the Last Days in the earlier part of his writing —"In the last days the mountain of [Yahweh] will be established... Come let us go up to the mountain of [Yahweh], to the house of the God of Jacob. He will teach us his ways, so that we may walk in his paths... Come... let us walk in the light of [Yahweh]" (Isa 2:2-3, 5)?

David testified to the powerful voice of Yahweh, comparing it with thunder and lightning in Psalm 29. In response to this voice of Yahweh, the worshipers "in his temple cry, 'Glory!'" In the case of Isaiah's vision, in seeming response to "the sound of [the seraphs'] voices," the temple doorpost and thresholds shook as though Yahweh had entered the temple since "the temple was filled with smoke" (Isa 6:4). Just proclaiming Yahweh's holiness ushered in Yahweh's glory cloud in the temple. What was a rare phenomenon which had occurred only twice in Israel's history, Yahweh filling His dwelling place with His glory cloud, took place in this vision at the sound of the seraphs' proclamation and praise.

Likewise, when God's word, the gospel is preached, may the worshipers experience God's powerful voice in the sanctuary! And in response to His word, may the congregation all cry out in one voice, "Glory!" And as the result of their praise, may the worshiping congregation witness God's presence in their midst.

Countless offerings and sacrifices were made in Isaiah's days—"The multitude of your sacrifices—what are they to me?" But all their religious ritual practices and observances had "become burden to" Yahweh (Isa 1:11, 14). The people of Judah were under Yahweh's judgment because of the breach between their acts of worship and their way of life (vv. 16-17). And the root of all sins was traced back to idolatry—"You will be ashamed because of the sacred oaks in which you have delighted; you will be disgraced" (v. 29).

Through the prophet Isaiah's own vision experience of God's forgiveness (Isa 6:5-7), the people of Judah were to repent of their ways (Isa 1:18). But they continued to insist on going their own way with the idols in their hearts. Therefore, as a nation, Yahweh would give them the delight of their hearts and what they have "chosen" to serve (Isa 1:29). Yahweh God had already spoken and warned through David that "those who make [idols would] be like them, and so [would] all who trust in them" (Ps 115:8).

Unlike the prophet Isaiah who, as his spiritual eyes were opened, saw and heard in his vision the voices of Yahweh and the seraphs, the idolaters of Judah would be judged with spiritual deafness and blindness, and like Pharaoh (Exod 4:21), their hearts would be hardened (Isa 6:9-10). And this hardening of the heart would continue until they placed their faith in Christ Jesus.

The apostle Paul spoke concerning this hardened heart's condition, describing it as a veil covering Israel's heart—"But their minds were made dull... [the veil] has not been removed, because only in Christ is it taken away... when Moses is read, a veil covers their hearts. But whenever anyone turns to the Lord, the veil is taken away" (2 Cor 3:14-16).

In response to God's judgment on the nation of Judah, the discouraged prophet Isaiah asked in verse 11, "For how long, O Lord?" But God's answer was only more discouraging since His judgment could not be partial but rather had to be complete; the idolaters would have to be completely judged—"Until the cities lie ruined... until [Yahweh] has sent everyone far away and the land is utterly forsaken" (vv. 11-12). Even those who were left behind in the land and not taken into the Babylonian captivity like the northern kingdom of Israel (Hos 4:12-13, 16), the remnant in the land would be unwilling to turn from their stubborn idolatry—"And though a tenth remains in the land, it will again be laid waste. [And] as the terebinth and oak leave stumps when they are cut down, so the holy seed will be the stump in the land" (Isa 6:13). Just as the nation's idolatry was depicted with "oaks" (Isa 1:29), the remaining people of Judah would become like the idols ("stumps") losing their spiritual senses (vv. 9-10).

The solution to such spiritual deafness and blindness and the hardened heart is having our "guilt... taken away and... sin atoned for" (Isa 6:7). For this reason, Jesus Christ was crucified, and on the cross, God's judgment was completed and His justice, satisfied. And through Christ's resurrection, the new covenant people are raised to new life. The apostle Paul wrote to the church in Ephesus and prayed that "the eyes of [their] heart[s] may be enlightened in order that [they] may know the hope to which he has called [them]... and his incomparably great power... That power is like the work of his mighty strength, which he exerted in Christ when he raised him from the dead" (Eph 1:18-19).

David wrote in Psalm 24:3, "Who may ascend the hill of [Yahweh]? Who may stand in his holy place?" In other words, who can worship Yahweh? David answered in the following verse 4, "He who has clean hands and a pure heart, who does not lift up his soul to an idol." Here, the pure heart is connected with a heart that does not have an idol. Jesus said, "Blessed are the pure in heart, for they will see God" (Matt 5:8). One of the goals in worship is to encounter God, that we "may dwell in the house of [Yahweh]... to gaze upon the beauty of [Yahweh] and to seek him in his temple" (Ps 27:4).

May we never allow idols in our hearts that dare compete against the Lord as the Holy Spirit convicts us of our sin of idolatry so that we, too, could behold the beauty of Yahweh and see Jesus highly exalted as we worship. Therefore, as we enter into worship, we ought to pray that the Holy Spirit would enlighten our minds so that through the cross and resurrection of Christ our commitment to Him alone would be renewed.

PART VI - WORSHIP IN CHRIST JESUS WITHOUT AN ALTAR, TABERNACLE, OR TEMPLE BUILDING

17

JESUS CHRIST AS THE LAST PROPHET, GOD'S FINAL WORD

The people in Jesus' days, especially His followers, commonly known as "disciples," called Him "teacher" (*rabbi*). Those who knew of him in Nazareth where He grew up, on the other hand, though "gracious words ... came from his lips" (Luke 4:22), could not recognize Him as a teacher (v. 29) since they just knew Him too well. The apostle Paul shared regarding his own prior misunderstanding of Christ—"So from now on we regard no one from a worldly point of view. Though we once regarded Christ in this way, we do so no longer" (2 Cor 5:16).

Yet the Jews were impressed with Jesus' teaching in two respects: His knowledge and His authority. When Jesus taught out in the open in the temple courts in John 7:15, the people were impressed with His knowledge —"The Jews were amazed and asked, 'How did this man get such learning without having studied?'" Some might have been impressed with Jesus' knowledge, but the general audience overall, especially the religious leaders, could not accept Jesus' teaching because His background was not especially distinguished and the content of His teaching was offensive. In this way,

Jesus was a "stone that causes men to stumble and a rock that makes them fall" (1 Peter 2:8).

Another reason for the people's amazement was His authority. People went to the temple to pray and worship, but the place of learning was the synagogue. Therefore, the people went to a synagogue to be taught. As a rabbi, it was expected of Him to teach in the synagogue (although most of His teaching actually took place outside of synagogues). On one occasion, "Jesus went into the synagogue" in Capernaum "and began to teach. The people were amazed at his teaching, because he taught them as one who had authority" unlike other teachers they were used to (Mark 1:21-22). The temple guards who were sent by the Pharisees to arrest Jesus came back without Him since they were amazed at Jesus' teaching, and they said, "No one ever spoke the way this man does" (John 7:46). Of course, that did not mean the people were willing to become His disciples; like the audience of any magic show, they were just impressed with the rabbi from Nazareth.

One of the ways God spoke under the old covenant was through His messengers, known as "prophets." "Teachers" taught God's word, while "prophets" proclaimed/prophesied a message based on God's revealed written word as the Spirit came on them in the prophetic anointing. Often God spoke and revealed His will to prophets through the means of visions and dreams (Num 12:6).

"A miraculous sign and wonder" did not solely determine the authenticity of a prophet but rather who or what the prophet proclaimed should be the object of worship attested to whether or not the person was a prophet of Yahweh (Deut 13:1-5). A true prophet was recognized by the people if what he spoke of came to pass. And sometimes what the prophet spoke of had to do with miracles. Therefore, often signs and wonders followed the prophets. For this reason, Jesus was known not only as a teacher but also as a prophet.

On one occasion, Jesus comforted a widow who had lost her only son, telling her not to weep, and then He brought her son back to life from the dead. In response to this miracle, the people "were all filled with awe and praised God" and said, "A great prophet has appeared among us" (Luke 7:12-16).

Not all the prophets' ministries were authenticated by miracles. At one time, Jesus was at the place "where John had been baptizing in the early days," and many came to believe in Him. On placing their faith in Jesus, the people said of John, the last prophet under the old covenant, "Though John never performed a miraculous sign, all that John said about this man was true" (John 10:40-42). In a way, the people only came to realize John was a true prophet of God after placing their faith in Jesus, because when they met Jesus, they saw in Him the fulfillment of John's prophetic words, that they had come true. And like those people, anyone who comes to believe that Jesus Christ is Lord and Savior will also realize that all that the prophets of the Old Testament prophesied/proclaimed/bore witness to was true.

Different religions may wrongly speculate on the identity of Jesus, considering Him merely a good moral teacher or just one prophet of God among many prophets. In many parts of Asia, Jesus could be regarded as an "enlightened one."

Yet at the very beginning of the Epistles to the Hebrews, it says, "In the past God spoke to our forefathers through the prophets at many times and in various ways, but in these last days he has spoken to us by his Son [Jesus Christ] ... sustaining all things by his powerful word" (Heb 1:1-3). Jesus Christ, the Son of God, is the Last Prophet, the Final Word of God. All the prophets under the old covenant either testified to or foreshadowed through their prophetic ministries the coming Christ. In this sense, Jesus is the fulfillment of the Old Testament.

Therefore, if the people in Jesus' days had had eyes to perceive and hears to hear, they would have seen that what Jesus did and taught was the fulfillment of what the prophets had done and testified—"These are the Scriptures that testify about me" (John 5:39). Jesus said clearly that the old covenant was about to be fulfilled and replaced with a new covenant by His death and resurrection. Everything the Scriptures testified was about to be fulfilled in Christ—"For all the Prophets and the Law prophesied until John" (Matt 11:13). And since many of the Old Testament prophets testified against false worship, it is not surprising to find that Jesus, who was the fulfillment and the Final Prophet, taught about true worship during His earthly ministry.

Foretasting the Heavenly Rest

To this day, keeping the Sabbath day holy, observing the dietary laws, and celebrating certain Jewish holidays are important for the Jewish people. But what does it mean to keep the Sabbath holy? By the time of Jesus, as they went from one interpretation to another over the course of Jewish history and development of tradition, the people had moved away from the very essence of the Law. Therefore, Jesus, in describing the religious culture and practice of His own days, referred to what Isaiah had prophesied—"These people honor me with their lips, but their hearts are far from me. They worship me in vain; their teachings are but rules taught by men" (Mark 7:6-7).

The people's understanding of the Sabbath law was so narrow and focused on "not doing" rather than God's intent for the Sabbath to be something to be experienced since "The Sabbath was made for man, not man for the Sabbath" (Mark 2:27). In the creation, the first thing man experienced after man was created was the Sabbath since man was created on the sixth day. Just as God, after He completed His work of creation, entered into rest, so did man, who was created in God's own image to resemble God, at the same time also enter into the Sabbath (Exod 20:20:10-11). One can say that one of God's calling upon man was to enter the rest.

When Jesus drove out demons, since the Pharisees did not want to come to the conclusion that He was the Christ, they made an accusation, "It is by the prince of demons that he drives out demons" (Matt 9:34); however, as serious as the accusation was, interestingly, this was not the "crime" (of which Jesus was falsely accused) that would lead them to the point of plotting to actually kill Jesus.

Although one of Jesus' ministries was healing people on a regular basis, there were times when He healed the sick on the Sabbath day even though He knew it would bring controversy among the Jews. In fact, it would be Jesus' healing people on the Sabbath and His claiming to be God that would come to serve as the Jews' justification for plotting to kill him—"the Jews tried all the harder to kill him; not only was he breaking the Sabbath, but he was even calling God his own Father, making himself equal with God" (John 5:18).

Just as it was at the creation, that man was to model himself after God since "in the image of God he created him" (Gen 1:27), Jesus, being the Son of God, was simply doing what His Father did—"the Son can do nothing by himself; he can do only what he sees his Father doing" (John 5:19). Jesus would heal people on a Sabbath all the more since God the Father had never ceased to heal and restore people from the very beginning—"My Father is always at his work to this very day, and I, too, am working" (v. 16). In this way, Jesus taught that keeping the Sabbath holy was not just about ceasing from doing regular work but that true rest came when man was restored.

God did not rest because He was so tired from creating the world in six days that He really needed to rest. But rather, just as God was preparing the place, the Land and the Garden, for five days so He could put man to rest in the Garden, in the same way, all six days served as a preparation for the seventh day, the Sabbath. Likewise, God's people were to "do all [their] work" for six days so they could consecrate the Sabbath day (Exod 20:8-9).

Therefore, the emphasis is placed on finishing all their work as a preparation during the six days as they look forward to the Sabbath rather than on just looking forward to ceasing from work. This is different from when a person works hard and saves up all his sick days in order to go somewhere for vacation in the modern day cultural understanding of rest. But rather, just as Adam was placed in the Garden, in the sanctuary, after God created him, so God's people were to work for six days so they would not be distracted from worshiping the Lord and experiencing God's presence in the temple courts. For this reason, the author of the Epistles to the Hebrews was alluding to the entire Christian life as a preparation to enter the ultimate, true Sabbath, heaven—"There remains, then, a Sabbath-rest for the people of God... Let us, therefore, make every effort to enter that rest" (Heb 4:9. 11).

During Jesus' earthly ministry years, the old covenant was still in effect until it was fulfilled by the new covenant through His crucifixion and resurrection—"God sent his Son, born of a woman, born under law" (Gal 4:4). Since the old covenant stipulations, including the Sabbath laws, were still binding in Jesus' days, if "His disciples... [picking] some heads of grain" was considered "work," then certainly the Pharisees' accusation that they were "doing what [was] unlawful on the Sabbath" was valid (Matt 12:1-2).

But Jesus' response that was much more startling than the disciples' apparent breaking of the Sabbath law helps us to understand the complete and full meaning of *sabbath*. Once we have the true biblical understanding of *sabbath*, what the people under the new covenant in Christ should anticipate as they come together to worship on Sunday, the first day of the week and day after the Sabbath, becomes clearer.

The two events that took place on a Sabbath day in Matthew 12:1-14 give us three important connections between the Sabbath and worship that need to be considered: 1) David and his companions foreshadowing the Son of David, Jesus Christ, and His disciples, 2) Jesus being greater than the temple, and 3) doing good on the Sabbath.

Matthew 12 comes immediately after Jesus' invitation—"Come to me... I will give you rest... you will find rest for your souls" (Matt 11:28-29). What does it mean to find rest? Since Jesus is the "Lord of the Sabbath" (Matt 12:8), what are we to experience when we heed His invitation?

Just as David and other prophets testified, "Sacrifice and offering you did not desire... Here I am, I have come—it is written about me in the scroll" (Ps 40:6-7), the sacrificial system under the old covenant would be fulfilled by the perfect sacrificial death of the Christ, and what David did by taking "the consecrated bread—which was not lawful for them to do, but only for the priests" (Matt 12:4) foreshadowed what the followers of the Son of David, Jesus Christ, would one day do.

The prophet, Samuel, anointed David as king while King Saul was still in power, showing how in the eyes of God, Saul had already been rejected as king. From that time on, David and his followers continually fled from Saul until Saul met his end in 1 Samuel 31. David wrote many psalms during those years. Until he actually became king, David and his followers spent most of their years in the wilderness.

We see a parallel between David and the Son of David, Jesus, since humanly speaking, Jesus was anointed by the Holy Spirit after He was baptized by John (Matt 3:16-17) though He would not become the King until later, through his death and resurrection. Both had a period of waiting between anointing and coming into kingship, and in this way, David's time in the wilderness on his way to becoming king parallels Jesus' three and a half years of earthly ministry on his way to becoming the King through facing and overcoming the cross.

David and his companions' eating the consecrated bread took place when they were running away from Saul (1 Sam 21:3-5). We do not know exactly where they ate the consecrated bread which only the priests were allowed to eat, whether it was while they were in the house of God (the tabernacle) or outside of it. But one thing that was certain was that Jesus was fulfilling what David had foreshadowed. Although both David and Jesus were under the Mosaic Law, eating the consecrated bread was not "unlawful" for David and his followers according to Jesus' interpretation of that event. In the same way, it was not unlawful for Jesus, who had been anointed by God to be the Lord and Savior, to "pick some heads of grain" on the Sabbath, and this act, rather than being one that breaks the Sabbath law actually ends up showing how Jesus would fulfill the Sabbath law and its intent.

If the priests were partially fulfilling the Sabbath law by ministering (working) in the temple on the Sabbath day, making preparations for the sacrifices (Matt 12:5, cf. Num 29:9-10), then how much more were Jesus' disciples who were "in Christ" actually fulfilling the Sabbath law since Jesus, the "one greater than the temple" (Matt 12:6), was there with them.

The teachers of the law and the Pharisees, in the name of keeping the law, "tie[d] up heavy loads and put them on men's shoulders, but they themselves [were] not willing to lift a finger to move them" (Matt 23:4). Jesus confronted such people with what the prophet Hosea proclaimed, "I [God] desire mercy, not sacrifice" (Matt 12:7).

As God's children were to imitate their Father, for God's people, the Sabbath ought to have been a day more for showing mercy than for just very intentionally not doing any work. But the sad truth was that they would try to save one of their sheep if it fell "into a pit on the Sabbath" but were unwilling "to do good" unto others (Matt 12:11-12). Jesus, however, who is Lord of the Sabbath, was doing good on the Sabbath by healing and bringing restoration to people, thus fulfilling the true meaning of *sabbath*—

"Which is lawful on the Sabbath: to do good or to do evil, to save life or to kill" (Luke 3:4)?

God's work of new creation began when His Son Jesus was crucified and resurrected—"Therefore, if anyone is in Christ, he is a new creation; the old has gone, the new has come" (2 Cor 5:17), and upon the second coming of Christ, God's new creation will be completed and its order established once and for all. Until then, we the believers in Christ are called to "make every effort to enter that rest" (Heb 4:11).

We need to be faithful in the everyday, in the area where God has placed us throughout the week, but especially on Sunday, when we as a church come together to worship God and fellowship with one another, we need to experience and foretaste the true rest in heaven when God will be making all things new (Rev 21:5). We worship in God's presence. Coming together on Sunday to worship reminds us of Christ's resurrection that began the new creation. Therefore, we anticipate healing and restoration in Jesus Christ who is Lord of the Sabbath. It is only in Christ that we are able to find the true rest of our souls, and through worshiping Him, we enter the rest and foretaste entering the true unabridged rest in heaven.

The Word Ministry and the Lord's Supper

There were two religious places in the life of Israel: the temple and the synagogues. The place of worship always had been at the temple. The people gathered together corporately to worship God, and people also went up to the temple to pray individually (Acts 3:1). But on a Sabbath day, people, especially those who lived outside of Jerusalem where the temple was, gathered together in their local synagogues to read and learn about God's word (Acts 15:21). The temple courts, not limited to worship and prayer, were also a main place for the religious leaders to discuss and teach God's word. Therefore, Jesus not only taught God's word in synagogues but also in the temple courts (Matt 26:55). It was natural for religious debates to be held regularly in the temple courts since a majority of the religious leaders would spend a great amount of time at the temple. For this reason, the early church met together regularly in the temple courts (Acts 2:46) until the persecution broke out in connection with Stephen (Acts 8:1).

Like the prophets of the Old Testament, in the Gospel writings, Jesus spoke on the essence, the heart of worship, rather than the form or order of the worship service. Therefore, rather than gathering Jesus' teaching on worship, we want to understand what worship to God entails based on Jesus' interactions with people, their momentary encounters with Christ. After all, worship is about approaching God, being in His presence, and serving Him because of His worthiness.

Although the event that took place on the road to Emmaus in Luke 24:13-35 does not give a direct teaching on worship and its format, it touches upon two types of ministries that take place during the worship service—the ministry of the Word and the Lord's supper. In a way, what the two disciples experienced from encountering the risen Christ foreshadowed what would take place when the new covenant community of believes would come together to worship.

On one occasion, when the disciples were in the boat, struggling because the boat was "buffeted by the waves," they failed to recognize Jesus at first and thought they were seeing a ghost (Matt 14:24-26). To some degree, it is understandable since they could not have imagined that Jesus, their rabbi, as powerful as He may have been, would be coming to them, walking on water. Their logical mind kept them from perceiving Christ.

Even through the virgin birth, divine confirmation and announcements from the angelic visitations, the testimony of the shepherds, from Jesus' own words—"Didn't you know I had to be in my Father's house?" we can see that while "his mother [had] treasured all these things in her heart," some unknown reason kept her and others from believing and remembering that Jesus was the Son of God (Luke 2:19, 51; John 7:5). His earthly parents continued to forget that Jesus was the Son of God. Humanly speaking, their failure to believe was perhaps from their own expectation of what the Son of God was supposed to be and be doing. But from a theological perspective, no human can perceive and believe Jesus is the Son of God without Christ's death and resurrection. It is only through the gospel message that having faith in Jesus Christ is possible (Rom 10:17).

The passage of Luke 24:13-35 took place after the resurrection but prior to His ascension and sending of the promised Holy Spirit (Acts 2:33). Initially, Mary also failed to recognize the risen Christ (John 20:14-15).

Again, humanly speaking, for Mary, perhaps it was because she was so filled with sadness and tears that she could not recognize Jesus. But from a biblical theology perspective, unless God reveals Himself through the Holy Spirit, no one can know God or recognize Christ in His divine-human glorified state. Therefore, what the two disciples experienced foreshadowed what would take place in the life of the Christian community after the day of Pentecost.

Even though the two disciples had been with Jesus for three and a half years, the text says, "Jesus… walked along with them; but they were kept from recognizing him" (Luke 24:16). Throughout the Bible, when there was a divine visitation, it was usually an angelic being. The three men visiting Abraham in Genesis 18 were angelic beings, which Abraham did not know—"some people have entertained angels without knowing it" (Heb 13:2). But at the same time, reading from the text, the one who stayed with Abraham while the other two visitors went down to Sodom, was Yahweh Himself (Gen 18:16-22). Later, Abraham's grandson, Jacob, would one night wrestle with one who perhaps was an angelic being in Genesis 32, but Jacob later realized that the man, the angelic being, was none other than God Himself—"I saw God face to face, and yet my life was spared" (Gen 32:30, see also Hosea 12:3-5).

After going through the cross and conquering death in His resurrection, Jesus was no longer in His humiliation state but coming to His disciples as their Lord and Savior. Therefore, His disciples and those who would come to follow him later needed to relate to Jesus in faith—"Though you have not seen him, you love him; and even though you do not see him now, you believe in him and are filled with an inexpressible and glorious joy" (1 Peter 1:8). So the two disciples on their way to Emmaus were foretasting how they would need to relate to Jesus Christ going forward.

The spirit of revelation when the two disciples encountered the risen Lord was twofold: in the speaking of the Scriptures and the breaking of the bread.

The bible is not a book full of magic spells (i.e., verses) that if memorized and quoted in the appropriate situation release some kind of power. This mistake is commonly made when referring to the temptation of Jesus in the wilderness account (Matt 4:1-11). We all know that power is not in the knowing but in obedience. The true Israel, the Son of God, perfectly obeyed in submission to the Father's will what the Israelites could not and failed to do in the wilderness for forty years. Therefore, God's word needs to be more than just head-knowledge—"Blessed is one who reads... are those who hear it and take to heart" (Rev 1:3).

The gospel message—Christ's crucifixion and resurrection, should be the central focus of the Scriptures (Luke 24:25-27). Not only in Judaism but also in the early church of the New Testament context, the apostle Paul instructed his spiritual son, Timothy, in regard to the Scriptures and the spiritual gift of ministry—"devote yourself to the public reading of Scripture, to preaching and to teaching. Do not neglect your gift" (1 Tim 4:13-14). Most likely, Timothy's gifts were not limited to the word ministry, but as a leader, that was supposed to be the primary ministry he was to devote himself to, just as the Twelve devoted themselves and prioritized the word ministry as their primary responsibility—"and will give our attention to prayer and the ministry of the word" (Acts 6:4).

Therefore, when the risen Christ was taking the two disciples who were "slow of heart to believe all that the prophets have spoken," explaining "what was said in all the Scriptures concerning himself," their hearts were burning within them (Luke 24:25-27, 32).

When a teacher "correctly handles the word of truth" and as a preacher, faithfully proclaims and applies it to the congregation in the worship service in hopes that the Holy Spirit would honor His servant's delivery of God's word, the congregation could testify to one another—"were not our hearts burning within us?"

From the very beginning in the Garden, God spoke to Adam and Eve. We do not know how exactly God spoke, but one thing was certain, the Garden, being God's sanctuary where God chose to dwell, when they were in the very presence of God, God spoke. When God's glory cloud filled the tabernacle (Exod 40:35), Yahweh "called to Moses and spoke to him from the Tent of Meeting" (Lev 1:1). During the days when worship was being profaned by Eli's two sons and "the word of [Yahweh] was rare [and] there were not many visions," God raised up the prophet Samuel to speak through him so "the lamp of God" would not be put out in Israel (1 Sam 3:1-4).

Today, God continues to speak from the place where He has chosen to dwell, the new covenant community gathered in worship. When we gather together to worship, we do not just assume, without having any kind of discernment, that any kind of "spiritual" phenomenon is a word from the Lord or God's work when we have God's perfect written revelation, God word that is "centered around Christ." The real issue is, "Is there a ministry of God's word in worship?" Has God word been preached faithfully to the text that testifies Christ crucified and resurrected? David once said, "I will bow down toward your holy temple and will praise your name for your love... for you have exalted above all things your name and your word" (Ps 138:2). Therefore, when a preacher honors God's word by faithfully proclaiming it to the worshipers in the sanctuary, we can expect that God would honor the proclamation and bring a certain divine conviction within the hearts of the people. And then, without a shadow of a doubt, the worshipers' commitment to Jesus Christ would be renewed since God's voice was heard in His sanctuary.

The two disciples did not know fully at the time when their risen Lord "opened the Scriptures to" them. So it could be like this with us also. As the preacher preaches God's word, we may understand intellectually that the gospel makes sense. But it should not end there; there has to be a conviction from the Holy Spirit, even though at that moment we may not fully understand and grasp what is really happening in our hearts other than that "our hearts [are] burning within us." Yet once we encounter Christ in worship, we will look back in retrospect and be fully assured, it was Jesus all along; God's voice was heard in the sanctuary.

In the passage, it is interesting to note, that although the two disciples were the ones who invited Jesus to stay for the evening, Jesus was actually hosting them—"at the table... [Jesus] took bread, gave thanks, broke it and began to give it to them" (Luke 24:30). At the table, an expectedly ordinary meal became an extraordinary sacred meal when "they recognized him" (v. 31).

The last time the two disciples had had a meal like that with a "rabbi" was three days prior when they had had the Passover meal with their rabbi. The two disciples did not recognize Jesus because they were able to put those two different events together and concluded that it had to be their

Lord. But from the very beginning (vv. 16, 25) and throughout to the climax of the event (v. 31), the subject matter was about the heart to understand, the eyes to perceive, and the ears to hear (Isa 6:10) in the context of a sacred meal.

Some regard the Lord's Supper, the Communion, as an ordinary religious ritual that aides the worshipers to remember Christ's death so that they could give thanks; to them, the Communion meal is nothing more than remembering Christ's death that is symbolized by the bread and the wine. To some degree, it is indeed about doing (ritual) "in remembrance of" Christ (Luke 22:19). But what happened at the Emmaus village over a simple evening meal was more than a remembrance.

The event foresees what will happen as God's word is faithfully preached to the worship congregation. Just as long ago, Christ, in the Spirit, preached through Noah, "a preacher of righteousness" (2 Peter 2:5), "when God waited patiently in the days of Noah while the ark was being built" (1 Peter 3:20), so does God speak in the preaching of the gospel to the congregation gathered to worship. The Word ministry in the worship service is a must in order for the congregation to be taught, rebuked, corrected, and trained for righteousness (2 Tim 3:16).

Putting all different views of the Communion aside, one thing was certain, Jesus chose to reveal Himself in the context of a meal. How much more when we prepare a Communion table and say, "A man ought to examine himself before he eats of the bread and drink of the cup. For anyone who eats and drinks without recognizing the body of the Lord eats and drinks judgment on himself" (1 Cor 11:28-29).

When everything is said and done, at the conclusion of the worship service, we long for God's voice to have been heard and for us to be able recognize, "surely God [was] really among [us]" (1 Cor 14:25).

Preaching the Word goes beyond just an intellectual reasoning or seminar; the God of the universe Himself could be speaking to us. Participating in the Lord's Supper goes beyond remembrance; through it, when the moment of revelation of Christ occurs, we rely no longer on what we are able to see but rather our faith in Christ is renewed—"We live by faith, not by sight" (2 Cor 5:7).

The moment they finally recognized Him, Christ "disappear[ed] from their sight" (Luke 24:31) as though to remind that we need to "fix our eyes not on what is seen, but on what is unseen. For what is seen is temporary, but what is unseen is eternal" (2 Cor 4:18). Maclaren's comment is helpful:

"...when Christ's Presence is recognized sense may be put aside... You and I... need no visible manifestation; we have lost nothing though we have lost the bodily Presence of our Master... The earthly manifestation was only the basis and the platform for that which is purer and deeper in kind... when the platform has been laid, then there is no need for the continuance thereof. And so, when He was manifested to the heart He disappeared from the eyes; and we, who have not beheld Him, stand upon no lower level than they who did." (Alexander Maclaren, *Expositions of Holy Scripture, St. Luke*, p.360)

Being Justified by God

Although God is omnipresent, He had at one time chosen to dwell in His temple when His people gathered together to pray and worship. Our subject matter is worship, and just as music and worship are inseparable, so it is with prayer and worship. For this reason, upon the completion of the temple construction, prayer was the dominant theme of Solomon's prayer of dedication—"Hear the supplication of your servant and of your people Israel when they pray toward this place. Hear from heaven, your dwelling place, and when you hear forgive" (1 Kings 8:30). Much prayer was offered while sacrifices from the worshipers were made.

Since different sacrifices were connected with different aspects of the worshipers' relationship with God, it would not have made sense if they just made sacrifices without a prayer of supplication, confession, thanksgiving or commitment. Unlike worship, God did not require the prayer to be done in the temple. Yet, it was and is to this day a good spiritual discipline to set a certain time and place to pray. For this was the regular practice of the apostles—"Peter and John were going up to the temple at the time of prayer" (Acts 3:1).

Against this background of Israel's religious culture, on one occasion Jesus told a parable in order to unmask "some who were confident of their own righteousness and looked down on everybody else" (Luke 18:9). One can immediately notice that something is not quite right with this picture, especially when we read this statement in connection with the parable that follows. But if we read this statement in isolation, we may be able to relate it to ourselves since all of us, to some degree, are somewhat confident in what we do when we are doing (what we feel is) the right thing. We may not look down on "everybody," but since we do have people that we look up to, it means that we have a system, whether conscious or subconscious, of putting people into different classes, and there may be people who are less fortunate than us that we easily look down on without thinking much of it.

Just as there is a cultural diversity in our society, so are there social and economic diversities that we cannot deny. Just because the early church practiced generosity in giving does not mean that the church had a socio-economic uniformity—"There were no needy persons among them. For from time to time those who owned lands or houses sold them" (Acts 4:34). The people were more aware the need of others in the church, and when they saw the need, either for church or some individuals in the church, they gave generously.

The difference between the two people in the parable of Jesus in Luke 18:9-14, however, was not in socio-economic status but moral and religious practice. Jesus was not saying that there was no need for moral uprightness —"Religion that God our Father accepts as pure and faultless is this: to look after orphans and widows in their distress and to keep oneself from being polluted by the world" (James 1:27). The real problem with having confidence in one's own righteousness in the parable was that it was righteousness according to one's own standard, which was based on moral goodness and religious practices. If we are not careful, we, too, may be vulnerable to falling into this kind of attitude and perception as devout religious people, like the Pharisee in the parable, can be especially susceptible to such.

Another problem with this self-righteousness was being its relative and comparative; the Pharisee's moral standard was based on comparing himself with the tax collector in the parable. The Pharisee's prayer sounds like that of some religious men who thank God daily for not making them Gentiles and for making them men rather than women.

With such diversity amongst the people, how is unity possible? As a new covenant community, we have yet to achieve it, and how can we when we currently reflect more the existing secular society than the people belonging to God?? It has become almost a cliché that the most segregated hour in America is Sunday morning in church. Going from ethnic to other social barriers, if there is any semblance of unity, i.e., a variety of ethnic backgrounds represented in a single congregation, then it is because they are united by their cultural, social, or economic similarity and anything but the spiritual reason—"Make every effort to keep the unity of the Spirit through the bond of peace" (Eph 4:3).

There was nothing insincere or hypocritical about the Pharisee's prayer in the parable (Luke 18:11-12); all he was doing was acknowledging how he had been living before God. There was no pretense or exaggeration in his prayer. Most likely, the listeners of the parable did not have any problem with the Pharisee's prayer or attitude towards the social scum, a tax collector. But to their utter surprise, Jesus concluded the parable with an unexpected answer, and perhaps confused some people—"I tell you that this man [the tax collector], rather than the other [the Pharisee], went home justified before God" (v. 14).

What does it mean to be "justified before God"? Does moral uprightness not have a place in the religious practice of prayer and worship? Are we not supposed to thank God by acknowledging God's goodness in our lives, but rather, no matter how we have tried to live a life that pleases the Lord, just have to acknowledge that we are just sinners? Can anyone who lives like the tax collector during the weekdays and then goes to God in worship on Sunday and humbles himself, "be justified before God"?

The "two men went up to the temple to pray" to God (v. 10). What was the Pharisee's reason for praying to God? Just as worship has to primarily be about God, so does prayer. And this was the very reason behind the Pharisee's shortcoming before God. It was all about himself—"The Pharisee stood up and prayed about himself" (v. 11); apart from his thanking of God as he begins, God was absent from the man's prayer. A person used to say that she did not have many prayer requests to share and did not see the need of being desperate in prayer since her life was comfortable and she had no specific need other than to thank the Lord.

Just as it is with worship (Heb 11:6), prayer is lot more than us just simply approaching God and making supplication. It is about God, not a monologue but us dialoging with God, seeking to listen to obey, spending time with Him, communing with Him, and being in God's presence (Matt 6:5-8). The Pharisee in the parable was just full of himself, and his confidence came not only from what he had been doing but also from how he compared himself with others. There was no vertical relationship with God but only a comparative relationship with others.

Both the Pharisee and the tax collector "went up to the temple to pray." But the one left that temple only with exactly what he brought to the temple—his self-righteousness, while the other "went home justified before God"—having received God's mercy.

The question is not, "How bad one does have to be" to receive mercy from God? The real issue is, "Who needs God's mercy?" The longer a person is a Christian, the more vulnerable one can become to a diminishing appreciation of God's grace. Although the gospel message is one and the same, everyone has a different conversion experience; externally, even the degree of emotion and the depth of understanding of the gospel would vary from person to person. But in our sanctification, our road to Christian spiritual maturity, we do not walk away from the cross as though the cross were needed only to receive God's forgiveness and mercy for conversion. Instead, in our Christian experience, especially as we experience God's presence in worship, His holiness and His nearness, we realize that we are worse sinners than we thought we were. This is so, not because we become worse than before. No, it is quite the opposite. Just as a person moving out of darkness and coming closer to the light comes to see himself better, so do we; the more we approach Him, the closer our communion with God who is pure and holy, the more we are aware of our sinful state. Just as the prophet Isaiah cried out after experiencing God's holiness, "Woe to me... I am ruined! For I am a man of unclean lips, and I live among a people of unclean lips" (Isa 6:5). Ironically, perhaps the only member of Isaiah's body that could possibly have been considered holy or "clean" was his lips, since it was with his lips, as a prophet, that he would have preached God's holiness. How true it is, "All of us have become like one who is unclean, and all our righteous acts are like filthy rags" (Isa 64:6). It has been said that our sin scorches us the most under the scrutinizing light of God's holiness.

An attempt to comprehend the parable from a humanistic perspective —by looking at how others perceived and evaluated the two men based on what they did, can make the parable confusing and seem somewhat unfair —"Why does the Bible tend to regard respectable and morally good people like the Pharisee and religious leaders as bad, while people like the tax collector and others known as sinners always walk away scot-free?"

Could it be that the Pharisee looked at himself and others more than he looked at God? Yet was he not supposed to look to God in prayer and worship—"I lift up my eyes to you, to you whose throne is in heaven. As the eyes of slaves look to the hand of their master... so our eyes look to [Yahweh] our God, till he shows us his mercy" (Ps 123:1-2).

But unlike the Pharisee, the tax collector "would not even look up to heaven... God, have mercy on me, a sinner" (Luke 18:13). Was the tax collector being melodramatic? Or did he seek God and look up to Him in prayer and worship? Anyone, regardless of whether they are just the "average" sinner or worse, in the presence of God's holiness would quickly realize that the only legitimate response is humbly asking for God to be merciful. And what is amazing about this parable is that God did show mercy, even to a well-known sinner; at the very place God had promised to dwell and put His Name, God met a tax collector.

What do we actually bring to church on Sunday to the worship? What are we to look for in worship? Knowing that Jesus Christ, Son of God, is in the midst of our congregation, leading us to worship God, what should be our confession? Jesus, who is not ashamed to call us His brothers and sisters (Heb 2:11), said through David long ago, "I will declare your name to my brothers; in the congregation I will praise you. You who fear [Yahweh], praise him" (Ps 22:22-23).

Worship in Spirit and Truth

Many have taken the event in John 4 as a method of evangelism. This is one way of looking at it since the Samaritan woman did go to her village and say to the people, "Come, see a man who told me everything I ever did. Could this be the Christ?" (John 4:29). But this perspective may come from an underlying assumption that the goal of evangelism is "conversion" rather than seeing someone become a member of a worshiping community through evangelism.

The event and dialogue that took place between Jesus and a Samaritan woman in Sychar, a village of Samaria, was significant in regard to worship and Jesus' self-disclosure. A conversation that started with Jesus asking for a drink ended with Jesus' teaching on worship. The direction the conversation went was not because the woman was avoiding an issue, feeling uncomfortable and so therefore trying to evade questions she felt were rather too personal. But it was Jesus, from beginning to end, who was leading the whole conversation to worship and His self-disclosure. To the Samaritan woman, Jesus initially was just a Jewish stranger. Yet at the end of their dialogue, Jesus became more than a prophet; He was the Christ whom the woman longed for.

The apostle John in his Gospel writing presented Jesus as being, from the beginning, the Eternal Word, Creator, and God manifest in glory. The prophet John testified to Jesus as "the Lamb of God, who takes away the sin of the world" (John 1:29). Philip, who later became one of Jesus' disciples, referred to Jesus as "the one Moses wrote about in the Law, and about whom the prophets also wrote" (v. 45). The Jews had been waiting for someone like Moses, the Second Moses—"[Yahweh] your God will raise up for you a prophet like me from among your own brothers" (Deut 18:15). The apostle John, towards the end of his Gospel, wrote that he had been selective in terms of which of Jesus' miracles he had included in his writing; although "Jesus did many other miraculous signs... If every one of them were written down... even the whole world would not have room for the books that would be written" (John 20:30; 21:25).

In a way, the apostle John was saying that Jesus was the Prophet that the last book of Moses, Deuteronomy, had anticipated—"Since then, no prophet has risen in Israel like Moses, whom [Yahweh] knew face to face, who did all those miraculous sings and wonders [Yahweh] sent him to do in Egypt... For no one has ever shown the mighty power... in the sight of all Israel" (Deut 34:10-12).

As the second Moses, the first miraculous sign that Jesus performed was changing water into wine at a wedding banquet in Cana in Galilee. For the prophet Moses, turning the waters of the Nile to blood was a sign of God's judgment upon the Pharaoh and his people's unbelief. For Jesus, it was a blessing anticipating "the wedding of the Lamb... Blessed are those who are invited to the wedding supper of the Lamb" (Rev 19:7, 9).

The prophet, Moses, and the Israelites "all ate the same spiritual food" (1 Cor 10:3) called "manna" that served as a sign of "the true bread from heaven" (John 6:32). For this reason, Jesus fed over five thousand people with five loaves and two fish in the most unlikely setting, the wilderness, to show that He was the Prophet that Moses wrote about, and that He was the bread of life (John 6:35).

Earlier, in the days of Jesus' ministry, the true temple He was referring to was His body (John 2:21). Later, not only would His body the true temple but also every believer who would drink the water Christ could give (John 4:13-14) would become the temple. In His conversation with the Pharisee, Nicodemus (John 3:1-10), Jesus spoke of spiritual birth from what the prophets, especially Jeremiah and Ezekiel, prophesied (Jer 31:33-34; Ezek 36:25-27).

With the Samaritan woman at the well, Jesus promised the Holy Spirit, the living water, "Indeed, the water I give him will become in him a spring of water welling up to eternal life" (John 4:14). Later, Jesus would elaborate on the Holy Spirit in the believers by making a connection with the prophet Ezekiel's vision of the temple. The altar and the temple from which the living water was flowing out (Ezek 47:1-12) was the heart and the body of every believer under the new covenant—"Whoever believes in me, as the Scripture has said, streams of living water will flow from within him" (John 7:38).

Even though Nicodemus was a teacher of Israel, he did not have a clear understanding of the spiritual birth by the work of the Holy Spirit under the new covenant. How much less would a Samaritan woman? For her, she was at best familiar with the prophetic ministry (John 4:19) and somewhat waiting for the Messiah (v. 25) just as all the Jewish people had been for thousands of years.

To the woman's best knowledge, a prophet was one who could know what was really going on in someone else's life; a prophet was able to perceive and know beyond the surface level of a person. For some odd reason, as she was conversing with Jesus, she felt there was no need for pretense. For the first time, she became vulnerable and truthful to a Jewish stranger, saying to Jesus, "What you have just said is quite true," as Jesus spoke of what the woman had gone through regarding her relationships with men (vv. 17-19).

Once the woman became true to herself and realized that the Jewish man was a prophet, she wanted to know about what had been a controversial topic for hundreds of years, most likely based on Deuteronomy 27, regarding Mount Ebal and Mount Gerizim—"Our fathers worshiped on this mountain, but you Jews claim that the place where we must worship is in Jerusalem" (John 4:20). The woman probably assumed that if the prophet she was talking to knew her deep inner struggle, then this prophet could also possibly shed some light on issue of where the people should worship, regardless of whether they were Jews or Samaritans. It seemed like their same God, Yahweh had designated only one location as the place to worship Him. Yet the sad thing was that the Samaritans were not able to worship in Jerusalem, if indeed that was place of worship, because of social and ethnic barriers.

Why was the woman concerned about the right place to worship or worshiping correctly? Had she forgotten about the living water that the prophet had offered? Could it be that if she was a worshiper of Yahweh, the only place she could be true to herself was before Yahweh, before whom she did not have to worry about being criticized like she did before the people from her village? The woman had just had a moment of experiencing what truth is from Jesus who is the truth (John 14:6).

There is something about worship before God that could either bring the person to truthfulness, since there is no need for pretense, or could bring about no change at all, like with the Pharisee in the parable of Luke 18:11-12. From the man she assumed to be a prophet, unlike Jeroboam's wife had before the prophet Ahijah in 1 Kings 14:4-5, the Samaritan woman experienced that pretense was unnecessary before God.

If there is going to be any true fellowship in the Christian community, it has to begin with believers relating to God in truthfulness, without any guile, as Jesus described Nathaniel (John 4:47) in worship. Intimate fellowship with the Father God in Christ Jesus will enable His children to be free from any hypocrisy—"so that you also may have fellowship with us. And our fellowship is with the Father and with his Son, Jesus Christ" (1 John 1:3). Perhaps the reason some of us still have a hard time being "real" in the community of believers is because we have not experienced worshiping in spirit and in truth (John 4:23).

Jesus said that more than at a particular place, people would be able to truly worship at God's designated time—"a time is coming… salvation is from the Jews" (John 4:21-22). The prophets of the Old Testament had prophesied about worship one day not being limited to a particular designated place, "For the earth will be filled with the knowledge of the glory of [Yahweh], as the waters cover the sea" (Hab 2:14).

The particular time Jesus was referring to was in relation to His death and resurrection. In other words, this particular time was when the new covenant redeemed people, made alive as they are spiritually born from above because of Christ's death and resurrection, could truly worship the Father who is spirit.

Yet in the next verse 23, Jesus said, "Yet a time is coming and has now come when the true worshipers will worship the Father in spirit and truth." Here, what Jesus said about worship was twofold: prophetically foretasting what was to come, and relating to God the way He is in worship.

First, although Jesus had yet to accomplish and fulfill the redemptive work of God through His death and resurrection, the Samaritan woman, like the guests at the wedding banquet in Cana (John 2:1-11), experienced what it meant to worship God in spirit and truth. In the same way, God's people under the new covenant in Christ, while they "eagerly await a Savior… the Lord Jesus Christ, who… will transform [their] lowly bodies so that they will be like his glorious body" (Phil 3:20-21), will experience worshiping God without the temple or a particular place to worship "because the Lord God Almighty and the Lamb are its temple… The nations will walk by its light, and the kings of the earth will bring their splendor into it" (Rev 21:22, 24). Therefore, the new covenant worshipers should study what will be fully actualized and fulfilled in the consummation; they seek to experience God's holiness, purity, fullness of light and truth in their worship as they are living the Last Days. God in His grace will help His worshiping community to foretaste whatever belongs to the future now. In this way, His people will continue to look up to the Lord in heaven.

Second, we need to worship God in the way He is, spirit, invisible and how Jesus is—"The Word became flesh... full of grace and truth... No one has ever seen God, but God the One and Only, who is at the Father's side, has made him known" (John 1:14, 18). We worship Jesus Christ who is the visible manifestation of the invisible God in humanity. The spiritually born people under the new covenant in Christ need to worship God, not in fleshly desire but in spirit—"Christ, our Passover lamb, has been sacrificed. Therefore, let us keep the Festival, not with the old yeast, the yeast of malice and wickedness, but with bread without yeast, the bread of sincerity and truth... let us draw near to God with a sincere heart in full assurance of faith" (1 Cor 5:8; Heb 10:22). Carson's comment is helpful in regard to who God is and how His worshipers ought to worship:

"'God is spirit' means that God is invisible, divine as opposed to human... unknowable to human beings unless he chooses to reveal himself ... now become flesh, he may be known as truly as it is possible for human beings to know him (1:1-18)... unless they are born from above... they cannot worship God truly... This God who is spirit can be worshipped only *in spirit and truth*... the one preposition 'in' governs both nouns... essentially God-centered... The worshippers whom God seeks worship him out of the fullness of the supernatural life they enjoy ('in spirit'), and on the basis of God's incarnate ... Christ Jesus himself, through whom God's person and will are finally and ultimately disclosed ('in truth'); and these two characteristics form one matrix, indivisible." (D. A. Carson, *The Gospel according to John*, pp.225-26)

After listening to what the Jewish prophet said about true worship and worshipers, the Samaritan woman expressed her hope in the Messiah, "I know that Messiah... is coming. When he comes, he will explain everything to us." To this Jesus responds by revealing Himself (John 4:25-26). This is another prophetic event that the new covenant worshipers would experience later, God revealing Himself in the context of worship as they long to see Christ who will appear in heaven in all of His splendor and glory.

Since we worship God the way He is, invisible but revealed in the person of Jesus Christ, the way we worship must reflect who God is in

Christ who is "the image of the invisible God" (Col 1:15). This was the very will of God for mankind in creation when He created man in His own image. In the Garden, the sanctuary of God, Adam and Eve were to truly reflect the invisible God. And when the image of God was marred due to sin, the only way man could worship the true living God was to first be redeemed by the blood of Christ, who is the invisible God in visible human flesh. When we are redeemed, we "worship by the Spirit of God" (Phil 3:3) in our spiritually renewed life — no pretense, not out of legalism, no show-manship, not in uncertainty, but 'in spirit and truth,' true freedom in Christ, like the Samaritan woman who foretasted such freedom before Christ.

18

THE NEW COVENANT WORSHIPING COMMUNITY ACCORDING TO THE EPISTLE TO THE EPHESIANS

In Ephesians 1, the apostle Paul praises God for blessing God's people "with every spiritual blessing in Christ" (v. 3) which he describes as the following: (1) to be holy and blameless (v. 4); (2) adoption (v. 5), redemption, the forgiveness of sins (v. 7); (3) lavishing the "riches of his grace" in all wisdom and understanding (v. 8); (4) revealing the mystery of his will (v. 9). In sum, God chose the apostle Paul and other believers so that they "might be for the praise of his glory" (v. 12). Not only the leaders but also all true believers in Christ have come to realize the same ultimate calling from God—"the praise of his glory" when they accepted "the word of truth" in faith (vv. 13-14).

Although having received every spiritual blessing in Christ, no one can fully comprehend these blessings all at one time. Therefore, prayer is needed for God to pour out "the Spirit of wisdom and revelation, so that [we] may know him better" (1:17). Prayer is needed in order that: (1) "the eyes of [our] heart may be enlightened" to "know the riches of God's glorious inheritance... and his incomparably great [resurrection] power for" the believers (vv. 18-19); (2) the community of believers would know Christ's authority over "all rule and authority, power and dominion, and every title" (vv. 20-21). Christ rules primarily through the church, which is the fullness of Christ (vv. 22-23).

Therefore, the church is the visible manifestation of the invisible fullness of Christ. Because Christ's full presence is in the church, it is the church's responsibility to properly exercise Christ's invisible heavenly authority on this earth—"whatever you bind on earth will be bound in heaven... For where two or there come together in my name, there am I with them" (Matt 18:18, 20).

Doing the Gospel Ministry as Good Works

People are incapable of serving God because they are spiritually dead in their sins (Eph 2:1). The natural person does not have to do sinful things in order to die spiritually—"through the disobedience of the one man [the first man Adam] the many were made sinners" (Rom 5:19), and as the result "in Adam all die" (1 Cor 15:22). Therefore, natural people are not sinners because they have sinned, but because they are in a sinful state—"gratifying the cravings of [their] sinful nature and following its desires and thoughts" (Eph 2:3).

For this reason, if natural people are to have any hope, God must newly create them—"if anyone is in Christ, he is a new creation... All this is from God" (2 Cor 5:17-18). God's people are totally a work of God—"God's workmanship" (Eph 2:10). For people who are spiritually born from above in Christ, God has done the following: [God] "made us alive with Christ... seated us with him in the heavenly realms" (vv. 5-6). Our spiritual state, position, and authority are in heaven with Christ Jesus. Therefore, we are called to struggle and engage in a battle not of this world. Although many of our battles seem to take place in this world—"The weapons we fight with are not the weapons of the world. On the contrary, they have divine power to demolish strongholds" (2 Cor 10:2-4).

God's purpose for saving us—not by the result of our works but by God's new created work—is so that we may "do good works" (vv. 8-10). These good works can refer both to moral goodness and to gospel ministries. With respect to moral goodness, our lives should be transparent before the world so that God's goodness is evident—"In the same way let your light shine before men, that they may see your good deeds and praise your Father in heaven" (Matt 5:16). Good deeds are to be the result of Christ's work of redemption in us so that redeemed people should be "eager to do what is good" (Titus 2:14).

Doing "good to others" has been emphasized as part of a Christian's responsibility to his/her neighbor and city. Moreover, this emphasis often ended up in a social gospel and humanitarianism. However, when "works" is used in the context of God's creation, Paul was likely referring to Adam (Genesis 1 and 2) who was placed in the Garden to work. Now, the redeemed people under the new covenant in Christ, are ministering in the new temple of God. For this reason, Paul mentions the temple in the following section (Eph 2:11-22).

The first man, Adam was in a testing period in the Garden. If he passed the test, Adam would have entered into glory but he had broken the covenant with God and failed. Nevertheless, "God, who is rich in mercy" created and seated us with Christ in the heavenly realms because Christ, who is the Last Adam, was "obedient to death... on a cross... Therefore God exalted him to the highest place" (Phil 2:8-9; cf. Luke 24:26).

By placing Adam in the Garden, God's purpose for the first man was "to work it [Garden] and take care of it" (Gen 2:15). And now because of Jesus Christ's perfect work of obedience, God's purpose for those who are in Christ, like the first man, is "to do good works" (Eph 2:10). Before sin entered and affected every aspect of humanity and creation, whatever Adam did in the Garden was considered to be ministry (serving God). In the Garden, there was no distinction between what was ministry and secular. Now, God saves and newly creates His people in Christ, for the purpose of doing good works. God had placed His people in the sanctuary (church) and their primary responsibility is to minister, which Paul elaborates in Ephesians 4.

Approaching God as One Community in Christ

One characteristic of a major city is socio-economic diversity. This is due to the fact that a city can provide different opportunities for all types of work and business. Likewise, the church should also reflect such diversity of people with different socio-economic backgrounds, coming together to form a community of one faith in Christ—"Make every effort to keep the unity of the Spirit through the bond of peace. There is one body and one Spirit... one Lord, one faith" (Eph 4:3-4). However, not many churches in the city reflect such diversity. Why? Will a social gospel or liberation theology, or racial reconciliation break down barriers of hostility?

Some years ago, a well-known evangelical author and speaker was the keynote speaker at an Asian-American Promise Keeper Conference. At an informal luncheon meeting with only predominantly Asian Christian leaders, there was much discussion concerning racial reconciliation. The speaker proposed that recognizing each ethnic group's strengths would help to accomplish true reconciliation in a ministry context. In response to the speaker's comment, a question was raised, "What does it meant to work together as one body of Christ?"

The speaker shared what he thought would occur in the next twenty years or so in America and perhaps around the world: 1) African-Americans would be making their greatest contribution to preaching/speaking while the Latinos would be providing music. 2) Asians Christians in America will promote the value of family being raised in and having the Eastern background. One person from the audience asked, "What about the Caucasians?" Without any hesitation, the speaker made a statement as though it was an obvious truth, "We will continue to provide the biblical scholarship!" Some of us could not believe what our ears had just heard.

How is unity possible in the midst of diversity? We all bear, to some degree, prejudices toward those who differ from us in respect to ethnicity and/or socio-economic status. To those who are less fortunate than us, we are willing to help, support, teach and lead them as long as they become the object of our "mission." To those who are wealthier, more intellectual and more authoritative than we are, we are afraid to reach out to them with the gospel. There is this fear and assumption that they would not be interested in the gospel. As a result, most of the local churches in the city seldom reflect the city's diversity.

At the time when the apostle Paul wrote his Epistle to the Ephesians, the ethno-centricity was worse as it was based on faulty theology and traditions of the Jews in the First Century. Even some of the prominent Jewish Christian leaders had difficulty with accepting the gentiles unless they kept all of the traditions which they believed to be derived from the Pentateuch (Acts 15:5). Even after the Gentiles were converted to the Christian faith, the Jewish Christians were uncomfortable with having table fellowship with the Gentile converts (Gal 2:1-13).

There were many significant differences that made it almost impossible for the Jews to be united with the gentles in their relationship to God and their worship (Eph 2:11-12). In the beginning of his letter, Paul elaborated what it means to be "blessed... in the heavenly realms with every spiritual blessing in Christ" (Eph 1:3). It was never enough for Paul to intellectually know God's election love for His people. Rather, Paul was led to pray for the believers in Ephesus for "the Spirit of wisdom and revelation, so that [they] may know [the glorious Father] better" (Eph 1:17). It is never sufficient to know, understand, and comprehend God's love simply by reading. Much prayer is also needed for "the Spirit of wisdom and revelation" and for a deeper knowledge of God's love.

In chapter two, Paul states the reason why God "made us alive with Christ"—in order that in the coming ages he might show the incomparable riches of his grace, expressed in his kindness" (Eph 2:5, 7). This revelation of God's incomparable riches of his grace was to be expressed through God's new covenant people in Christ who were the objects of God's great mercy by doing "good works" (the gospel ministries) in verse 10.

There is a parallel between the two sections, 2:1-10 and 11-22. The latter section elaborates based on the first one: 1) the former state and life without Christ (vv. 1-3 and 11-12), 2) through Christ's resurrection the redeemed people are also were made alive (vv. 4-6) while in the next section through Christ's death He "[created] in himself one new man out of the two" (vv. 13-17), and 3) God's purpose of redeeming His people in Christ (vv. 7-10 and vv. 18-22).

Making an attempt to find commonality or compliment one another based on the humanitarian reason would only utterly fail. But rather, each person's identity in the community of faith should be based not on the religious traditions or ethnic background (or in our days, socio-economic status), but on the person's relationship with Christ and life with God (2:11-13).

In practice, within a diverse group of people, unity is only possible when the primary purpose for coming together as the new covenant community in Christ is realized. Paul used the phrase "far away... brought near... far away... were near" (vv. 13, 17); near to what though?

In the wilderness, the Israelites were "to camp around the Tent of Meeting some distance from it," but the Levites were "to set up their tents around the tabernacle... so that wrath will not fall on the Israelite community" (Num 2:2; 1:53). For people under the old covenant, there was a limitation with respect to how close they could approach God. This was expressed by the visible Tabernacle and the different sites for the manifestation of the glory cloud (e.g., courtyard, altar, Holy Place, and Most Holy Place).

When the temple was renovated and expanded by king Herod, there were more divisions in the temple courts—courts for priests, women, and the outer courts for the Gentiles (Acts 21:28). In the apostle John's vision, the same divisions were made except for the vision of the outer court where gospel ministry took place outside of the covenant community—"Go and measure the temple of God and the altar and count the worshipers there. But exclude the outer court; do not measure it, because it has been given to the Gentiles" (Rev 11:1-2).

In Revelation, which concerns both the future consummation and the here and now for the new covenant community, Israel is the true spiritual Israel (John 1:47) made up of all peoples (Jews and Gentiles who placed their faith in Christ Jesus).

If Paul was using the temple as an analogy for God's people serving/worshiping God, then the concept of being "near" is the referent for the following in the Old Testament: the Garden, tabernacle and temple. It is in the act of approaching the throne of God, the sanctuary at the temple courts, when Asaph confesses, "it is good to be near God" (Ps 73:28).

When Jesus was crucified, not only "the curtain [that separated the Most Holy Place from the Holy Place] of the temple was torn in two from top to bottom" (Matt 27:51) which symbolized an obsolete old covenant priesthood (Heb 8:13), but also "the barrier, the dividing wall of hostility" (Eph 2:14-15) which distinguished Israel from the Gentiles, was destroyed by Jesus.

When the apostle Paul was writing the Epistle to the Ephesians, the physical temple building of the old covenant was still standing. However, it was eventually destroyed in 70 A.D. The redeemed people of Christ, who were predominantly made up of Gentiles in Ephesus, would have been familiar with distinctions amongst worshipers in the temple courts. Just imagine the excitement and greater appreciation for the cross by worshipers under the new covenant in Ephesus; there were no distinctions amongst the worshipers. Just as the Law was fulfilled in Christ, now the new covenant worshiping community, as "a royal priesthood" was able to approach God as one corporate body in worship—"For through [Christ] we both [Jews and Gentiles] have access to the Father by one Spirit" (Eph 2:18).

Through the cross, Christ "made the two one... His purpose was to create in himself one new man out of the two" (vv. 14-15). Just as it was in the Garden when "it [was] not good for the man to be alone" (Gen 2:18) since the will of God for mankind was to reflect who Yahweh was—the Triune God, the community of Godhead. Now, under the new covenant in Christ, the redeemed people would "become one" (Gen 2:24).

In the name of equality between man and woman, countless arguments have been made amongst those who support egalitarianism and others who hold to complementary/hierarchical views. The biblical revelation of two becoming one is not a product of a life philosophy such as the idea of looking at every aspect of life in the perspective of "Yin-Yang", opposites complementing each other.

But for now, we will put those different views aside, and consider Paul's primary usage of creating "one new man out of the two" in the context of worshiping community. Just as it was in the Garden, the sanctuary of God, where Adam and Eve who had been created in God's image were supposed to reflect the God of community (Gen 2:25), the worshiping community under the new covenant in Christ is called "to live a life worthy of

the calling [we] have received... [Making] every effort to keep the unity...
There is one body... one God" (Eph 4:1, 3-4, 6), as Christ "himself [has
become] our peace, who has made the two one and has destroyed the barrier... in his flesh" (Eph 2:14-15).

This unity must have the death and resurrection of Christ as its foundation, expressed in the new covenant worshiping community, and should
influence every community that we are part of, mainly church (Eph
5:17-21) and family (vv. 22-33). For this reason, the apostle Paul commanded believers to "be imitators of God... as dearly loved children" (v.
1). Even in our marriage relationships must reflect who God is and the relationship between "the church" and Christ (vv. 22-30).

What God has instituted in the creation (Gen 2:24) was fulfilled
through Christ's death in the community of believers (Eph 2:14-18), and
His death made it possible to reflect God and Christ's relationship with
church even in the marriage relationship—"For this reason a man will leave
his father and mother and be united to his wife, and the two will become
one flesh... so they are no longer two, but one" (Matt 19:5-6).

The apostle Paul calls Genesis 2:24 as "a profound mystery" in Ephesians 5:32. "Mystery" in the Bible is not in the sense of "weird" but rather it
means that the gospel that "was not made known to" the previous generations (Eph 3:5), had been "revealed by the Spirit to God's holy apostles and
prophets". In other words, from the beginning of creation, what God had in
mind with regards to creating Adam and Eve went beyond simply marriage.
God's intent was to send His Son, Jesus Christ, taking the form of human
flesh, paying the penalty of sin for the church, and purchasing His people
with His own blood in order for the church to be a pure bride for the Bride-
groom, Christ (2 Cor 11:2).

Therefore, when God revealed, "they will become one flesh" (Gen
2:24), it foreshadowed our relationship with Christ. Because of Christ's
death we need to "make every effort to keep the unity of the Spirit" amongst
the new covenant community (Eph 4:3). Our effort to be one in Christ
means living out God's image that had been restored and newly created
within the redeemed people and with one another through Christ's death.
And the "two becoming one" in creation has finally been fulfilled in Christ's
death and expressed when His redeemed people come together in worship

and experience God's indwelling presence more and more what began in the Garden as church continue to experience maturity (Eph 2:21-22).

Depending on one's eschatology, countless attempts have been made to identify the future temple that the Messiah will build. The purpose of God's revelation of the temple to the prophet Ezekiel was not meant for the temple to be built, but rather that Israel may be ashamed of their idolatry— "if they are ashamed of all they have done, make known to them the design of the temple...so that they may be faithful to its design and follow all its regulations" (Ezek 43:11). What good was the meticulous design of the tabernacle or the temple when true worship was not taking place?

The prophet Ezekiel was to "look with [his] eyes and hear with [his] ears and pay attention to everything [what God would] show [him]" and Ezekiel was supposed to tell everything that he saw to the house of Israel (Ezek 40:4). Just as the tabernacle was the copy of what Moses saw on the mountain and the earthly tabernacle had its significance in the worship regulations and what it stood for—God's indwelling presence.

Therefore, just as Jesus Christ is God Himself—the perfect temple and the fullness of God's presence—the temple in Ezekiel 40-44 was to be the new covenant worshiping community. This community was experiencing the following: "In him the whole building is joined together and rises to become a holy temple in the Lord... you too are being built together to become a dwelling in which God lives by his Spirit" (Eph 2:21-22), when the Holy Spirit came upon the first believers on the day of Pentecost which marked the beginning of the Last Days (Acts 2:1-5, 17).

As God's children in Christ, we are called to "be imitators of God" (Eph 5:1) and reflect who God is in every aspect of our lives: 1) in the new covenant community in Christ; 2) in family relationship (5:22-6:4); 3) and in the working environment of a secular world (6:5-9). In order to experience and reflect the image of the God of community, the following is needed primarily in the context of worship: 1) *praise* and *prayer* that reveals and experiences God's blessing from the heavenly realms (1:3-23), 2) *God's indwelling presence* as the new covenant community engages in worship (2:1-22), 3) revelation and display of God's manifold wisdom through *proclamation* and *prayer* (3:1-21), 4) serving God through *gospel ministry* primarily within the covenant community (4:1-16), 5) flowing life out from *worshiping* God (4:17-32) and from living the life worthy of God's calling as His children (5:1-21), 6) relationships in life that flow out from the *worshiping community* (5:22-6:9), and 7) being equipped with *God's word* and *prayer* to be "strong in the Lord" in order to overcome daily spiritual struggles (6:10-20).

Displaying God's Manifold Wisdom

God's purpose of saving us "because of his great love for us" is to "show the incomparable riches of his grace" in the coming ages (Eph 2:4, 7). When redeemed people gather together as a church, God's purpose for the church is to display His redemptive work, which was accomplished through His Son's death and resurrection. In this way, the new covenant community in Christ would be displaying "the manifold wisdom of God... to the rulers and authorities in the heavenly realms" (3:10-11).

What is this "manifold wisdom of God" that is to be displayed through the church? The "mystery" was made known to Paul (3:3), and by reading his letter to Ephesians, one would "be able to understand [Paul's] insight into the mystery of Christ (v. 4). This mystery is what Paul had said earlier in chapter two—the distinction between ethnic Israel and the Gentiles was no longer made under the new covenant in Christ (v. 6). And through the proclamation of the gospel, the Gentiles and Israel alike would be experiencing one body, one community, one family of God, and true citizenship in the spiritual Israel.

Through preaching of the gospel, God is forming a new covenant community, the church. God's intent for revealing the mystery in Christ from the preaching of the gospel is that through the community of the redeemed people, "the manifold wisdom of God [would] be made known to the rulers and authorities in the heavenly realms" (vv. 9-10). God redeems people through the proclamation of the gospel. But the goal of evangelism must go beyond saving souls. Through the preaching of the gospel, people are saved and become part of a new covenant community in order to fulfill God's purpose of preaching of the gospel, which is making God's manifold wisdom known to the rulers.

The place of "the heavenly realms" connects with where God the Father and the Son rule (1:3, 20; 2:6). However, in 6:12, the place of the heavenly realms is where "the rulers ... the authorities ... powers of this dark world and ... the spiritual forces of evil" dwell or operate. Therefore, "the rulers and authorities" of 3:10 (and also in 2:2) are the spiritual forces of evil.

Before the people were redeemed, they were following "the ways of ... the rule of the kingdom of the air" (Eph 2:2). The message of the cross, the gospel is "foolishness" in the eyes of the world. The cross of Jesus was not a mistake or failure but "in the wisdom of God ... God was pleased through [preaching of the gospel] to save those who believe" (1 Cor 1:18, 21).

Therefore, when the new covenant community comes together with people of diverse backgrounds in order to worship as "one new man out of the [many]" (Eph 2:15), the church displays the true spiritual unity which was accomplished through the death of Christ on the cross. The devil's plan from Creation, was to incite skepticism towards God's good intentions towards those who were created in God's image. Now, through the cross, many are delivered from the world. They have become members of Christ's body and by calling on the Name of God in worship and in one spirit, they make the manifold wisdom of God known to the spiritual world.

When priests under the old covenant entered the tabernacle to minister, they wore a breastpiece over their priestly ephod, and in the breastpiece was "the Urim and the Thummim" (Exod 28:30). Whenever Aaron entered into the presence of Yahweh, the Urim and the Thummim were "the means for making decisions for the Israelites". Different commentators suggest various interpretations on these stones— whether the two stones symbolically represented the twelve stones or whether the way the light reflected or transmitted through these stones affected the decisions that were made. However, it was clear that the priest was able to know God's will through the Urim and Thummim.

God continued to reveal His will through various means for the people under the old covenant. When king Saul rebelled, God withdrew His presence from him—"[Saul] inquired of the Lord, but the Lord did not answer him by dreams or Urim or prophets" (1 Sam 28:6). The priests continued to minister with the Urim and Thummim in the priestly breastpiece even after coming back from the exile (Ezr 2:63; Neh 7:65). All of this took place in the presence of Yahweh, in the sanctuary.

What took place in the sanctuary did not only involve the priests wearing the ephod and the breastpiece but through their ministry, God would reveal His will to the ministering priest. In Rev 21:15-21, we are reminded of this kind of priestly ministry and the ephod that was worn to minister. However, in Revelation 21, rather than a particular building or city, what the apostle John witnessed in his visionary experience was "the bride, the wife of the Lamb... the Holy City, Jerusalem," and the city "shone with the glory of God, and its brilliance was like that of a very precious jewel, like a jasper, clear as crystal... [John] did not see a temple in the city, because the Lord God Almighty and the Lamb are its temple" (Rev 21:10-11). The materials for the city were "jasper... pure gold decorated with every kind of precious stone" (vv. 18-19).

If the ministering priest could discern God's will by the Urim and Thummim, then in the new heaven/ new earth, the wisdom of God would no longer be a hidden mystery because of God's glory and His presence in the midst of His redeemed people. The ultimate mystery and wisdom of God was that through the cross of Jesus, there would be one humanity serving one God, one Savior and Lord Jesus Christ as forming one community, which will be the bride of the Lamb, the Holy City.
What began through Christ's death and resurrection, "the whole building is joined together and rises to become a holy temple... being built together to become a dwelling in which God lives by his Spirit" in these Last Days (Eph 2:21-22; cf. Rev 21:5).

Therefore, what God will accomplish and fulfill in the consummation, He has already started in the new covenant people. And when the redeemed come together as the new covenant community in unity, they are actually experiencing and displaying "the manifold wisdom of God... to the rulers and authorities in the heavenly realms" (Eph 3:10) and foreshadowing what God will accomplish in the new heaven and the new earth.

In our local churches, despite cultural, socio-economic, and ethnic differences, are we truly experiencing the cross and the power of His resurrection that brings the community as one under one head, Jesus Christ (Eph 2:22)? Has our worshiping community tasted even a little glimpse of "the fullness of [Christ] who fills everything in every way" in our worship

(2:23)? When we come together as church to worship, are we displaying the wisdom of God in His sanctuary (3:10)?

Countless movements in the name of Christ have risen and died throughout history. However, a church, "a city on a hill cannot be hidden" (Matt 5:14) situated in a cultural diverse city that comes together in Christ, will endure in history and make known to the invisible world, what God started in the Garden has been fulfilled through the cross and the resurrection of Christ, "two shall be one." After all, only what Christ does will remain forever—"I will build my church" as Jesus said (Matt 16:18).

Experiencing Unity through the Gospel Ministries in the New Covenant Community

The more the new covenant community experiences spiritual maturity, the more of the fullness of Christ will be experienced (Eph 1:23; 2:21-22). Just as praising God for blessing "us in the heavenly realms with every spiritual blessing in Christ" (1:3) led the apostle Paul into prayer for "the Spirit of wisdom and revelation (1:17), God's intent "was now, through the church, the manifold wisdom of God should be made known… according to his eternal purpose" (3:10-11), led Paul again to prayer that they "may be filled to the measure of all the fullness of God" (3:19).

It should never be enough for us to know God intellectually or to praise God for His blessings upon His people; there has to be prayer for: 1) "the Spirit of wisdom and revelation," and 2) "being filled" to "the fullness of God."

In the light of what God accomplished through Christ's death and resurrection, and how God blessed His people with every spiritual blessing in Christ, Paul "urge[d] [the church]… to keep the unity of the Spirit" in the body of Christ, church (4:1, 3). How does a church "keep the unity of the Spirit?" In chapter four, the new covenant community is to keep and experience the unity in the following ways: 1) by being equipped for the gospel ministry (v. 12) for the purpose of 2) reaching "unity in the faith and in the knowledge of the Son of God" (v. 13). When the members of the body of Christ are doing the gospel ministries, church will experience her maturity by having the sound doctrinal stability (v. 14) and "speaking the truth in love" (v. 15).

How is one trained to do the gospel ministries? What are the gospel ministries? Just as the Levites and the priests were ministering in the tabernacle and the courtyard under the old covenant, now God's newly redeemed people in Christ are to minister in the new covenant community. Just as the different ministries that took place in the tabernacle and the courtyard were all related to offering sacrifices, worship to God, in the new covenant community, the gospel ministries should relate primarily to the worship matters, and flow out from the worship to different areas of ministries.

While in Romans 12:6, the emphasis is on different gifts according to the grace given to the members of the new covenant community in general, Ephesians 4:7, 11-12 speak of Christ giving grace to the different leaders as listed in verse 11, who ministered at the Ephesian church at that time "to prepare God's people for" the gospel ministries (v. 12).

Throughout church history, arguments have been made whether the leaders of verse 11, who were known in the apostle Paul's days, were limited to the apostolic period or whether these leaders continue to exist and function in our days. If the apostles and prophets of verse 11 are the same apostles and prophets mentioned earlier in 2:20, then the two titles, offices cannot exist today based on the argument since God is (or was) building His church "on the foundation of the apostles and prophets," and the foundation is laid only once, while building on that foundation is an ongoing construction.

Moreover, if the major role of apostles and prophets was to write God's written word (assuming that the "prophets" here were the Old Testament writing prophets), then what about the rest of the apostles? Since in the New Testament, not all of the apostles in the time of the writing the New Testament, were used by God to write His word.

Therefore, although the apostles and prophets were the ones who wrote the majority of the Bible, the emphasis should not be placed on their unique role to write His holy word. Rather, the emphasis should be on their ministry of teaching and application—how their lives and gospel ministry affected the life of church.

By placing too much emphasis on their office in connection with the laying of the foundation of the early church, and the writing of the New Testament, one could miss what the author of the Epistle to the Ephesians intended. In what ways did those leaders mentioned in verse 11 prepare God's people to do the gospel ministries in the local churches that would result in unity and maturing the church? The works of the gospel ministries should continue. They are ongoing ministries since no church on this earth or church as a whole, collectively, has matured enough to attain "to the whole measure of the fullness of Christ" (v. 13).

The act of Christ giving grace is mentioned two times: 1) to each one of us (v. 7) and 2) to the community of God's people to prepare them to do ministries (v. 11). Verse 7 has to do with Christ giving grace to the ministry leaders. In verse 12, Christ gives ministry leaders to the church in order to equip the members of the body of Christ. Therefore, while the overall emphasis is on Christ giving grace, verse 7 is about Christ giving "grace" to individual leaders, and verse 11 is Christ giving "the individual leaders" to church to equip the saints for the gospel ministries.

This order of God giving grace is emphasized in Numbers 3, 8, and 18. Yahweh had "taken the Levites from among the Israelites" (Num 3:12) and gave them "as gifts to Aaron and his sons to do the work at the Tent of Meeting on behalf of the Israelites" (8:19, and also in 18:6). God also gave the priestly ministry as a gift to Aaron (18:7). Once this order was established, Yahweh said, "From now on the Israelites must not go near the Tent of Meeting... It is the Levites who are to do the work at the Tent of Meeting," (18:22-23). On behalf of the Israelites, the Levites were to fulfill "the obligations... by doing the work of the tabernacle" (3:7-8) while Aaron and his sons, as priests, were to serve God in the sanctuary (v. 10).

Why were the Israelites not allowed to fulfill their obligations to do the works of ministry at the Tent of Meeting? Perhaps the Israelites had broken their covenant with Yahweh (the golden calf; Exodus 32). In Exodus 19, Yahweh said, "Now if you obey me fully and keep my covenant, then out of all nations you will be my treasured possession... you will be for me a kingdom of priests and a holy nation" (vv. 5-6). This may be debatable since, based on Solomon's prayer for foreigners (1 Kings 8:41-43), Israel might have continued to understand their role as a God-serving nation to the surrounding nations which was promised to Abraham—"all peoples on earth will be blessed through you" (Gen 12:3).

Or it could have been after the golden calf incident when Moses said, "Whoever is for [Yahweh], come to me," and then all the Levites came forward and they killed off the idolaters (Exod 32:26-28). In response to such commitment and zeal for Yahweh, Moses said to them, "You have been set apart to Yahweh today, for you were against your own sons and brothers, and he has blessed you this day" (v. 29). It is clear that sin separates and keeps a distance from the very presence of Yahweh.

For this reason, Yahweh took the Levites as gifts for the rebellious Israelites. The Levites were set apart as gifts to "to do the work at the Tent of Meeting on behalf of the Israelites" (Num 8:19). It was a privilege and blessing to serve Yahweh in the temple courts and be closer to Yahweh's presence in His sanctuary.

David wrote Psalm 68 in relation to worship in God's holy dwelling place (v. 5), His sanctuary (v. 35), in the great congregation (v. 26). The date for this psalm was around three hundred years after the wilderness journey of the Israelites, looking back at the history of how Yahweh fought for His people in the wilderness (v. 1) and at the times of the Judges in the Promised Land (vv. 7-10).

As David spoke about "the mountain where God [chose] to reign, where [Yahweh] himself [would] dwell forever" (v. 16), he looked back in the books of Exodus and Numbers how Yahweh came down "from Sinai into his sanctuary... received gifts from... the rebellious—that... [Yahweh] God, might dwell there" (vv. 17-18). David also foresaw what later another prophet Micah would speak on—"In the last days the mountain of [Yahweh's] temple will be established as chief among the mountains.... And peoples will stream to it. Many nations will come and say, 'Come, let us go up to the mountain of [Yahweh]... He will teach us his ways'" (Micah 4:1-2).

As strange it may seem, after speaking of God's dwelling place, David immediately praised God for being their Savior, "who daily [bore their] burdens" (v. 19). What relationship is there between God receiving gifts from the rebellious and His dwelling place with God being the Savior "who daily bears our burdens" (vv. 18-19)?

If David were mainly referring to Exodus 19, 32 and Numbers 3, 8, 18 (with the list of rebellious incidents from chapters 11 to 14, and 16-17), then Yahweh chose to dwell in the midst of His people ministering in relation to worshiping and serving God at the Tent of Meeting. Somehow, David as a prophet foresaw that a person has to receive a gift from Yahweh in order to do ministry, since the priestly ministry of Aaron and his sons, was given from Yahweh as a gift. That gift would be received when the Lord God, the Savior would take the burden of sins of His rebellious people. Yet, we do not see God taking the burden of their sins other than the animal sacrifices, which foreshadowed and anticipated one perfect sacrificial death of God's Son, Jesus Christ.

Perhaps through God's revelation of Himself in acts of history, the prophet David not only foresaw Christ's resurrection, but also the son of David being "exalted to the right hand of God, [Christ] would receive from the Father the promised Holy Spirit and [had] poured out what" God-fearing Jews saw and heard on the day of Pentecost (Acts 2:31, 33). The apostle Peter concluded his message with "Repent and be baptized... in the name of Jesus Christ... and you will receive the gift of the Holy Spirit" (v. 38).

Psalm 68 anticipates how Yahweh will have the ultimate victory over sin through His Son becoming man, dying on the cross, resurrected, exalted, and becoming the baptizer of the Holy Spirit (Matt 3:11), in order to prepare God's people to do the gospel ministry. This equipping is to be done in the new covenant church community by leaders, who have uniquely received the grace from God "as Christ apportioned it"—to be apostles, prophets, evangelists, and pastors-teachers for the church in Ephesus (Eph 4:7, 11).

Psalm 68 was looking back to the history of Israel, with respect to the worship and God's dwelling place. Based on such a written revelation of God, the Scriptures, the prophet David foresaw how Christ, David's Lord, would give gifts to God's people by accomplishing the redemptive work. This was for the purpose of doing the works of ministry in the church, Christ's body, where God had chosen to dwell.

For this reason, the apostle Paul was writing to the church in Ephesus —how God the Father has been preparing and working from eternity (Eph 1:11) to send Christ in order for "[His will] to be put into effect when the times will have reached their fulfillment" (v. 10), "which was not made known to men in other generations" (3:5).

When God came down from Sinai, He took out the Levites from the rebellious idolaters, the twelve tribes of Israel, in order to do ministry at the tabernacle. In a way, the Levites were gifts not only to the priests but also to the Israelites since they were not allowed to be near the tabernacle. Therefore, only the Levites, on behalf of the Israelites, served God at the sanctuary of God.

According to David in Psalm 68, all these events took place in order to prophetically foreshadow how Christ would fulfill and restore what had been lost because of man's rebellion against God, since the creation. This breach of the covenant between God and Adam brought alienation from God's presence for the entire human race, and for the Israel as a nation.

Just as Yahweh came down and received the Levites in order to give them as gifts to Aaron and to the Israelites, to do the works of ministry at the Tabernacle, likewise, the Son of God came down from heaven, as "the Lamb of God who [took] away the sin of the world" (John 1:29) on the cross. Christ was raised to life and "ascended higher than all the heavens, in order to fill the whole universe" (Eph 4:10). Christ has already begun this "filling" of the "fullness of God" by giving leaders who have received God's grace, to the new covenant church community in order to prepare every member of the body of Christ to do the works of the gospel ministry (vv. 11-12). This is so since "Christ… gave himself up for [church] to make her holy, cleansing her by the washing with water through the word" (5:26). So, what had been foreshadowed in Psalm 68 has been fulfilled through Christ who "daily bears our burdens" through the cross once and for all.

The Five Types of Gospel Ministry Leaders Influencing the Worshiping Community

By looking at how the five different ministry leaders, listed in Ephesians 4:11, ministered to the local churches in the time of the apostle Paul, we will have a better understanding of how people were trained/discipled in the community of faith in Christ.

Just as the term "disciple" was not limited to the Twelve, but included anyone who followed a rabbi's teaching, the term "apostles" could have been used referring to other leaders beside the Twelve and Paul. When "a great persecution broke out against the church at Jerusalem... all except the apostles were scattered" (Acts 8:1). From that point on, what we know of the Twelve, the apostles mainly ministered in the church at Jerusalem (at least up to Acts 15). Rather than trying to identify "who" were the apostles, the focus should be on "how did apostles and prophets minister to local churches?"

Since our main subject is not about apostles or other leaders, but is about worship and worshipers who were equipped by those leaders in a local church, we will limit our discussion to a few people and the church in Antioch along with the Ephesian church.

Barnabas, a Levite from Cyrus, first appears in the book of Acts as someone who generously gave along with many other members of the church in Jerusalem (Acts 4:34-37). Barnabas, along with Paul, were referred to as "apostles" in Acts 14:4. The question is not "at what point were they given the title?" The focus should be on their gospel ministry.

When "a great number of [Greeks] believed and turned to the Lord" in Antioch, the church in Jerusalem needed someone, who was reliable to find out perhaps about the legitimacy of the gentiles' faith in Christ and they chose Barnabas (Acts 11:20-22). Barnabas is introduced as "a good man, full of the Holy Spirit and faith" (v. 24), which was the same determining factor to be fit to serve the widows in the church (Acts 6:3). It could be possible that one of Barnabas' ministry responsibilities was to administrate "the daily distribution of food" to the widows.

As the church at Antioch continued to grow, Barnabas' primary ministry along with Paul was focused on maturing the church not by sharing and preaching the gospel to nonbelievers which the church was already doing, but teaching God's word to the believers, Christians (v. 25). Therefore, we see the community of faith experiencing 1) God's grace through conversion (the ministry of evangelism), 2) spiritual growth through learning (the ministry of teaching), and 3) financial support through giving by obedience to the prompting of the Holy Spirit (the ministry of prophetic) in verses 27-30.

We see how Barnabas, who assumed the title of apostle, was constantly being sent out: 1) to oversee and evaluate local church matters (Acts

11:22); 2) to deliver support (v. 30); 3) to do the work of evangelism; 4) to edify churches under his (and also Paul's) ministry and spiritual influence (Acts 13:2-3; 14:21-28). Therefore, apart from the Twelve and Paul, the apostolic ministry ranges from being sent out from a church for a special task to having a spiritual influence over a church or churches, which could distinguish them from teachers according to 1 Corinthians 4:15 (if the "guardians" are seen as teachers or counselors in our days).

Whatever has been written in the Bible is not necessarily prescriptive. At the same time, certain things, like the work of the Holy Spirit could only be known by how He *worked* in the hearts and midst of His people (John 3:8). Man cannot duplicate or mimic the miraculous work of God. Similarly, our interpretation, which systematically fits concepts into our own logical framework, has its limitations.

Only God's written revelation, the Bible, His word, is absolute and objective, while our experiences can only be personal, relative, and subjective. God's word gives the context in which the Holy Spirit operates. Just as the Son of God submitted to the will of God and did only what His Father did (John 5:19), the Holy Spirit chose to "limit" Himself to speak and do within the context of Christ's word and work (John 16:12-15).

Therefore, when the Bible states, "In the church at Antioch there were prophets and teachers... While they were worshiping the Lord and fasting, the Holy Spirit said..." (Acts 13:1-2), we do not know exactly how the Holy Spirit spoke to people in the church. However, it is certain that what was heard was not something that the church expected, even though the church was equipped to hear the voice of God through the prophetic ministry that was based on Christ's word. The important thing is that there were two types of leadership in the church of Antioch: prophets, who proclaimed what they were convicted of based on God's word, and teachers who taught God's written word.

Although new Christians were experiencing ministries of evangelism (Acts 11:21), only two types of leadership are mentioned in Acts 13:1— prophets and teachers. These two different types of leadership shared the same foundation for their ministry—God's written revelation of His word.

Under these two types of leadership, the church continued to grow and mature. Therefore, the church was equipped by being able to hear and obey what the Spirit said to the church. The church had already been ministered by Barnabas, who was sent from the church in Jerusalem. By the prompting of the Holy Spirit (Acts 13:2–3), the church in Antioch was the first church to send off their two most important leaders for the gospel ministry.

Moreover, under such leadership, the Antioch church continued to grow, experiencing the fullness of God in their worship, as God's word was being faithfully taught. By being sensitive to the prompting of the Holy Spirit, they were prepared to release Barnabas and Saul "for the work to which [the Holy Spirit had] called them" (Acts 13:2). Through this four or fivefold ministry of Ephesians 4:11, the church continued to grow and it witnessed what God was doing beyond Antioch (Acts 14:21-28).

We do not worship God's word, but we worship God in the way He reveals Himself in Scripture.

Preaching God's word should be one of the main activities in worship but not the focus of worship, since preaching is what the preacher does with God's word—praying through the message in his preparation and expecting God to bless the faithful exposition of His word. While the preacher should limit his preaching to God's word, he should also expect to submit to the leading of the Holy Spirit who speaks and works in the context of God's word and its proclamation. The preacher should be open to the Spirit's prompting in the hearts of both the preacher and the worshipers.

The apostle Paul in his letter to the Ephesians not only explained what it meant for the new covenant community to be equipped for the works of the gospel ministry in different areas of their lives, but he also explained specifically how the different leadership ministries should affect the worship and how the worship was to be conducted in the life of the new covenant community church (Eph 5:18-21).

Just as church is "[Christ's] body, the fullness of him who fills everything in every way" (1:23), so are the worshipers ought to seek the fullness of the Holy Spirit in worship (5:18). Pagan religions have their own way of worshiping their gods through rituals and religious regulations. Wine, strong drink or a special potion was used in order to "help" pagan worshipers to be "spiritual" and have spiritual experiences with some types of spirits. Just as it was prevalent in the time of the apostle Paul, this practice of drinking as a part of worshipping pagan gods has not been foreign in our Western culture.

The "speaking the truth in love" (4:15) is applied in the way the new covenant worshipers ought to worship by "[speaking] to one another with psalms, hymns and spiritual songs" (4:19). Under the filling of the Spirit, four different aspects of worship are highlighted: 1) speaking to one another, 2) making music, 3) giving thanks, and 4) submission.

Paul does not limit one type of song or music in worship. Mostly, the psalms may refer to the Old Testament collection of psalms. Before a psalm is incorporated into a worship service, the worship leader must understand the background and exegete the text in connection with God and the Lamb of God, Christ.

Often hymns were based on one's experience of God's word in his or her real life. In that respect, hymns are similar to many of the psalms. But the difference lies in the following: the book of Psalms is what had been written as God's word, while hymns are similar to any other songs which are based on the written word of God. "Spiritual songs" could be any songs or music that may not be categorized into one of the two previous categories.

This reminds us that worship, singing, and music involve more than just an intellectual mental knowledge but our emotions are touched in a way that cannot be systematically theorized. Perhaps this was what Paul had in mind when he states, "make music in your heart to the Lord" (v. 19). Just as one cannot sing without engaging emotionally, worshiping God goes beyond the intellectual understanding of our minds—"Love the Lord your God with all your heart and with all your soul and with all your mind and with all your strength" (Mark 12:30).

While different types of songs and music may be used for the congregation to worship God, these songs must come from our 1) hearts, 2) thankful attitudes (v. 20), and 3) submissive hearts (v. 21). Paul starts with speaking "to one another" (v. 19) and concludes with submitting "to one another" (v. 20). In worship, much of "the communion of saints" takes place. If the primary purpose for the church meeting is edification, then there is no greater activity for Christians than coming together in worship.

Presently, many people have generalized and oversimplified the fellowship of believers. Any activity or gathering of a group of Christians tends to be called fellowship. But just as the early church "broke bread in their homes" (Acts 2:46) did not replace the Lord's Supper (Acts 2:42), just because Christians gather together to do some types of activities does not make it a true fellowship.

Being ministered by the five different types of leadership should affect the way we worship. In a way, worship releases worshipers to be more: 1) apostolic in the sense of a willingness to leave comfort zones for the sake of the gospel; 2) prophetic in the area of prayer and sensitivity to the Holy Spirit's leading in worship; 3) evangelistic by having the heart for the lost; 4) shepherd-like in having the heart to love and care for God's people; 5) firmly grounded in God's word through heartfelt worship.

It was very clear that God had given "grace as Christ apportioned it" to the leaders for preparing "God's people for works of service... until we all reach unity in the faith and in the knowledge of the Son of God" (Eph 4:7, 11-13). Primarily, the equipping starts in the church since Christ gave those five different leaders/ministries to church. Moreover, the purpose is so that "the body of Christ may be built up" (v. 12), which again, is the edification of the church (to be more specific, a local church).

Since most people, who live in the city, have lost the sense and importance of community, it is very important to keep in mind the local church. The backdrop of such a "non-communal mindset" is that many contemporary Christians tend to gravitate towards doing the "ministry" itself, serving God with their "giftedness," and being "spiritually blessed" from one meeting to another without seeking to edify and be committed to a local church, and without any spiritual accountability to the leaders whom Christ has given to the church as gifts. After all, what good are the five different leadership ministries if they only promote people who are hungry for religious experiences, seeking one conference after another and consequently, the local church is not edified?

Regardless of whether a church is a large "mega-church" or a small "house church," every church worships. This is one of the primary ways to define church. Therefore, the primary purpose for the gathering of a community of believers is: edification through worship. Out of worship, some Christians are ready to be sent out for the proclamation of the gospel and to go beyond where they are—"Our hope is that, as your faith continues to grow, our area of activity among you will greatly expand, so that we can preach the gospel in the regions beyond you" (2 Cor 10:15-16); it is mainly through the influence of apostolic and evangelistic ministries that God's people will reach out to their neighbors.

But sadly, the concept of community has been lost for many people living in the city. Many city dwellers have become so comfortable practicing their Christian faith by attending church services once a week and participating in their small groups on weekdays. This has been the trend partly because of the "busyness" of their daily life activities. Many have lost the need and sense of community in the church. Many have become indifferent and oblivious to their neighbors.

Often the famous story of the parable of the Good Samaritan have been misinterpreted and misapplied by preachers. Jesus told the parable of the Good Samaritan in response to loving God and our neighbor (Luke 10:27-28). Many assume that loving God means to love and care for those who are in need; therefore, the parable is primarily applied to "mercy ministry." However, loving God can be understood in Deuteronomy 6:5 as only worshiping God only (Deut 6:13). For this reason, Luke describes Mary sitting "at the Lord's feet, listening to what he said" (Luke 10:39) in order to show that love for our neighbor must flow out from worship, which is the primary expression of loving God. Like Mary, we need to gaze long enough to be influenced by the beauty of the Lord and listen to what He has to say through worship.

Not much has changed for the modern day religious Christians from the Jesus' days. Although in a different context, the people in the city could be asking the same question as the experts of the law, "Who is my neighbor" (Luke 10:29)? Could it be that modern evangelical worshipers have lost the sense of seeing the church as a worshiping community? Perhaps, because we still have not experienced true worship in a local church community of faith, we are still asking the same question after two thousand years, "Who is my neighbor?"

Through worship, the Holy Spirit convicts some worshipers to engage in prayer and intercede for the various needs of the church. Others may be convicted to have a greater hunger for God's word. When a church is influenced by these four/five different leadership ministries, there will be: 1) a deep hunger for God's word; 2) a passion for God's dwelling place; 3) a desire to seek Him in prayer, interceding for the church to influence across boundaries and comfort zones into the lives of neighbors as well as beyond the city, to the world.

In our days, the church often focuses on the preaching of God's word so that the worship service becomes no more than a teaching seminar. When there is worship that "appeals" to many people in our culture, this worship is often in the context of a worship-concert or a conference outside of the local church. Therefore, many churches in the city are characterized by diversity and individualism without spiritual accountability. These are the characteristics of a typical city culture, which are not distinguishable from a secular culture.

Without realizing the influence of our secular culture, many Christians continue to seek out relevant messages and/or some type of spiritual experiences through musical worship concerts. The Lord Jesus said this to an immoral woman, who was far from the religious community in her life, "Yet a time is coming and has now come when the true worshipers will worship the Father in spirit and truth, for they are the kind of worshipers the Father seeks" (John 4:23).

True satisfaction in life, whether one may be morally upright or immoral according to our cultural norm, comes not as a longing or wishful thinking but a reality in Jesus Christ who is the baptizer of the Spirit, pouring the Spirit into our hearts—the Spirit that is like "a spring of water welling up" to eternal life (John 4:14). Through true worship in spirit and truth, the Holy Spirit, who is described as "streams of living water [which] flow from within [us]" (John 7:38)(cf. Ezekiel 47:1-12) will flow through worshipers, touching and influencing the city so that people in the city will break away from their "private-ism", emptiness and loneliness and become part of a worshiping community of faith, speaking to "one another with psalms, hymns and spiritual songs" (Eph 5:19).

The challenge and struggle to regain biblical worship and to put it into practice in "a city on a hill that cannot be hidden" (Matt 5:14) can be daunting. Yet, we look forward to our city being overcome by another city, "the Holy City," in which the "dwelling of God is with men," where the apostle John "did not see a temple in the city, because the Lord God

Almighty and the Lamb [were] its temple" (Rev 21:2-3, 22). It is through our present worship, which takes place at a small miniature scale, that we experience what it would be like to be in the city where a temple building will not be necessary as there will be no barriers between God and His worshipers, as they enjoy the fullness of God in the Holy City.

As we look "forward to the city with foundations, whose architect and builder is God" (Heb 11:10), we are called to worship in church, a true city within a city, in order to experience a foretaste of the true city, "the city that *really* never sleeps," the city where there is no pretense, the city that "does not need the sun or the moon to shine on it, for the glory of God gives it light, and the Lamb is its lamp" (Rev 21:23). Therefore, God's people are called to set themselves apart from secular culture by having fellowship with Christ in worship—"Let us, then, go to [Christ] outside the camp, bearing the disgrace he bore. For here we do not have an enduring city" (Heb 13:13).